PREDICTING THE MARKETS
TOPICAL STUDY #3

Fed Watching
for Fun & Profit

A Primer for Investors

Edward Yardeni

YRI PRESS

Predicting the Markets Topical Study #3:
Fed Watching for Fun & Profit: A Primer for Investors

Copyright © 2020 Edward Yardeni

ISBN: 978-1-948025-06-5 (paperback)
ISBN: 978-1-948025-07-2 (eBook)
Library of Congress Control Number: 2020902591

Published by YRI Press, a division of Yardeni Research, Inc.
68 Wheatley Road, Suite 1100
Brookville, New York 11545

Contact us: **requests@yardeni.com**

For my children
Melissa, Sarah, Samuel, David, and Laura

Watch and learn.

Author's Note

This book is another in a series of Topical Studies examining issues that I discussed in my book *Predicting the Markets: A Professional Autobiography* (2018), but in greater detail and on a more current basis. Previous studies in this series include:

Stock Buybacks: The True Story (2019)
The Yield Curve: What Is It Really Predicting? (2019)

The charts at the end of this study were current as of January 2020. Updates (in color), as well as linked Endnotes and Appendices, are available at **www.yardenibook.com/studies**.

Institutional investors are invited to sign up for Yardeni Research's service on a complimentary trial basis at **www.yardeni.com/trial-registration**.

The idea that the business cycle can be altogether abolished seems to me as fanciful as the notion that the law of supply and demand can be repealed.

—William McChesney Martin,
Fed chair from 1951 to 1970

If we ask too much of monetary policy, we will not only fail but we will also discredit this useful, and indeed indispensable, tool for shaping our economic development.

—William McChesney Martin

Introduction

Watch the Fed

I started my career on Wall Street in 1978 as an economist at EF Hutton & Co. I spent the prior year at the Federal Reserve Bank of New York in the economics research department after receiving my undergraduate degree in economics and government from Cornell University in 1972 and my PhD in economics from Yale University in 1976. Over the past 40-plus years, I've worked as both the chief economist and the chief investment strategist at several firms on Wall Street. Since January 2007, I've been the president of my own consulting firm, Yardeni Research, Inc.[1]

My job continues to be to predict the financial markets, particularly the major stock, bond, commodity, and foreign exchange markets around the world. To do this job well, I've learned that nothing is more important than to anticipate the actions of the Federal Reserve System's Federal Open Market Committee (FOMC), which sets the course of monetary policy in the United States.

By controlling the interest rate in the federal funds market and other key monetary variables, the FOMC has an enormous impact on the financial markets and economy. The federal funds rate equilibrates the supply and demand for overnight commercial bank reserves and significantly affects the longer-term interest rates that influence the supply and demand for credit throughout the economy.

More specifically, here's how that works: The FOMC meets on a regular basis to discuss, vote on, and set the federal funds rate. The committee issues a directive to the Trading Desk ("the Desk") at the Federal Reserve Bank of New York to target the determined rate with the open market operations that it conducts—buying and selling fixed-income securities in the System Open Market Account (SOMA).[2] These targeted transactions in the open market accordingly affect bond prices and yields, making them highly sensitive to US monetary policy. Less directly but just as surely, prices in the stock and commodity markets, foreign exchange rates, and financial markets generally are highly sensitive to US monetary policy.

Watching the Fed closely are not only Wall Street's economists and investment strategists but also reporters and commentators at the major financial news organizations. In fact, anyone involved in investment matters and business activities anywhere in the world needs to watch the Fed, because its policies have powerful impacts not only on the US economy but also on the global economy. For participants in the financial markets, anticipating a policy change by the Fed and positioning an investment portfolio or speculative trade accordingly can result in big gains. Conversely, failing to anticipate a move by the Fed can result in big losses or missed opportunities for gains.

Economists on Wall Street—who spend most of their professional lives scrutinizing Fed officials' words and actions for clues to the outlook for monetary policy—are "Fed watchers." I am one of them, though my approach to forecasting the financial markets is much broader than Fed watching alone.

Don't Fight the Fed

I learned early in my career that Martin Zweig was right when he famously said, "Don't fight the Fed." Zweig was a highly respected analyst and investor. He started his newsletter in 1971 and his hedge fund in 1984. On Friday, October 16, 1987, in a memorable television appearance on *Wall Street Week with Louis Rukeyser*, he warned of an imminent stock market crash.

It happened the following Monday, and Zweig became an investment rock star. His newsletter, *The Zweig Forecast*, had a stellar track record, according to Mark Hulbert, a panelist on the show who tracked such things. I appeared several times on the widely watched show, which was the pacesetter for financial television programs. Louis was a class act, and so was Marty.

In his 1986 book, *Winning on Wall Street*, Zweig cogently elaborated on his oft-quoted saying:

> Monetary conditions exert an enormous influence on stock prices. Indeed, the monetary climate—primarily the trend in interest rates and Federal Reserve policy—is the dominant factor in determining the stock market's major direction. . . . Generally, a rising trend in rates is bearish for stocks; a falling trend is bullish. Let's see why. First, falling interest rates reduce the competition on stocks from other investments, especially short-term instruments such as Treasury bills, certificates of deposit, or money market funds. . . . Second, when interest rates fall, it costs corporations less to borrow. . . . As expenses fall, profits rise. . . . So, as interest rates drop, investors tend to bid prices higher, partly on the expectation of better earnings. The opposite effect occurs when interest rates rise.[3]

Unlike Zweig's objective approach, many Fed watchers spend too much time criticizing the Fed. It's easy to do. Anyone can play the game; you don't need a PhD in economics. Attacking the Fed is like shooting at sitting ducks: Fed officials can't respond directly given their public role. The most vocal Fed critics are the reformers who want to change the Fed system or even end it. Most Fed watchers are macroeconomists who would jump at the opportunity to be the Fed chair or at least a Fed governor. Many would even settle for the presidency of one of the 12 regional banks of the Federal Reserve System. So naturally, they feel compelled to pontificate on what the Fed is doing wrong and what they would do differently. Their fault-finding and sermonizing are subjective. They are preachers rather than objective observers.

As an investment strategist, my approach to Fed watching isn't to preach but to analyze and inform. Investors want to know what the Fed is going to do next. So my aim is to anticipate whether monetary policy will be bullish or bearish for stocks, bonds, commodities, and currencies and advise my accounts accordingly. That requires a good read on the Fed chair and the other FOMC participants as well as a good read on the economy.

In this study, I explore the art of Fed watching for fun and profit. It's fun because it's interesting and relevant to our financial and business lives. It can be quite profitable once you get the hang of it. Profiting from anticipating what the Fed will do requires dispassionate and rigorous analysis of the most powerful economic policymaking organization in the US economy.

Judging the Fed can be fun too, I admit. Despite my best intentions, I occasionally stray, and do so in the following chapters. It's a hard habit to break because most of the monetary policy decisions of Fed officials are their judgment calls based on limited data, and on theories and models that are often controversial. An occupational hazard of Fed watching is that you tend to form your own opinions about their calls.

You'll see.

So take it from a longtime Fed watcher: Don't judge the Fed. Don't fight the Fed. Watch the Fed. And learn how to profit from your insights.

Chapter 1

The Committee: Talking Heads

Profiling the Fed Chairs

Predicting monetary policy is obviously important for predicting financial markets. To do so, I learned early in my Wall Street career the importance of thinking like the Fed chairs, who head up the Board of Governors of the Federal Reserve System and preside over the Federal Open Market Committee (FOMC). I've had to think like Paul Volcker, Alan Greenspan, Ben Bernanke, Janet Yellen, and Jerome Powell. As I explain below, Volcker was the Great Price Disinflator, Greenspan was the Great Asset Inflator, and Bernanke was the Great Moderator. Yellen was the Gradual Normalizer. Jerome Powell, the current Fed chair, has been the Pragmatic Pivoter—so far, as of December 2019.

To anticipate their policy moves, I've had to be their profiler, analyzing their professional thought processes and decision making. Assessing their latest thinking requires careful reading of their speeches and congressional testimonies. By law, the Fed must submit the *Monetary Policy Report* semiannually to the Senate Committee on Banking, Housing, and Urban Affairs and to the House Committee on Financial Services; that happens in February and July. The report discusses the conduct of monetary policy along with recent economic developments and the economic outlook. The Federal Reserve Board chair reviews the report during two days of testimony, involving the delivery of prepared remarks and a Q&A session with lawmakers.[4] Occasionally, he or she may use the opportunity to address Congress on other Fed-related matters as well. Additionally, most Fed chairs speak in various public forums about monetary policy, usually to explain the FOMC's policy decisions and the rationale behind them.

When reading Fed chairs' prepared remarks, I pay particular attention to the academic articles they cite in footnotes to see who is influencing their thinking—which is an excellent way to stay current in the field of monetary macroeconomics. In addition, I often reread their previous pronouncements to monitor the evolution of their thought process. I even count the number of times a keyword, such as "inflation" or "unemployment," appears in their prepared remarks and compare it with their previous remarks on monetary policy. Changes in the counts, as well as additions and deletions of keywords along the way, can sometimes shed light on whether the Fed chair is turning more hawkish (favoring tighter monetary policy) or more dovish (favoring an easier policy stance).

Some Fed chairs left long paper trails revealing their thinking before they were chosen to run the Fed. Volcker hadn't written much before he became the Fed chair, and he didn't give many speeches after he assumed the top post. However, Volcker wasn't hard to figure out. He kept things simple, maybe because he isn't a PhD economist like the more loquacious Drs. Greenspan, Bernanke, and Yellen. These three already had lots in print before heading up the Fed and had many more speeches under their belts when they assumed the role of Fed chair. Getting up to speed on how each of them thought required a fair amount of ongoing effort.

The three PhDs testified in Congress more often than did Volcker. They also relished applying their favorite macroeconomic theories to managing the economy, a bit like mad scientists conducting experiments in a lab. In fact, Bernanke regularly expressed his admiration for President Franklin Roosevelt (FDR) because of

FDR's willingness to experiment with new policies during the Great Depression. Giving occasional speeches before groups of fellow economists provided opportunities for the three PhDs to toss around their professional jargon as they theorized aloud about the policy issues they confronted.

Powell doesn't have a PhD, but he spent roughly six-and-a-half years as a Fed governor surrounded by PhD macroeconomists. He has learned to think like them, essentially earning an honorary PhD in macroeconomics from "Fed University." No amount of studying in a university can beat on-the-job training when it comes to learning the ropes of monetary policymaking.

Powell has been the most publicly loquacious of the four PhD chairs. Whereas Bernanke in April 2011 instituted the practice of holding press conferences following four of the eight FOMC meetings each year, Powell in 2019 increased the frequency to press conferences after every FOMC meeting.

Looking back, I was fortunate that my career on Wall Street so far has coincided with Fed leadership by these five extraordinary individuals. They contributed greatly to the remarkable bull markets in both stocks and bonds since the early 1980s (Fig. 1 and Fig. 2). The three Fed chairs prior to Volcker allowed inflation to rise rapidly, which led to a collapse in bond prices and weighed on stock prices, whereas Volcker decided to stop inflation no matter what. By doing so, he set the stage for the "long good buys," as I affectionately call the great secular bull markets in stocks and bonds during my career so far.

When Volcker became the Fed chair, on August 6, 1979, the S&P 500 was 104.30 and the 10-year US Treasury bond yield was 8.91%. Forty years later, by August 6, 2019, the S&P 500 had soared 2,663% to close at 2881.77, and the bond yield was down to 1.73% from a record high of 15.84% on September 30, 1981. Over this same period, the Dow Jones Industrial Average rose 2,968% from

848.55 to 26029.25. I stayed bullish on stocks and bonds for most of that time, because the five Fed chairs adopted policies that I saw as bullish for both asset classes.

FOMC Basics and the Dual Mandate

Monetary policy is determined by the FOMC, headed by the Fed chair. Here is some important background information:

- **Origin.** The Panic of 1907 convinced Congress that the country needed a central banking system.[5] The Fed, which began to operate in 1914, was created by the Federal Reserve Act of 1913 "to furnish an elastic currency, to afford means of rediscounting commercial paper, to establish a more effective supervision of banking in the United States, and for other purposes."[6]

  The Act provided for the establishment of up to 12 Federal Reserve Banks (district banks), with the Federal Reserve Board in Washington, D.C. consisting of seven members appointed by the President of the United States. Each regional bank had various branches, a board of directors, and district boundaries.

  All nationally chartered banks are required to be members of the Federal Reserve System, while state-chartered banks can join if they meet certain requirements. Commercial banks that are members of the System are required by law to hold stock in the district Reserve Banks, which are not operated for profit.

- **Dual mandate.** Following World War II, it was widely feared that the US economy could fall into another depression. Congress passed the Employment Act of 1946, directing the federal government to promote maximum employment, production, and purchasing power. Back then, liberals wanted to call it "The Full Employment Act," but conservatives resisted. In early 1975, Congress adopted Resolution 133, instructing the Federal Reserve to, among other things: "maintain long run growth of the monetary and credit aggregates commensurate with the economy's long run potential to increase production, so as to promote effectively the goals of maximum employment, stable prices, and moderate long-term interest rates."[7]

In 1977, Congress amended the Federal Reserve Act to incorporate the provisions of Resolution 133 in the Full Employment and Balanced Growth Act, known informally as the "Humphrey–Hawkins Full Employment Act." It was signed into law by President Jimmy Carter on October 27, 1978. This act calls on the federal government to strive for full employment, production growth, price stability, and balanced trade and budget accounts. The Fed is specifically mandated to maintain long-run economic growth and minimize inflation.

Fed officials believe that this legislation imposes a dual mandate on the Fed to keep the unemployment rate low and consistent with full employment, while achieving inflation so low that it amounts to price stability.[8] The law requires the semi-annual congressional testimony and monetary policy report by the chair.

- **Governors.** After the President picks a candidate for an open position on the Board, he or she must then be confirmed by the full US Senate.[9] Governors serve 14-year terms and may not be reappointed. However, they can serve longer than 14 years if they are appointed to serve another member's uncompleted term, then subsequently appointed to a full term themselves. The nominees for chair and vice chair may be chosen by the President from among the sitting governors for four-year terms; these appointments are also subject to Senate confirmation.

Once appointed, governors may not be removed from office for their policy views. The appointments of governors are staggered so that one term expires on January 31 of each even-numbered year. The Fed's website notes: "The lengthy terms and staggered appointments are intended to contribute to the insulation of the Board—and the Federal Reserve System as a whole—from day-to-day political pressures to which it might otherwise be subject."[10]

While those protections are good to have in place, Fed chairs have resisted formidable political pressure from various Presidents. They've managed to maintain the Fed's independence reasonably well, in my opinion, though it's not a spotless record.

- **FOMC.** The Banking Act of 1933 amended the Federal Reserve Act. It created the FOMC, which consists of the seven members of the Board of Governors of the Federal Reserve System and five representatives from the Federal Reserve Banks. All seven governors get to vote at every meeting of the FOMC, as does the president of the Federal Reserve Bank of New York. Four of the remaining 11 Reserve Bank presidents serve one-year terms on a rotating basis.[11] Nonvoting Reserve Bank presidents attend the meetings of the Committee, participate in the discussions, and contribute to the Committee's assessment of the economy and policy options.[12] In other words, when all positions are filled, there are up to 19 participants on this committee, who attend each of the eight regularly scheduled meetings per year, with up to 12 of them being voting members.

I do my best to follow what all these FOMC participants say publicly. However, the viewpoints of some are more important than those of others. The ones who seem to be most aligned with the views of the chair tend to provide more insights into the views of the majority, or the emerging majority, of the voting members. The Fed chair tends to spend a fair amount of time lobbying the other FOMC members to develop as much of a consensus as possible going into FOMC meetings.

Volcker and Greenspan tended to lord over the FOMC as an assertive corporate board chairman might over a board of directors. Given their academic backgrounds, Bernanke and Yellen were more collegial in their approaches to managing the FOMC, seeking to build consensus as if they were the chairs of a college economics department. Bernanke was especially committed to ending Greenspan's cult of personality. Powell also seems to be a consensus-builder and more prone to influence by Fed colleagues.

The public comments of all Fed officials are picked up by the press and sometimes move financial markets. That's especially so if those comments signal an unexpected change in policy. In some cases, the officials are purposely trying to align market expectations with the course that policy will likely take at an upcoming FOMC meeting. When more than one official does that, the markets tend to get the message, especially if the officials are the chair and like-minded FOMC members. Sometimes, the Fed's message will be conveyed in an article in the financial press—especially *The Wall Street Journal*—that undoubtedly came from authoritative but unidentified sources inside the Fed.

At times, Fed officials simply float their own ideas as trial balloons. That's become annoyingly commonplace in recent years. FOMC participants, especially the regional bank presidents, seem all too happy to appear on televised financial news programs as well as to provide on-the-record interviews for the print and digital media. This makes for lots of chatter with scant import on policymaking. I occasionally call the Fed's talking heads "the Federal Open Mouth Committee."

Thankfully, we all get a regular break from the gabfest. Federal Reserve policy prohibits FOMC participants and staff from speaking publicly or granting interviews during blackout periods, which begin the second Saturday preceding an FOMC meeting and end the Thursday following a meeting. But once that quiet time is over, the yacking resumes. Sometimes, the chatty officials feel compelled to clarify the committee's latest message if they perceive that the markets haven't properly understood it.

The FOMC's message is formally provided in a short statement released immediately after the latest meeting. The few paragraphs start with a description of how the economy has performed since the previous meeting and how that compares to the Fed's ideal scenario. There might be a sentence or two on how the committee expects the economy to perform over the short term. The focus is always on the Fed's dual mandate, which is to keep the economy at "maximum sustainable employment" while maintaining "stable prices." Specific longer-run goals are developed by the Fed around these concepts. Then the statement announces whether the committee has decided to make policy adjustments to achieve its goals. At the tail end is a list of which members voted for or against the policy decision, sometimes including a line explaining the objections of any dissenters.

The statement is so important that *The Wall Street Journal* has a "Fed Statement Tracker" to help pundits and traders do what they have always done. It parses the statement, comparing the latest one with the previous one to see how the wording has changed and what that might imply. If economic growth is upgraded from "moderate" to "solid," for example, but rates were not increased at the meeting, the markets might adjust rapidly to reflect an increased chance of a Fed rate hike at the next meeting. In the past, the appearance or disappearance of words like "uncertain," "measured," "gradual," "balanced," and "risks" have moved markets. Fed officials do their best not to surprise the markets by providing lots of verbal "forward guidance" prior to a blackout period.

The first time the FOMC issued a statement immediately after a meeting was on February 4, 1994 to explain its first tightening decision since 1989.[13] Before then, no communication was provided on what federal funds rate target was decided upon at the FOMC meetings. Market participants had to guess the rate based on the SOMA's trading activity by the Desk at the Federal Reserve Bank of New York and its impact on the federal funds rate.

After each policy meeting, the FOMC issues an Implementing Note to the SOMA manager, which outlines the approach to monetary policy that the FOMC considers appropriate for the period between its meetings. The directive contains the interest rate at which the FOMC would like federal funds to trade over the coming intermeeting period.[14] Before 1994, changes in the discount rate at which commercial banks could borrow funds from the Fed provided clearer signals of a change in the federal funds rate. The Board of Governors approves these changes in response to FOMC decisions on the federal funds rate and in response to requests for doing so by the district banks.[15]

In February 1995, the committee decided to issue statements only to announce changes in the stance of monetary policy, specifying the changes in the federal funds rate target. Beginning in May 1999, statements were issued after every FOMC meeting, always including the federal funds rate target and forward guidance on the balance of risk. If risk is deemed to be weighted to the upside for economic growth and inflation, that usually indicates that the Fed is in credit-tightening mode. If risk is perceived as weighted to the downside, then the Fed is usually in an easing or neutral mode.

The FOMC meets roughly every six to eight weeks; the schedule is posted on the Fed's website.[16] The Fed chair conducts a press conference after FOMC meetings (Powell doing so after every meeting versus Bernanke's and Yellen's quarterly schedule, as I mentioned previously). The chair starts with prepared remarks that tend to be a longer version of the statement just issued by the FOMC. The press conference ends with an informative Q&A

session with members of the financial press who cover the Fed on a regular basis. The chairs' answers to the reporters' questions have often moved the financial markets more than the prepared remarks.

The seven members of the Board of Governors and the 12 presidents of the Federal Reserve Banks, all of whom participate in the deliberations of the FOMC, submit individual economic projections in conjunction with four FOMC meetings a year, a practice that began with the October 30–31, 2007 FOMC meeting. The Summary of Economic Projections (SEP) is circulated to the FOMC participants without any attributions showing whose projections are whose. It is also made available to the public as an addendum to the minutes that are released three weeks after each meeting. Since April 2011, an advance version of the SEP table, showing the ranges and central tendencies of the participants' projections, also has been released to the public in conjunction with the chair's post-meeting press conference.

The chair typically discusses the SEP during both the prepared introductory comments and the Q&A session. The SEP includes the consensus economic projections of all the participants, whether they are voters or not. The projections reflect each participant's independent view of the economic and policy outlooks. The dispersion of the projections is one way to assess whether there is a consensus or disagreement within the FOMC on the future course of monetary policy.

The SEP starts with a table showing the medians, central tendencies, and ranges of the forecasts for real gross domestic product (GDP) and the unemployment rate. Similar forecasts are shown for the "headline" inflation rate and the "core" inflation rate, excluding food and energy price inflation. The table then shows projections for the current year and the next three years. At the bottom of the table is a similar set of forecasts for the "projected appropriate policy path" for the federal funds rate. The fun continues with the so-called "dot plot" chart that shows the federal funds rate forecasts of each of the unidentified participants for the current year, the next three years, and the longer run.[17]

Like everyone else who closely watches the Fed, I carefully read the minutes of the FOMC meetings, which are released three weeks after the Fed's policy-setting committee meetings.[18] They are a bit stale, with their key points often overshadowed by the post-meeting statements, by the chair's post-meeting press conference, and by the latest comments of the Fed's various talking heads. But importantly, the minutes often identify the general views attributed to unidentified members (who vote) and unidentified participants (nonvoters). That provides some insight into the breadth of the consensus view on key issues, as well as where the risks are deemed to be. The minutes often specify whether a few, some, or many of the participants held various views or expressed various concerns.

The minutes are organized around a standard outline, with the second-to-last section covering the views of all participants and the last section reserved for the voting members only:

- **Developments in financial markets and open-market operations.** In this section, the deputy manager of the SOMA reports on developments in financial markets and open-market operations since the committee's previous meeting.

- **Staff review of the economic situation.** In this section, the staff economists at the Board of Governors report on the latest developments in the major components of real GDP, focusing on monthly economic indicators that shed light on these developments. Of course, given the Fed's dual mandate, the staff also reports on employment, unemployment, and inflation.

- **Staff review of the financial situation.** Financial conditions are reviewed by the staff in this section of the minutes. This overview covers credit availability, the quality of credit, interest rates, and the stock market. The dollar is rarely mentioned.

- **Staff economic outlook.** Instead of a quantitative presentation of the staff's economic projections, the minutes provide qualitative guidance on the likely direction of key economic variables. In addition, the staff provides an assessment of whether risks to the economic growth and inflation projections are likely to be on the downside or upside.

- **Participants' views on current conditions and the economic outlook.** This section covers the views of the FOMC's official participants (i.e., all seven Board governors, if all the positions are filled, and the 12 regional Fed bank presidents).

- **Committee policy action.** This section discusses only the views of the FOMC's 12 voting members (the seven governors, the Federal Reserve Bank of New York president, and the four currently voting regional presidents in the rotation of the 11 regional presidents), never mentioning the word "participant" (which also includes the nonvoting regional presidents). This last section ends with the same summary statement that is released to the press at 2:00 p.m. following the FOMC meetings.

On my firm's website, we post and update all the FOMC statements going back to 1997.[19] That allows me to search for keywords and phrases when I'm watching for changes in Fed policy or trying to keep track of how long a keyword appeared in the statements. The site also provides links to all the FOMC minutes over that same period, which I also scan for keywords and phrases.

Beyond their official meetings, Fed officials tend to meet professionally on a regular basis. The Fed district banks often organize symposiums to discuss working papers by both Fed and academic economists on matters deemed relevant to monetary policymaking.

One of the most important confabs is sponsored by the Federal Reserve Bank of Kansas City. The annual event started in 1978 and officially became known as the "Jackson Hole Economic Symposium" in 1982, when the location became a tradition. At Jackson Hole, Wyoming, over a long weekend in late August, monetary policy experts gather to discuss a specific topic (e.g., "Fostering a Dynamic Global Economy" in 2017, "Changing Market Structure and Implications for Monetary Policy" in 2018, and "Challenges for Monetary Policy" in 2019). Top officials from the Federal Reserve System and the major central banks around the world participate. The Fed chair usually does so as well and presents a speech that is widely followed. (See Appendix 1, Jackson Hole Economic Symposium Themes, 1978–Present.)

By the way, before 1982, the Kansas City Fed's symposium was held in different places in the district. It was a low-key, academic sort of event. Fed Chair Paul Volcker was invited in 1982 to enhance the gathering's stature. To convince him to come, Jackson Hole was picked because it has lots of good fly fishing, which Volcker enjoyed greatly. Volcker accepted the invitation, and tradition has kept the conference at Jackson Hole ever since.

Another event that Fed chairs attend is a regular get-together with the heads of the world's other major central banks. They meet at the Bank for International Settlements in Basel, Switzerland to discuss monetary policy and enjoy a fine dinner together.

Additionally, the central bank heads often host conferences for one another in their respective countries.

There's never a dull moment for Fed officials, or for Fed watchers.

Chapter 2
William M. Martin: Punch Bowl

Hundreds of Macroeconomists

From my undergraduate days at Cornell University through my graduate education at Yale University, the courses I took in economics prepared me to be either a professor or a policymaker. My interest in managing the economy was only stoked by majoring in macroeconomics as a graduate student at Yale under Nobel laureate James Tobin. This education trained me to meddle. Macroeconomists are professional meddlers who feel a calling to make the world a better place. Our ingrained conceit is that without our meddling, the economy would perform pitifully, stumbling into recessions on a regular basis. It might never regain its footing without our help. Like the Hulk, we are superheroes with the power to lift economies out of ditches. We set economies back on the road to prosperity with just the right mix of fiscal and monetary policies to fine-tune the economy's performance to perfection—or close to it.

I often remind myself that my day job is to predict how the policy wonks will do their job, not to tell them how they should be doing it. I still struggle against the temptation to meddle since I view myself as a recovering macroeconomist.

Janet Yellen and I both received our PhDs from Yale University and studied macroeconomics under Professor Tobin. She graduated in 1971. I graduated in 1976. Despite our similar training, we do not share political views. She's a liberal. I'm a conservative. When she presided over the FOMC, she was powerful and could move markets. I wrote about her power to move the stock market higher, though that isn't technically a Fed mandate.

Bloomberg's Rich Miller posted an interesting October 31, 2013 article about Yellen.[20] He wrote, "As a teaching assistant, Yellen was so meticulous in taking notes during Tobin's macroeconomics class that they ended up as the unofficial textbook for future graduate students." I studied from those wonderfully useful Xeroxed notes. I must thank Yellen for helping me get through Yale's graduate program.

I still fondly recall the IS-LM Model from Yellen's notes. It's a model based on the teachings of John Maynard Keynes that works great on paper but not so well in practice. Also known as the "Hicks–Hansen Model," it is usually shown in a chart where the vertical axis is the economy's interest rate and the horizontal axis is real GDP.[21] These two variables are determined by the intersection of the downward sloping "investment–saving" (IS) line and the upward sloping "liquidity preference–money supply" (LM) line. Stimulative fiscal policy (i.e., deficit-financed government spending or tax cuts) can be used to shift the IS curve to the right, thus boosting real GDP when it is depressed or not growing fast enough to lower the unemployment rate. Alternatively, stimulative monetary policy can shift the LM curve to the right to boost the economy.

The model is extremely simplistic, and macroeconomists have moved on to more complex ones. However, the simple one still seems to drive lots of policy thinking. The model appeals to demand-side macroeconomists who believe, as Keynes did, that demand sometimes needs to be lifted by more government spending or easier monetary policy, or both. It appeals to policymakers' need to meddle, since it posits that when the economy isn't performing well on its own, a dose of fiscal and/or monetary stimulus should do the trick.

In recent years, particularly since the Great Recession of 2008, monetary policy has been doing most of the heavy lifting around the world. That's because the stimulative impact of fiscal policy has been limited by government deficits that have been widening for many years to fund swelling social welfare programs. Most macroeconomists, at least the conservatively inclined bunch, deem that government debt is already too high relative to GDP. Besides, fiscal policy is messier than monetary policy. The former involves working with politicians, who tend to see proposed legislation aimed at boosting economic growth as a wonderful opportunity to add pork-barrel spending that benefits their own constituencies.

On November 18, 2008, as the Great Financial Crisis intensified, Rahm Emanuel, the chief of staff for President-elect Barack Obama, famously stated, "You never want a serious crisis to go to waste. . . . This crisis provides the opportunity for us to do things that you could not before."[22] Lots of politicians and policymakers, not only the ones trained in macroeconomics, follow "Rahm's Rule for Politicians," as I call it.[23]

On the other hand, the Fed and the other major central banks are politically independent, at least in theory. They certainly have more centralized control of their policymaking than do fiscal authorities. Not surprisingly, central bankers have been more than willing to take the leading policy role. That's because in recent years, the central banks have been mostly overrun by macroeconomists, who were trained to play this role. Among top Fed officials, there has been a noticeable shift in backgrounds from businesspeople to economists with PhDs, especially professors from top-ranked universities. In the past, there were more commercial bankers and business executives running monetary policy. They tended to be more conservative and less convinced that monetary policy could work as well as expected and promised by most macroeconomists.

The Fed's website includes a page titled "Meet the Economists." It notes that the Fed employs over 400 PhD economists, adding that:

> [They] represent an exceptionally diverse range of interests and specific areas of expertise. Board economists conduct cutting-edge research, produce numerous working papers, and are among the leading contributors at professional meetings and in major journals. Our economists also produce a wide variety of economic analyses and forecasts for the Board of Governors and the Federal Open Market Committee.[24]

The website categorizes the Fed's economists under five fields of interest: Finance, International Economics, Macroeconomics, Mathematical and Quantitative Methods, and Microeconomics. Not surprisingly, macroeconomists form the clear majority, with only one-third of the Fed's economists specializing mainly in microeconomics.

Justin Fox, a *Bloomberg View* columnist, wrote an interesting article, "How Economics PhDs Took Over the Federal Reserve," for the February 2014 *Harvard Business Review*.[25] He asked former Fed Vice Chair Alan Blinder, a Princeton economics professor, whether an economics PhD basically had become a prerequisite for running the Fed. Blinder responded by email as follows: "I think the answer is 'probably yes' these days. Otherwise, the Fed's staff will run technical rings around you." Fox also observed that "the Federal Reserve System is almost certainly the nation's largest employer of PhD economists." In addition to the ones working at the Board of Governors in Washington, D.C., there are plenty scattered around the research departments and the executive offices of the 12 regional Federal Reserve Banks.

How did the Fed evolve from an organization run by businesspeople to one run by economists? It was a transformation that started with the Banking Act of 1933. Congress reorganized the Fed after it was blamed for bungling monetary policy at the start of the Great Depression.

During its formative years, Fed policy was strongly influenced by Benjamin Strong, Jr. He was the first president of the Federal Reserve Bank of New York. He served for 14 years, from October 5, 1914 to October 16, 1928. He was an extremely effective leader. He was the de facto equivalent to a Fed chair. His premature death in 1928 left a leadership vacuum at the Fed. In a November 8, 2002 speech, then-Fed Governor Ben Bernanke observed that under Strong's successor, George Harrison, "power became diffused; worse, what power there was accrued to men who did not understand central banking from a national and international point of view, as Strong had."

According to Bernanke, "The leadership vacuum and the generally low level of central banking expertise in the Federal Reserve System was a major problem that led to excessive passivity and many poor decisions by the Fed in the years after Strong's death."[26] The Banking Act of 1933 created the FOMC to give the chair in Washington more power.

The Fed's power shift toward Washington continued with the Banking Act of 1935. It changed the name of the "Federal Reserve Board" to the "Board of Governors of the Federal Reserve System." It renamed "members" of the Board as "governors," and increased the number of them from six to seven. The act required the President of the United States to designate one of the persons appointed as "chairman" of the Board and one as "vice chairman" of the Board, each to serve in such roles for a term of four years.[27]

Treasury-Fed Accord Liberates the Fed

The first chair under this new structure was Utah banker Marriner Eccles. His term started February 1, 1936 and ended January 31, 1948. His title was chairman of the Board of Governors of the Federal Reserve Board. The others prior to 1935 were chairman of the Board of Directors of the Federal Reserve System, with much more limited power. (See Appendix 2, Chairs of the Fed's Board of Governors, 1936–Present.)

Perversely, Eccles believed that fiscal policy was much more effective than monetary policy. So the Fed didn't do much to stimulate the economy in the 1930s under his leadership. During World War II, the Treasury Department forced the Fed to buy US government securities to keep interest rates low. In effect, the Fed was running an easy monetary policy to finance the war and continued to do so after the war.

Once World War II was over, the Fed continued its wartime commitment of pegging interest rates. The Treasury-Fed Accord, announced March 4, 1951, freed the Fed from that obligation. A 2001 article in the Federal Reserve Bank of Richmond *Economic Quarterly* reviewed the story.[28] In April 1942, after the United States entered the war, the Fed publicly committed itself to maintaining an interest rate of 3/8% on Treasury bills. In practice, it also established a ceiling for long-term government bonds at 2.50%. In the summer of 1947, the Fed raised the peg on the Treasury bill rate. However, the Treasury insisted that the bond yield stay put.

After the war, policymakers in the Truman administration feared that the economy might fall back into a depression and leaned on the Fed to keep monetary policy easy. Fed officials became increasingly concerned about inflation and wanted their independence back. Indeed, the primary economic problem after the war turned out to be inflation rather than depression. There was a brief bout of inflation when wartime price controls ended during the summer of 1948. Inflation heated up again after the outbreak of the Korean War. Meanwhile, five years of relative economic stability had greatly reduced the fear of falling into another depression. According to the Richmond Fed article:

> The prospect of a prolonged war [in Korea] created the likelihood of government deficits and the issuance of new government debt. Additional debt would force down the price of debt unless the Fed monetized it. That is, to prevent yields from rising above the 2½ percent rate peg, the Fed would have to buy debt and increase bank reserves. Banks would then fuel an inflationary expansion through increases in credit and the money supply.

This led to a momentous change in the way Fed officials viewed their job. They came to believe that they had to control money creation to keep a lid on inflation.

In early 1948, after Eccles retired, President Harry Truman appointed Thomas McCabe, the president and chief executive officer of Scott Paper Company, to run the Fed. McCabe pushed to regain the Fed's power over monetary policy and succeeded in doing so with the Treasury-Fed Accord of 1951. He negotiated the deal with Assistant Treasury Secretary William McChesney Martin. McCabe returned to Scott Paper, and Martin took over as chair of a re-empowered Federal Reserve on April 2, 1951, serving in that position until January 31, 1970 under five Presidents.

The March 1951 Accord freed the Fed and marked the start of the modern Federal Reserve System.

Under Martin, the Fed's overriding goals became price and macroeconomic stability. In his aforementioned article, Fox observed that under Martin's leadership, "regulating the economy through monetary policy pushed aside bank regulation to become the central bank's No. 1 job. So hiring economists, and bringing people with serious economic backgrounds onto the FOMC, became a priority." That's ironic because Martin really didn't like economists much. According to *The Economists' Hour*

(2019) by Binyamin Appelbaum, Martin, who was a stockbroker, told a visitor to the Fed's headquarters, "We have fifty econometricians working at the Fed. They are all located in the basement of the building, and there is a reason why they are there." Martin then acknowledged that they ask good questions, but "they don't know their own limitations, and they have a far greater sense of confidence in their analysis than I have found warranted."[29]

Martin believed that the Fed's job was to be a killjoy, removing the "punch bowl" just when the party was getting hot. His famous metaphor seems to trace back to this part of an October 19, 1955 speech:

> In the field of monetary and credit policy, precautionary action to prevent inflationary excesses is bound to have some onerous effects—if it did not it would be ineffective and futile. Those who have the task of making such policy don't expect you to applaud. The Federal Reserve, as one writer put it, after the recent increase in the discount rate, is in the position of the chaperone who has ordered the punch bowl removed just when the party was really warming up.[30]

In this speech, Martin also observed that monetary policy needs to work with fiscal and budgetary policies:

> But a note should be made here that, while money policy can do a great deal, it is by no means all powerful. In other words, we should not place too heavy a burden on monetary policy. It must be accompanied by appropriate fiscal and budgetary measures if we are to achieve our aim of stable progress. If we ask too much of monetary policy, we will not only fail but we will also discredit this useful, and indeed indispensable, tool for shaping our economic development.

In his 2018 memoir *Keeping At It*, Paul Volcker recalled that in the fall of 1965, Martin was intent on raising interest rates to head off inflationary pressures that were mounting as spending on the

Vietnam War escalated in an economy that was at full employment. The idea of a rate increase alarmed the Treasury secretary, Henry Fowler. Volcker, who was then on staff at the Treasury, noted, "Privately, I was sympathetic to Martin's argument and hoped to persuade the secretary into a compromise: perhaps a quarter-percentage-point increase instead of the planned half-point."

Martin, however, was determined to hike the discount rate by half a point—although he did yield on the timing at the request of President Lyndon Johnson. Johnson pleaded with Martin: "Bill, I have to have my gallbladder taken out tomorrow. You won't do this while I'm in the hospital, will you?" Martin responded, "No, Mr. President, we'll wait until you get out." In early December 1965, the Fed did act, voting to raise the discount rate from 4.0% to 4.5%.[31]

If he were alive today, no doubt Martin would be surprised to see the Fed full of so many macroeconomists committed to moderating the business cycle. In his October 19, 1955 speech, he said, "The idea that the business cycle can be altogether abolished seems to me as fanciful as the notion that the law of supply and demand can be repealed." Yet he unwittingly unlocked the gate, allowing the barbarians to seize the Fed's fortress with the intention of using its power to slay the business-cycle beast, or at least tame it.

Because Martin had refused to boost the economy by lowering interest rates, President Richard Nixon blamed the Fed chair for his 1960 presidential election defeat. Nine years was not too long for Nixon to harbor a grudge. So when Nixon did become President in 1969, he reportedly asked Martin to step aside. But Martin refused to retire early. When his term ended at the start of the following year, Nixon appointed Arthur Burns, someone more to his liking.

Chapter 3
Arthur Burns and G. William Miller: The Hapless Inflators

Fueling the Great Inflation

Arthur Burns served as Fed chair from February 1, 1970 to January 31, 1978 under Presidents Richard Nixon, Gerald Ford, and Jimmy Carter. Burns was an academic, and the first PhD macroeconomist to head the Fed. He taught economics at both Rutgers University (starting in 1927) and Columbia University (1945), having earned his PhD at the latter.

As a doctoral student at Columbia, Burns studied under Wesley Clair Mitchell, a founder of the National Bureau of Economic Research (NBER) and its chief researcher. Mitchell brought Burns into the NBER, where Burns began his lifelong research into the business cycle. Together, in 1946, they published *Measuring Business Cycles*, which introduced the characteristic NBER methods of analyzing business cycles empirically.[32] It was Burns who started the NBER's academic tradition of determining recessions—a role that has been continued by the organization's Business Cycle Dating Committee. The NBER remains the preeminent authority on dating recessions.[33]

Burns served as president and chair of the NBER at points throughout his teaching career. He also chaired the Council of Economic Advisers (CEA) from 1953 to 1956 under President Dwight Eisenhower. The CEA was established by the Employment

Act of 1946, which stated that it is the responsibility of the federal government to create "conditions under which there will be afforded useful employment for those able, willing, and seeking work, and to promote maximum employment, production, and purchasing power." The CEA was created to help President Eisenhower and successive Presidents make sure another Great Depression would never happen. The CEA provides the President with objective economic analysis and advice on the development and implementation of a wide range of domestic and international economic policy issues.

The council's chairman is nominated by the President of the United States and approved by the US Senate. The CEA members are also appointed by the President. The staff of the council includes about 20 academic economists, plus three permanent economic statisticians.

The council is one of the most prestigious destinations in Washington for academic macroeconomists to spend a couple of years as policymakers. An even more prestigious perch is the Board of Governors of the Federal Reserve System. Sometimes, the top CEA job leads to an even more powerful post, chair of the Fed. Arthur Burns, Alan Greenspan, Ben Bernanke, and Janet Yellen all had served as chairs of the CEA before becoming Fed chair. (See Appendix 3, Chairs of the Council of Economic Advisers, 1946–Present.)

When Nixon was elected President in 1968, he persuaded Burns to become his White House counselor, with the understanding that Burns would be appointed chair of the Fed when William McChesney Martin's term ended in early 1970.[34]

Burns assumed leadership of the Federal Reserve in the middle of what would later become known as the "Great Inflation," which lasted from 1965 to 1982 (Fig. 3).[35] During this period, the inflation rate, based on the year-over-year percent change in the consumer price index (CPI), rose from 1.0% in January 1965 to peak at a record high of 14.8% during March 1980. Over the next three years, it subsided remarkably quickly, to 2.5% in July 1983, thanks to the unprecedented moves by Burns' successor, Paul Volcker.

Many Americans who lived through the Great Inflation remember the worst of it as a time of gasoline rationing and long lines at the gas pumps. Paychecks didn't stretch nearly as far at the grocery store as they had before. It seemed to many that the inflation genie wreaking economic havoc could never be put back into the bottle.

Let's take a look at some of the reasons that US inflation spiraled out of control.

- **The dissolution of the Bretton Woods system of international currency management caused an immediate inflationary shock to the US economy in 1971.** On August 15, 1971, Nixon suspended the convertibility of the dollar into gold, which ended the Bretton Woods system that had kept the dollar's value at a constant $35 per ounce of gold since the system was established in 1944. All other currencies were pegged to the dollar, so other countries could present their dollars to the United States and receive gold in exchange.

  By the summer of 1971, this system was no longer viable because other countries collectively had three times more dollars than the United States held in gold. Theoretically, if they all had chosen to redeem their dollars at once, the United States would not have been able to come up with enough gold. That's because the United States was running a mounting balance-of-payments deficit.

  Facing a crisis of confidence within the global financial system, the United States simply closed the gold window, refusing to exchange the foreign central banks' dollars for gold. Foreign currencies were no longer pegged to the dollar or to gold. It was a free market. The value of the dollar in foreign exchange markets suddenly plummeted, causing spikes in import prices as well as the prices of most commodities priced in dollars (Fig. 4). Gold is such a commodity, and its price soared (Fig. 5).

- **Nixon's price-control measures were ineffective solutions.** In late July 1971, Nixon reiterated his adamant opposition to wage and price controls, calling them a scheme to socialize America. Yet less than a month later, he imposed the first and only peacetime wage and price controls in US history. Nixon's stunning reversal was driven by political considerations as the 1972 presidential election was approaching. A 90-day freeze was followed by nearly 1,000 days of measures executed in four phases. Price controls were applied almost entirely to the biggest corporations and labor unions, which were deemed to have price-setting power. However, when these companies and unions requested price increases, most of them were granted. The controls were lifted in 1973.

- **There were food, oil, and labor price shocks.** During the 1970s, several price shocks exacerbated inflation. During 1972 and 1973, for the first time since the Korean War, farm and food prices began to contribute substantially to inflationary pressures in the economy. Also, there was a major oil price shock during 1973 and again in 1979.

On October 19, 1973, immediately following Nixon's request for Congress to make available emergency aid to Israel for the conflict known as the "Yom Kippur War," the Organization of Arab Petroleum Exporting Countries (OAPEC) embargoed oil sales to the United States. On January 16, 1979, the Shah of Iran was forced to leave his country. He was replaced as leader soon after by Ayatollah Khomeini. The country's oil output plunged, and inflation soared around the world along with oil prices.

Together, the two oil price shocks of the 1970s caused the price of a barrel of West Texas crude oil to soar 11-fold from $3.56 during July 1973 to a peak of $39.50 during mid-1980, using available monthly data (Fig. 6). As a result, the CPI inflation rate soared from 2.7% during June 1972 to a record high of 14.8% during March 1980. Even the core inflation rate (i.e., the rate excluding food and energy) jumped from 3.0% to 13.0% over this period as higher energy costs led to faster wage gains, which were passed through into prices economy-wide. During the 1970s, strong labor unions in the private sector succeeded in quickly boosting wages through cost-of-living clauses in their contracts. The result was an inflationary wage-price spiral (Fig. 7).

- **The Fed's monetary response under Burns was inadequate too.** Monetary policy during this period helped spur a surge in inflation and inflation expectations. The Fed did raise interest rates, but the rate hikes were widely viewed as too little, too late to stop higher prices from spiraling into higher wages. The Fed was increasingly criticized for being behind the curve.

According to *The Economists' Hour* (2019) by Binyamin Appelbaum, "Burns told Congress he doubted the Fed had the power to control inflation, which he blamed on the excessive wage demands of labor unions." He also kowtowed to Nixon, who told Burns during one Oval Office meeting, "Err toward inflation."[36]

Under Burns, the Fed responded to the first oil price shock by raising the federal funds rate from a low of 3.18% during the week of March 1, 1972, to a then-high of 13.55% during the week of July 3, 1974 (Fig. 8). The discount rate, at which commercial banks could borrow funds from the Fed, was also raised to a then-record high of 8.00% on April 25, 1974 (Fig. 9). The prime rate offered by banks to their most creditworthy borrowers peaked at a then-record high of 12.00% on July 5, 1974 (Fig. 10). The result was a severe recession from November 1973 to March 1975 that caused the Fed to reverse course, lowering the discount rate from 8.00% to 7.75% on December 9, 1974. The discount rate was cut six more times to 5.25% by November 22, 1976. The federal funds rate fell from 9.00% to 4.75% over this same period.

At the end of his second term, late in 1977, Burns asked to be reappointed for another four years, but no such luck. I think President Carter didn't much like the Fed chair, maybe because he came across as an arrogant, pipe-smoking professor. Instead, Carter appointed G. William Miller, the chief executive of Textron Corporation.

Setting the Stage for Volcker

By some accounts, Arthur Burns poured gasoline on inflation, while G. William Miller lit the match. Miller succeeded Burns as Fed chair on March 8, 1978 but served only 17 months, until August 6, 1979. Inflation was accelerating again as the economy recovered from the first oil price shock. The second oil price shock hit the economy in early 1979, putting the wage-price spiral in overdrive.

Miller remained eerily laid back, believing that the inflation spiral was a transient phenomenon, so he resisted raising interest rates. The trade-weighted dollar dropped 5.4% during Miller's brief tenure (Fig. 11). In late 1978, the Carter administration responded with a "dollar rescue package" that included emergency sales from the US gold stock, executed by borrowing from the International Monetary Fund (IMF), as well as auctions of Treasury securities denominated in foreign currencies.[37]

Miller lacked the experience and the skills for his new job. Most observers were shocked that a few months after taking charge, Miller voted with the minority on the FOMC against raising interest rates. That quickly destroyed confidence in his leadership. The situation only got worse after he gave several interviews the day before the April 1979 FOMC meeting, expressing his view that there was no need to raise interest rates. Press leaks revealed that Miller's dovish stance against inflation was opposed by key administration officials who wanted the Fed to raise interest rates, including Treasury Secretary W. Michael Blumenthal and Charles Schultze, the chair of the CEA.

In any event, during Miller's brief tenure, the FOMC did raise the federal funds rate target from 6 3/4% to 10 5/8%. But that also was widely viewed as too little too late, as inflation continued to move higher while economic growth remained weak. The term "stagflation" was increasingly used by economists and the press to describe the economy's poor performance. The widespread view was that the United States was stuck with an intractable inflation problem.

On July 15, 1979, President Carter responded to the decline in his popularity with his famous "malaise" speech, in which he lamented that the country had not come together to solve its problems. Carter never actually used the word "malaise," but he did use the phrase "crisis of confidence," which was the title of the speech. Carter bemoaned, "The erosion of our confidence in the future is threatening to destroy the social and the political fabric of America."

In his speech, Carter never even intimated that monetary policy had allowed the inflationary price shocks of the 1970s to spiral into wages, which then spiraled back into prices. Instead, he blamed Americans for having become too dependent on foreign sources of oil:

In little more than two decades we've gone from a position of energy independence to one in which almost half the oil we use comes from foreign countries, at prices that are going through the roof. Our excessive dependence on OPEC [Organization of the Petroleum Exporting Countries] has already taken a tremendous toll on our economy and our people. This is the direct cause of the long lines which have made millions of you spend aggravating hours waiting for gasoline. It's a cause of the increased inflation and unemployment that we now face. This intolerable dependence on foreign oil threatens our economic independence and the very security of our nation. The energy crisis is real. It is worldwide. It is a clear and present danger to our nation. These are facts and we simply must face them.[38]

Carter called on Americans to travel less, to use carpools and public transportation, to obey the speed limit, and to lower their thermostats to save fuel.

While it is still widely believed that Carter delivered one of the most depressing speeches ever given to the nation by a sitting US President, the speech was well received, and Carter's poll ratings rose significantly.[39] Then he blew it just two days later when he fired five Cabinet members, including Blumenthal. Doing so suggested that Carter had lost control of his administration.

Carter convinced G. William Miller to leave the Fed to replace Blumenthal at the Treasury. Carter picked Paul Volcker to replace Miller as the new Fed chair. At 6-foot-7, Volcker was a towering personality, both physically and by reputation. A December 9, 2019 article in *The New York Times* on Volcker's death reported this anecdote: "Meeting Mr. Carter in the Oval Office, Volcker slumped on a couch, a familiar cigar in hand, and gestured at Mr. Miller, who was in the room. 'You have to understand,' Mr. Volcker said he told the president, 'if you appoint me, I favor a tighter policy than that fellow.'"[40]

The President was up for reelection in 1980 and was desperate to calm financial markets, which had responded badly to the White House meltdown. Carter knew that Volcker was highly respected in the investment community and in Washington. Indeed, Volcker was confirmed in the Senate with a unanimous vote.

Chapter 4
Paul Volcker: The Great Disinflator

Saturday Night Massacre

Paul Volcker chaired the Fed from August 6, 1979 through August 11, 1987. He is widely credited with ending the inflationary spiral of the 1970s. Rightly so, in my opinion. Volcker didn't have a PhD, but he had a great résumé. After earning his MA in political economy from Harvard University in 1951, he joined the Federal Reserve Bank of New York as a staff economist in 1952. He then became a financial economist with the Chase Manhattan Bank.

In 1962, he was hired by US Treasury Undersecretary for Monetary Affairs Robert Roosa, who had been his mentor in the research department of the New York Fed. Volcker started as the director of financial analysis and was promoted to deputy undersecretary for monetary affairs in 1963. He returned to Chase Manhattan Bank as vice president and director of planning in 1965. He was back at the Treasury from 1969 to 1974, serving as undersecretary for international monetary affairs.

When he was at the Treasury, Volcker was called to attend a meeting at Camp David during August 1971. President Nixon turned the meeting over to John Connally, his Treasury secretary, who laid out the plan to suspend dollar-gold convertibility, ending the Bretton Woods system. Volcker was charged with implementing the plan, which greatly contributed to the inflationary spiral of the 1970s. That's the height of irony, because it was also

Volcker who succeeded in breaking the back of inflation via bold and unprecedented monetary tightening when he took the Fed's helm in late summer of 1979. In his 1975 memoir, Nixon speech-writer Bill Safire wrote:

> Even as we kidded around, the men in the room knew that Volcker was undergoing an especially searing experience. He was schooled in the international monetary system, almost bred to defend it; the Bretton Woods Agreement was sacrosanct to him; all the men he grew up with and dealt with throughout the world trusted each other in crisis to respect the rules and cling to the few constants like the convertibility of gold. Yet here he was participating in the overthrow of all he held permanent; it was not a happy weekend for him.[41]

Volcker included this quote in his own 2018 memoir, *Keeping At It*.[42]

Fed Chair Arthur Burns developed a great respect for Volcker when Volcker was serving in the Treasury. In 1975, Burns picked Volcker to be the president of the Federal Reserve Bank of New York. That meant he sat next to Fed chairmen Burns and then Miller in FOMC meetings during the worst of the Great Inflation period. In his memoir, Volcker recalled, "I became increasingly concerned about monetary policy being overly easy during my time in New York." He began to dissent more forcefully after Burns was replaced by Miller.

Volcker was the president of the Federal Reserve Bank of New York when I worked there for a year and a half at the start of my career. I like to think of him as my first boss, though I obviously was at the bottom of the totem pole. I left in January 1978 to join EF Hutton. Volcker left at the end of July 1979 to head the Fed beginning in August. He was the first Fed chair of any meaningful duration in my career (given his predecessor G. William Miller's short stint).

I learned a simple and important lesson from Volcker early on about how to predict Fed policymaking: Don't second-guess the Fed chair. Volcker did what he said he would do, so betting that he would do so was a good bet and betting otherwise was a bad one. Reading Paul Volcker wasn't hard. He understood that part of his job was to communicate clearly and only as often as necessary to get his message across. He dominated the FOMC and either discouraged public speaking by other FOMC participants overtly or kept them in line subliminally.

The next four Fed chairs followed in Volcker's footsteps, doing exactly what they said they would do—no more, no less. I didn't have to spend much time predicting their next moves. I just had to pay close attention to what they said would be the likely course of monetary policy and make sure that my economic forecast and investment strategy were consistent. The trick was to avoid letting my own views of what they *should* do derail my focus from what they were *most likely* to do. Of course, I also had to predict the economic outlook the best that I could, since that would influence Fed decision-making.

When Volcker took the helm of the Fed, the Great Inflation was well underway. During the summer of 1979, oil prices were soaring again because of the second oil crisis, which started at the beginning of the year when the Shah of Iran was overthrown. Seven months later, in March 1980, the CPI inflation rate peaked at its record high of 14.8%. When Volcker left the Fed during August 1987, he had gotten it back down to 4.3%.

How did he do that?

Volcker didn't waste any time attacking inflation. Eight days after starting his new job, on August 14, 1979, he had the FOMC raise the federal funds rate by 50 basis points to 11.00%.[43] Two days later, on August 16, he called a meeting of the seven members of the Federal Reserve Board to increase the discount rate by half a percentage point to 10.50%. This confirmed that the federal funds rate had been raised by the same amount. Back then, as I previously noted, FOMC decisions about the federal funds rate weren't announced. The markets had to guess. However, the Board's discount rate decisions were announced immediately.

On September 18, 1979, Volcker pushed the Board of Governors for another discount-rate hike of 50 basis points to 11.00%. However, this time, the vote wasn't unanimous; the Board was split four to three. In his memoir, Volcker wrote that market participants concluded that "the Fed was losing its nerve and would fail to maintain a disciplined stance against inflation." The dollar fell and the price of gold hit a new record high.

Volcker, recognizing that the Fed's credibility along with his own were on the line, came up with a simple, though radical, solution that would take the economy's intractable inflation problem right out of the hands of the FOMC and the Board of Governors: The Fed's monetary policy committee would establish growth targets for the money supply and no longer target the federal funds rate.

This new procedure would leave it up to the market to determine the federal funds rate; the FOMC no longer would vote to determine it! This so-called "monetarist" approach to managing monetary policy had a longtime champion in Milton Friedman, who advocated that the Fed should target a fixed growth rate in the money supply and stick to it. Under the circumstances, Volcker was intent on slowing it down, knowing this would push interest rates up sharply.

On October 4, Volcker discussed his plan with the Board of Governors. In his memoir, he noted, "Even the 'doves' who had opposed our last discount-rate increase were broadly supportive, having been taken aback by the market's violent reaction to the split vote." A special meeting of the FOMC was scheduled for

Saturday, October 6.[44] After the meeting, Volcker held an unprecedented evening news conference in the grand boardroom at the Fed's headquarters on Constitution Avenue. It was the first time in memory that a Fed chair held a press conference. The Fed's staff scrambled to assemble the press corps. CBS said that it didn't have a spare camera crew because Pope John Paul II was visiting Washington. Volcker's spokesman persuaded the network to abandon the pontiff. "Send your crew here," he told a CBS producer. "Long after the pope is gone, you'll remember this one."[45]

Volcker proceeded to unleash his own version of the Saturday Night Massacre.[46] He announced that the FOMC had adopted monetarist operating procedures effective immediately. He said, "Business data has been good and better than expected. Inflation data has been bad and perhaps worse than expected." He also stated that the discount rate, which remained under the Fed's control, was being increased a full percentage point to a record 12.00%.[47] In addition, banks were required to set aside more of their deposits as reserves.

The Carter administration immediately endorsed Volcker's October 6 package. Press secretary Jody Powell said that the Fed's moves should "help reduce inflationary expectations, contribute to a stronger US dollar abroad, and curb unhealthy speculation in commodity markets." He added, "The Administration believes that success in reducing inflationary pressures will lead in due course both to lower rates of price increases and to lower interest rates."

The notion that the Fed would no longer target the federal funds rate but instead target growth rates for the major money supply measures came as a shock to the financial community. It meant that interest rates could swing widely and wildly.

And they did.

The economy fell into a deep recession at the start of 1980, as the prime rate soared to an all-time record high of 21.50% during December 1980.[48] The federal funds rate rose to an all-time record high of 20.00% at the start of 1981 (Fig. 12). During 1980, the discount rate was raised to 13.00% on February 15, then lowered three times by 100 basis points down to 10.00% on July 28, then raised again back to 13.00% on December 5, on the way to the all-time record high of 14.00% on May 5, 1981. The trade-weighted dollar index increased dramatically by 56% from 95 on August 6, when Volcker became Fed chair, to a record high of 148 on February 25, 1985.

The public reaction to Volcker's policy move was mostly hostile. Farmers surrounded the Fed's headquarters building in Washington with tractors. Homebuilders sent Volcker sawed-off two-by-fours with angry messages written on them. Community groups staged protests around the Fed's building. Volcker was assigned a bodyguard at the end of 1980. One year later, an armed man entered the Fed apparently intent on taking the Board hostage.

At my first job on Wall Street as the chief economist at EF Hutton, I was an early believer in "disinflation." I first used that word, which means falling inflation, in my June 1981 commentary, "Well on the Road to Disinflation." The CPI inflation rate was 9.6% that month. I predicted that Volcker would succeed in breaking the inflationary uptrend of the 1960s and 1970s. I certainly wasn't a monetarist, given my Keynesian training at Yale. I knew that my former boss wasn't a monetarist either. But I expected that Volcker would use this radical approach to push interest rates up as high as necessary to break the back of inflation.

Volcker must have known that would cause a severe recession. I did too. Back then, I called Volcker's approach "macho monetarism." I figured that a severe recession would bring inflation down, which in turn would force the Fed to reverse its monetary course by easing. Volcker had set the stage for a big drop in bond yields and a major bottom in the stock market.

Rise and Fall of Monetarism

Volcker was no born-again monetarist. He was a pragmatist. He understood the importance of credibility and psychology. He understood financial markets. In a 1982 interview with *The New York Times*, Volcker reviewed the events of late 1979:

> You had a sense in the summer of 1979 that psychologically and otherwise inflation was getting ahead of us. . . . [M]ore forceful action probably had to be taken, and it was only a couple of months after I was here that we adopted this new operating technique—I'm not sure we understood all the implications. You never do. But we understood some of them certainly. . . . What we did was not basically a new idea. I'd thought about it some, but I can't say I'd been an advocate of it. It had some problems. What persuaded me was the need to somehow get a grip on the situation, and on psychology, and this seemed to me a way to do it.[49]

Those were not the words of an ideologue. Monetarism was a means to an end for him. It allowed him to let interest rates soar to break the back of inflation. But first, soaring interest rates broke the back of the economy. During the 1960s and 1970s, interest rates only had to rise above the maximum ceiling rates paid on deposits to cause a recession. The Fed was granted the power to set maximum deposit rates for commercial banks under the Glass–Steagall Act of 1933. The Interest Rate Control Act of 1966 extended deposit rate ceilings to the thrift institutions, which included savings and loan institutions (S&Ls) and mutual savings banks.

When money-market interest rates soared above the ceilings imposed on deposit rates, depositors withdrew their funds from low-yielding, fixed-rate bank deposits and reinvested the proceeds in Treasury bills and other money-market instruments, which offered higher returns. That phenomenon was called "disintermediation," and Volcker's new approach caused lots of it and massacred the market value of the mortgages and other fixed-income assets held by the banks and thrifts. The resulting credit crunch depressed housing activity, sending the economy into a recession.

The thrift industry's representatives turned to Congress for help, which they promptly received. The Depository Institutions Deregulation and Monetary Control Act, signed by President Jimmy Carter on March 31, 1980, phased out "Regulation Q" ceilings for all types of bank accounts except demand deposits from 1981 to 1986. So thrifts could pay much higher interest rates on deposits. Congress also permitted investors to open an unlimited number of accounts, each insured up to $100,000. Previously, $40,000 had been the limit on insured deposits. This was the beginning of a wave of deregulation of the financial sector that had the unintended consequence of setting the stage for more financial crises in coming years.

At the beginning of 1982, my commentaries were growing more critical of the Fed and bearish on the outlook for stocks. In the January 29, 1982 issue, I called on the Fed to abandon monetarism and target real interest rates instead:

> Monetarism is the right idea, at the wrong time. We can't argue
> with the theory: if you want to bring down inflation, you must
> control and gradually lower the growth of the money supply.
> However, the theory is very difficult to operationalize. No one
> can determine which statistical measure of the money supply
> should be controlled.

I noted that monetarism might have worked better in the 1970s, when the financial markets were more rigidly regulated and offered fewer varieties of deposits and investment choices. I predicted that as the jobless rate continued to climb, the Fed would experience "overwhelming political pressure to junk monetarism and lower interest rates."

As an alternative to monetarist operating procedures, I promoted the Real Interest Targeting Approach (RITA) in my January 29, 1982 commentary. I wrote that the Fed should peg the federal funds rate at 300 basis points above the inflation rate. In my plan, this spread could be raised if inflationary pressures persisted or lowered if they eased. This approach would have targeted the inflation rate directly rather than targeting an intermediate variable such as the money supply, which was widely believed (especially by monetarists) to be the major driver of inflation.

As it turned out, I was 30 years early: The Fed finally did adopt an inflation-targeting approach, but not until the beginning of 2012! However, by then the problem was how to boost inflation back up to the Fed's 2.0% inflation target, not how to bring it down.

In a small way, I might have contributed to the political pressure on the Fed to lower interest rates. Dan Quayle (R-IN)—the 44th Vice President of the United States, from January 20, 1989 to January 20, 1993 under President George H.W. Bush—was a freshman conservative Republican senator from Indiana when he introduced a resolution on March 16, 1982 promoting my idea after I discussed it with him. We had been introduced to one another by Dan Murphy, who headed EF Hutton's equity division and was politically well connected. I was invited to explain my plan to the Senate Democratic Conference on July 27, after which Senate Democratic Leader Robert Byrd (D-WV) prepared a bill to force the Fed to abandon monetarism.

The episode was covered in the August 16, 1982 *New York Post* column by Rowland Evans and Robert Novak titled "Dems Move to Force Interest Rates Down." According to the column: "The lineal ancestor of the Democratic scheme is Dr. Edward Yardeni, chief economist of E.F. Hutton." They noted that in my January 29 newsletter, I predicted a 30% chance of a depression in 1982 unless the Fed abandoned monetarism. Just five years earlier, I had been a staff economist working near the bottom of the Fed's totem pole under Volcker.

The Fed was getting the message. On July 20, 1982, in his mid-year monetary policy report to Congress, Volcker indicated that the Fed soon would lower interest rates. Political pressure was a factor. More important, without a doubt, was a string of financial crises:

- **Drysdale.** In May, Drysdale Government Securities defaulted on interest payments due on Treasury securities that it had borrowed from other firms. Chase Manhattan Bank declared a pre-tax loss of $285 million as a result of Drysdale's failure. Chase had served as a middleman in Drysdale's transactions.

- **Penn Square.** In July, Penn Square Bank failed as a result of a large amount of poorly underwritten energy-related loans that it had sold to other banks. Losses on these loans led to significant financial problems for a number of those banks.

- **Lombard-Wall.** On August 12, Wall Street was shaken by the failure of a little-known government securities firm, Lombard-Wall Inc., and its wholly owned subsidiary, Lombard-Wall Money Markets. In a bankruptcy petition, the firm listed debts of $177.2 million to its 10 largest unsecured creditors. The two biggest were the Chase Manhattan Bank, which was owed $45 million, and the New York State Dormitory Authority, which was owed $55 million.[50]

- **Mexico.** Also on August 12, Mexico's Finance Minister, Jesus Silva-Herzog, declared that Mexico no longer would be able to service its debt. The steep rise in oil prices during the 1970s had flooded American banks with petrodollars (i.e., deposits from the oil exporters). The banks lent lots of those funds back to oil-exporting countries such as Mexico. Volcker's Saturday Night Massacre certainly massacred Mexican borrowers who no longer could afford to make their loan payments to the banks.

The discount rate, which had been hiked to a record high of 14.00% on May 5, 1981, was cut five times, by 350 basis points, to 10.50% by August 16, 1982. On that day—Monday, August 16, 1982—at the regularly scheduled 7:30 a.m. morning strategy meeting with my firm's sales force, I said that it was time to be bullish on stocks again. The lead story in my weekly commentary was "Fed-Led Recovery Now Seems Likely." I wrote, emphasizing with italics, *"We now believe that our upbeat forecast for 1983 is achievable and should positively influence both the bond and equity markets."* The Dow Jones Industrial Average (DJIA) subsequently rose 1,409% from a low of 777 on August 12, 1982 to peak at 11723 on January 14, 2000.[51] By the end of 2019, it was up above 28000.

The Fed's experiment with monetarist operating procedures lasted only three years, ending at the October 5, 1982 meeting of the FOMC.[52] I anticipated this might happen at the start of that year, writing in my January 29 commentary: "Should the Fed abandon monetarism? It may be forced to do so shortly." I observed that high interest rates combined with a severe recession were increasing the demand for liquidity, which boosted the growth rate of the M1 measure of the money supply. I added, "Once the unemployment rate hits 10%, as we expect it soon will, the Fed will experience overwhelming political pressure to junk monetarism and lower interest rates."

The unemployment rate rose from 8.6% at the start of 1982 to peak at 10.8% during November and December, the highest since the Great Depression (Fig. 13). On Thursday, October 7, *The Wall Street Journal* reported that the FOMC had decided at its meeting on October 5 to temporarily suspend its monetarist operating procedures. Volcker confirmed the change in a speech to the Business Council later that week on October 9. He said, "What is needed is market conviction that the fundamentals are consistent with lower interest rates, and I believe that is what we have been seeing for some months." He emphasized that lower interest rates are a "reward for success in dealing with inflation."

He reiterated his pragmatic approach, saying, "You have also heard me repeatedly express caution about the validity of any single [money supply] measure, or even all the measures in the short run." In his memoir, Volcker wrote: "The fact is that institutional developments, most importantly the end of interest-rate controls on bank deposits, had led to a revision of narrow money supply measurements and definitions." In other words, monetarism didn't work when the Fed couldn't measure, let alone define, the relevant monetary aggregate necessary to implement this approach.

My December 29, 1982 commentary was titled "Milton's Paradise Lost." I observed that in his December 27 *Newsweek* column, Milton Friedman, the father of monetarism, had sketched a terrible outlook for 1983 and 1984, clearly upset that the Fed had abandoned his approach. He warned:

> [T]he monetary explosion that started in July 1982 is almost certain to bring on a recovery starting within the next few months. As the recovery gathers steam, interest rates will erupt. The monetary explosion is then likely to end with a bang and be followed by negligible or negative monetary growth. As in 1982, that would abort the recovery and produce a renewed recession, probably starting in 1984.

I disagreed with what amounted to a "triple-dip recession" scenario. I argued in my year-end commentary that the evidence strongly suggested individuals were responding to the world economic crisis by building up precautionary balances of liquid assets: "So the increased demand for money actually reflects the effects of the recession; it does not foreshadow a super-hot recovery." I noted that my assessment was confirmed by the sharp decline in the ratio of nominal GDP to the M1 measure of the money supply (i.e., the so-called "velocity of money").

I didn't know it at the time, but I had sided with some members of the FOMC who, according to the November 16, 1982 transcript of the committee, believed that the falling velocity of money suggested "a distinct break from earlier postwar experience," resulting from "unusual economic and financial uncertainties." This was "inducing a greater desire to hold liquid assets than had been assumed in setting the annual [monetary] targets."[53] Here's more from my commentary at the end of 1982:

> In his November 24 testimony before the Joint Economic Committee, Volcker reiterated this view. In my year-end 1982 commentary, I concluded: Friedman's monetarism works best in Shangri-La, where the velocity of money is stable and predictable. In our economy, which is experiencing an infernal recession along with major structural and institutional changes, velocity is neither stable nor predictable. That's why the Fed abandoned "knee-jerk" monetarism in October and is now practicing "judgmental" monetarism. We think the new, more eclectic approach can deliver lower inflation and a sustainable recovery. That would be paradise.

Monetarism never recovered following its short heyday. A 2017 Federal Reserve Bank of Richmond working paper by Robert Hetzel was titled "What Remains of Milton Friedman's Monetarism?"[54]

Despite the author's best efforts to be constructive, I concluded that the answer to his question was "not much."

The CPI headline inflation rate dropped from a record high of 14.8% year over year during March 1980 to a low of 1.1% during December 1986. This was an extraordinary achievement for Volcker. Contrary to widely held belief, he proved that the inflation rate wasn't intractable but could be clipped in short order.

Volcker was reappointed by President Reagan during June 1983 for a second term. This time, the Senate confirmation vote was not unanimous. Eight Republicans and eight Democrats voted against Volcker, while 84 approved. By the start of his second term, the discount rate had been lowered to 8.50%. The recession had ended during November 1982.

On Thursday, May 10, 1984, there was a massive run on Continental Illinois National Bank and Trust Company, the seventh largest bank in the United States and the largest in the Midwest. It was triggered by rumors of the bank's insolvency after the bank reported a significant increase in nonperforming loans including speculative energy-related ones purchased from Penn Square Bank. It was the largest bank failure in US history, and it remained so until the Great Financial Crisis. On Friday, May 11, the bank borrowed $3.6 billion from the Federal Reserve Bank of Chicago. Though the Fed was not technically involved in the rescue beyond its discount window lending, the Fed was actively involved in discussions with the other bank regulators about bailing out the bank, which gave popular rise to the term "too big to fail."[55]

At the May 21–22 meeting of the FOMC, several participants favored tighter monetary policy. However, Volcker said that financial market fragility, from both Continental Illinois and the developing country crisis, ruled that out.[56]

On July 24, 1984, Volcker was summoned to meet with President Reagan in the White House. Reagan didn't say a word.

Instead, his chief of staff Jim Baker said, "The president is ordering you not to raise interest rates before the election." In his memoir, Volcker wrote that he was stunned because he had no plans for raising rates especially after the Continental Illinois bank bailout. He wrote: "I walked out without saying a word."

Volcker resigned on June 3, 1987. Reagan was ready to appoint him to a third four-year term, but he left for personal reasons, mostly to spend more time in New York City with his wife, Barbara. She struggled for much of her life from debilitating rheumatoid arthritis as well as diabetes and remained in New York to be near her longtime physician. After Volcker resigned from the Fed, his wife told a reporter: "I think he's really got mixed feelings about this. He thrives on work that he loves. I'm not sure that he will find something that will challenge him—like a hospital that's falling apart at the seams. He really needs something that's falling apart."[57]

Sure enough, after leaving the Fed, Volker became chairman of the prominent New York investment banking firm, Wolfensohn & Co., but remained active in his public service pursuits including investigations into the dormant Swiss bank accounts of Jewish victims of the Holocaust and possible corruption in the UN's Iraqi Oil for Food program. On January 21, 2010, President Barack Obama endorsed a set of bank regulations proposed by Volcker. The President dubbed them "The Volcker Rule." It would prevent commercial banks from owning and investing in hedge funds and private equity, and it would limit the trading they do for their own accounts.

Volcker was no fan of financial deregulation and innovation. He was a prescient financial conservative. In a February 2005 speech at Stanford University, he observed, "Baby boomers are spending like there is no tomorrow . . . and buying lots of houses at rising prices." He warned, "The capital markets which have been so benign in providing flexibility . . . can become a point of great vulnerability." He predicted, "Big adjustments will inevitably come . . . And as things stand it is more likely than not that it will be a financial crisis rather than policy foresight that will force the change."[58]

In fact, he made his aversion to innovation crystal clear at a conference in late 2009, just after the Great Financial Crisis. Railing against the ineffectual financial regulation and innovation that had catalyzed the crisis, he lamented: "I wish that somebody would give me some shred of neutral evidence about the relationship between financial innovation recently and the growth of the economy, just one shred of information." He even glorified the lowly ATM as the last of the useful financial innovations to underscore his point that new banking products, such as credit derivatives, effectively had turned Wall Street into a trillion-dollar casino:

> [T]he most important financial innovation that I have seen the past 20 years is the automatic teller machine. That really helps people and prevents visits to the bank and is a real convenience. How many other innovations can you tell me that have been as important to the individual as the automatic teller machine, which is in fact more of a mechanical innovation than a financial one?[59]

Volcker passed away on December 8, 2019. He was a truly great American hero.

Chapter 5
Alan Greenspan: The Great Asset Inflator

Ayn Rand's Disciple

President Reagan picked Alan Greenspan to succeed Paul Volcker as Fed chair. He served from August 11, 1987 until January 31, 2006. He was approved by a 91-to-2 vote in the Senate. Voting against the nomination were Senators Bill Bradley (D-NJ) and Kent Conrad (D-ND). Bradley presciently warned that Greenspan "will move too rapidly toward deregulation [of the banking industry], rather than showing the same caution as Chairman Volcker."

Another senator for whom Greenspan's stance on banking deregulation didn't sit well was William Proxmire (D-WI), chair of the Senate Banking Committee. Despite disagreeing with Greenspan's view that the banking industry needed more deregulation, Proxmire supported the nomination. He thought Greenspan would fight inflation as aggressively as Volcker did.[60]

Before he became chair of the Federal Reserve Board, Greenspan had his own economic consulting firm. He also served from 1974 to 1977 as chair of the CEA under President Gerald Ford. Greenspan had earned a PhD in economics from New York University (NYU) decades after leaving graduate school at Columbia to start his consulting firm. At Columbia, Arthur Burns had been one of his professors.

In his 2008 book, *Deception and Abuse at the Fed*, Robert Auerbach, a University of Texas professor, claimed that the PhD was only honorary, strongly implying that it was obtained in a few months just after Greenspan had completed a stint as chair of the CEA for Presidents Nixon and Ford.[61] Interestingly, Greenspan's dissertation was removed from the public shelves of NYU's Bobst Library at the author's request in 1987, the year President Reagan appointed him chair of the Federal Reserve Board. Upset that Auerbach was impugning NYU's reputation, Paul Wachtel, an NYU economics professor who was on Greenspan's thesis committee, provided a copy of the thesis to *Barron's* Jim McTague, who had reviewed the Auerbach book. The dissertation was unusual: a collection of Greenspan's previously published articles.[62]

The Fed chair's message has always been vitally important to investors and traders. Yet Greenspan was renowned for his "verbal obscurity and caution," noted Bob Woodward (renowned himself as an investigative reporter and co-author of *All the President's Men*); Woodward wrote a glowing book about Greenspan, *Maestro*, published in 2000. Greenspan was often asked to explain what he meant, Woodward observed, and left the questioner even more confused by his response. Greenspan once joked, "If I turn out to be particularly clear, you've probably misunderstood what I said."[63]

Around the time that the Fed chair famously questioned whether stock investors had become irrationally exuberant, he also haphazardly popped the marital question to television journalist Andrea Mitchell, his girlfriend of nearly 12 years:

> He later confided to one person that he actually proposed to Mitchell twice before she accepted, but either she had not understood what he was saying or it had failed to register. His verbal obscurity and caution were so ingrained that Mitchell didn't even know that he had asked her to marry him. . . . On Christmas Day [1996], Greenspan finally asked, flat out, "Do

you want a big wedding or a small wedding?" It was a message no one could miss.[64]

The trick to deciphering key messages in Greenspan's often convoluted lexicon was to think like a cryptographer, looking for repetitive phrases and themes in his frequent public statements. He enjoyed the limelight and gave many more speeches than his predecessors. I detected several themes along the way.

I knew that Greenspan was a proponent of free-market capitalism, having been strongly influenced by the views of Ayn Rand. In the early 1950s, Greenspan had become a member of Rand's inner circle, dubbed the "Ayn Rand Collective," who read her novel *Atlas Shrugged* (1957) as she was writing it. He contributed several essays for Rand's *Capitalism: The Unknown Ideal* (1966), including one supporting the gold standard. Rand stood beside him at his 1974 swearing-in ceremony as chair of the CEA, and they remained friends until her death in 1982.

Greenspan was a big believer in the invisible hand of competitive markets. He pushed hard for the deregulation of business, particularly of the financial industry. So he fit in well with the Reagan team during the first two years of his tenure as Fed chair. However, his policy moves on a few notable occasions showed that he wasn't averse to giving the stock market a visible hand when it seemed to need some help. Furthermore, he believed that it wasn't the Fed's job to stop asset bubbles because doing so might hurt the economy. In his view, it was better to let the bubbles pop and to clean up the mess afterward.

Greenspan's Put

During his long tenure at the Fed, Greenspan had great confidence in Wall Street, and Wall Street had great confidence in what came to be known as the "Greenspan Put," or actions Greenspan took to show investors he had their backs. That was quite different than Volcker's relationship with Wall Street. Volcker obviously was unperturbed by the bearish consequences of his policies on the stock market as he focused determinedly on breaking inflation. Nobody in the stock market thought he had their back.

Greenspan faced his first major test in office just two months after starting the job. The stock market crashed on Black Monday, October 19, 1987.

The stock market started heading lower after its 1987 peak was hit on August 25. Shortly after Greenspan joined the Fed, he fired a "preemptive strike" against inflation by raising the discount rate by 50 basis points to 6.00% on September 4 (Fig. 14).

It wasn't just the rate hike that hammered the stock market. The week before Black Monday, investors were further unnerved by news that the House Ways and Means Committee threatened to eliminate the tax deduction for interest paid on debt used in corporate takeovers. Equities had been boosted by some favorable tax treatments for financing corporate buyouts that included this deduction, which multiplied the number of potential takeover targets and pushed up their stock prices. At the time, big deals were driving stock prices higher.

Many investors and traders learned of this plan from a *Wall Street Journal* story on Wednesday, October 14. The day before, the Democrats on the committee agreed on a number of tax-raising measures, including the elimination of the deduction for interest expenses exceeding $5 million a year on debt from a takeover or leveraged buyout. The full committee approved the package on Thursday, October 15. Takeover stocks were pummeled late during the trading day. Several announced and unannounced deals were delayed. Arbitrageurs sold large blocks of the stocks.[65]

Also on Wednesday, October 14, the Commerce Department reported a record-high merchandise trade deficit for the United

States. A few days later, on Saturday, October 17, Treasury Secretary James Baker told German authorities to "either inflate your mark, or we'll devalue the dollar." The next day, Baker proclaimed on Sunday's television talk shows that the US "would not accept" the recent German interest-rate increase. Shortly thereafter, an unnamed Treasury official said we would "drive the dollar down" if necessary.

The S&P 500 plunged 20.5% on Black Monday. The market's freefall was exacerbated by "portfolio insurance" strategies that had backfired.[66] These strategies presumably provided insurance against a stock market decline in a process called "dynamic hedging" by selling more stock index futures contracts, with the resulting gains offsetting the losses in the stocks held in a portfolio.

Under Greenspan's leadership, the Fed immediately responded to the crash by issuing a statement affirming its readiness to serve as a source of liquidity to support the economic and financial system. The federal funds rate fell from 7.25% on October 19 to 6.50% in early 1988. Gerald Corrigan, the president of the New York Fed, pressured the major New York banks to double their normal lending to securities firms, enabling brokers to meet cash calls. Greenspan later told the Senate Banking Committee that the Fed's strategy during Black Monday was "aimed at shrinking irrational reactions in the financial system to an irreducible minimum."[67] That was the beginning of the Greenspan Put and affirmed my view that the financial crisis could mean buying opportunities in the stock market.

In response to the 1987 crash, President Reagan signed an executive order on March 18, 1988 that created the President's Working Group on Financial Markets, consisting of the Treasury Secretary, the Fed chair, and the heads of both the Securities and Exchange Commission and the Commodity Futures Trading Commission (CFTC). It came to be known colloquially as the "Plunge Protection

Team." Conspiracy buffs have suspected that from time to time it has coordinated covert measures to support the stock market.

I recognized early on that Greenspan had turned into an enthusiastic cheerleader for the bull market of the 1990s. My own bullishness was buttressed by Greenspan's unabashed enthusiasm. He promoted the notion that the technology revolution of the 1990s might be boosting productivity growth. As stock prices soared over the course of that decade, Greenspan made it increasingly clear that he didn't believe they were in a bubble. If the Maestro wasn't concerned about a bubble, many investors must have figured that they needn't be.

That's why a simple thought-provoking question Greenspan posed near the end of his speech on December 5, 1996 sent the investment community reeling. Greenspan famously asked, "But how do we know when irrational exuberance has unduly escalated asset values, which then become subject to unexpected and prolonged contractions, as they have in Japan over the past decade?"[68]

That sounded like he was concerned about a bubble in the stock market after all! Little attention was paid to the fact that he was just asking the question, not answering it. He was thinking out loud, essentially. Indeed, right before posing the question, he suggested that stocks were *not* irrationally exuberant given that "sustained low inflation implies less uncertainty about the future, and lower risk premiums imply higher prices of stocks and other earning assets."

Greenspan liked to muse out loud, as if he were chatting with an economist buddy over the phone and his words were not hung on by lots of people around the world and acted upon in global financial markets. The key to interpreting what Greenspan meant was to stick with his underlying themes and not get sidetracked by his occasional Hamlet-like "to be or not to be" musings.

In that 1996 speech, he was playing the "two-handed econo-mist," saying that on the one hand, the Fed shouldn't worry about bubbles that burst—as long as they didn't hurt the economy. He cited the example of the 1987 stock market crash. On the other hand, he said the Fed shouldn't be complacent about them either, because they might be big enough to do real damage when they burst.

He was at it again during his July 22, 1997 congressional tes-timony on monetary policy. He suggested that productivity was making a big comeback, but he also hedged that concept as follows:

> We do not now know, nor do I suspect can anyone know, whether current developments are part of a once or twice in a century phenomenon that will carry productivity trends nationally and globally to a new higher track, or whether we are merely observing some unusual variations within the context of an otherwise generally conventional business cycle expansion. The recent improvement in productivity could be just transitory, an artifact of a temporary surge in demand and output growth.[69]

Greenspan's thinking about bubbles evolved over time. During the Q&A segment of his congressional testimony on January 28, 1999, only two years after he first wondered out loud about irra-tional exuberance—when stock valuations were even more irra-tionally exuberant—he suggested that he now believed elevated valuations could be justified based on a "lottery principle":

> And undoubtedly some of these small companies, which . . . are going through the roof, will succeed. And they very well may justify even higher [stock] prices. The vast majority are almost sure to fail. That's the way the markets tend to work in this regard. There's something else going on here, though, which is a fascinating thing to watch, and it's, for want of a better term, the lottery principle. What lottery managers have

known for centuries is that you could get somebody to pay for a one-in-a-million shot more than the value of that chance. In other words, people pay more for a claim on a very big payoff, that's where the profits from lotteries have always come from. And what that means is that when you're dealing with stocks—the possibilities of which are either it's going to be valued at zero or some huge number—you get a premium in that stock price which is exactly the same sort of price evaluation process that goes on in a lottery. So the more volatile the potential outlook—and indeed, in most of these types of issues, that's precisely what is happening—you will get a lottery premium in the stock.[70]

Laurence H. Meyer was a Federal Reserve governor from June 1996 to January 2002. In his 2006 book *A Term at the Fed: An Insider's View*, he observed that during much of that period, he was involved in a debate with Greenspan about the outlook for productivity and inflation. He readily and graciously conceded that Greenspan won the debate.

According to Meyer, the Fed chair was convinced as early as 1996, if not earlier, that "the new economy was being fueled by the new computer and communications technologies, which were pumping up productivity." The data didn't confirm Greenspan's conviction until the late 1990s; nevertheless, he "passionately" supported the idea of the New Economy concept.[71] Meyer candidly admitted that, at first, he was the FOMC member most convinced that there was no evidence the economy could grow faster without stimulating inflation.[72] However, he came to doubt the validity of the Phillips curve model, which predicted rising inflation as the unemployment rate fell below the non-accelerating inflation rate of unemployment (NAIRU).[73]

As it turned out, Greenspan's hunch about productivity was on the money. During November 1999, the Bureau of Labor Statistics in the US Department of Labor revised productivity growth rates upward for the 1990–1998 period to 2.0% from 1.4%. The revised rate was even higher for the most recent three years of that span, 1995 to 1998: 2.6%, up from 1.9%.[74] These revisions put to rest the apparent disparity between the data and Greenspan's view.[75]

Meyer wrote, "We now had an explanation for the puzzling, apparent breakdown of the NAIRU model . . . if the NAIRU and the unemployment rate were falling simultaneously, it was possible that inflation could be stable—or even decline."[76]

Several years after the 1987 stock market crash and about a year before he won the productivity debate, Greenspan was put to the test again when the Russian government defaulted on its debt on August 17, 1998 and, more importantly, when Long-Term Capital Management (LTCM) blew up in September 1998. LTCM was founded in 1994 by renowned Salomon Brothers bond trader John Meriwether. Members of LTCM's board of directors included Myron S. Scholes and Robert C. Merton, who shared the 1997 Nobel Memorial Prize in Economic Sciences for a "new method to determine the value of derivatives."

The firm relied on quantitative models to generate eye-popping returns for a few years, attracting more investors. On a notional basis, the huge hedge fund had accumulated more than $1 trillion in over-the-counter (OTC) derivatives and $125 billion in securities on only $4.8 billion of capital. The spectacular returns popped during 1998, when the firm lost $4.6 billion in less than four months. LTCM's quant models worked until they didn't.

LTCM did business with nearly every major firm on Wall Street and was highly leveraged in various trading strategies that went awry. There was widespread fear on the Street that its failure could trigger a financial contagion, resulting in catastrophic losses throughout the financial system. The Federal Reserve Bank of

New York orchestrated a $3.63 billion bailout of the firm by its 14 OTC dealers, who had been clueless about LTCM's enormous bets.

In retrospect, the LTCM incident foreshadowed the global economy-wide blowup in 2008, holding advance warnings and cautionary lessons about derivatives, leverage, and risk—as well as quant models. That all fell on deaf ears.

Had the Fed not existed, Wall Street would have had to clean up its own mess—as J.P. Morgan did during the Panic of 1907. That scare prompted Congress to commission a 23-volume study on central banking that led to the formation of the Federal Reserve System. But in the case of the LTCM panic, the Fed was there to coordinate the cleanup efforts that contained the damage, avoiding contagion—at that time.

Once again, a financial crisis turned out to be a great buying opportunity thanks to the Greenspan Put. The FOMC lowered the federal funds rate three times, by a total of 75 basis points, from 5.50% on September 29, 1998 to 4.75% on November 17 of that year. The S&P 500 jumped 59.6% from its post-Russian-default low on August 31, 1998 through the March 24, 2000 peak. Over this same period, the Nasdaq soared by an astonishing 231.0%. Investors got the reassuring message that the Fed would come to the rescue every time the financial markets got into trouble.

Greenspan updated his hands-off approach to stock market bubbles during his June 17, 1999 congressional testimony:

> The 1990s have witnessed one of the great bull stock markets in American history. Whether that means an unstable bubble has developed in its wake is difficult to assess. A large number of analysts have judged the level of equity prices to be excessive, even taking into account the rise in "fair value" resulting from the acceleration of productivity and the associated long-term corporate earnings outlook. But bubbles generally are perceptible only after the fact. To spot a bubble in advance

requires a judgment that hundreds of thousands of informed investors have it all wrong. Betting against markets is usually precarious at best. While bubbles that burst are scarcely benign, the consequences need not be catastrophic for the economy.[77]

When the technology-led stock market bubble burst in 2000, the Fed once again responded quickly to contain the adverse financial and economic impact. A severe bear market ensued nonetheless, and so did a recession. Most of the so-called dot-com companies (i.e., Internet startups) had burned through their cash. Investors were no longer willing to provide more of it, and many of these companies either slashed their spending or simply went out of business. Investors lost lots of money.

The stock market downturn was exacerbated by accounting scandals revolving around Enron (2001), Haliburton (2002), Tyco (2002), and WorldCom (2002). They all had criminally cooked their books to boost their earnings. With the benefit of hindsight, investors wondered whether technology companies had done the same by pushing the limits of legitimate accounting practices. Doubts about the quality of earnings accelerated the plunge in valuation multiples. The bear market in stocks, especially technology stocks, was severe.

The economic recession from March through November 2001 wasn't that bad, despite the horrible shock of the 9/11 terrorist attacks. Yet Fed officials seemed traumatized by the events. They were particularly troubled by the sharp drop in the CPI inflation rate from 3.7% at the start of 2001 to 1.1% one year later. Deflation (i.e., falling prices) became a big worry. Fed Governor Ben Bernanke presented his famous speech "Deflation: Making Sure 'It' Doesn't Happen Here" on November 21, 2002.[78]

Although the economy started to recover at the end of 2001, the Fed delayed raising interest rates until the June 2004 meeting of the FOMC. In his premature mission-accomplished speech on January 3, 2004 before the American Economic Association, Greenspan concluded, "But we trust that monetary policy has meaningfully contributed to the impressive performance of our economy in recent decades."

But what about the recession that followed the bursting of the bubble in high-tech stocks only three years earlier? The experience confirmed in Greenspan's mind the logic of his approach to handling bubbles. In his speech, he bragged: "Instead of trying to contain a putative bubble by drastic actions with largely unpredictable consequences, we chose, as we noted in our mid-1999 congressional testimony, to focus on policies 'to mitigate the fallout when it occurs and, hopefully, ease the transition to the next expansion.'"[79] He said that just as one of the greatest bubbles of all time was starting to inflate, this time in the housing market.

Global Savings Glut

The federal funds rate was increased by 25 basis points to 1.25% at the June 29–30, 2004 meeting of the FOMC. That was followed by increases of 25 basis points at every one of the next 16 meetings, putting the rate at 5.25% after the June 29, 2006 meeting. It remained at that level through August 2007. Greenspan explained that the "measured pace" of tightening was necessary to sustain the recovery and avert deflation. That was a first: Such a cautious and predictable normalization of monetary policy had never happened before.

The predictability of the Fed's measured rate hikes also increased the gains from carry trades in which bonds could be financed with short-term borrowing as long as the trader was reasonably confident that those borrowing costs would remain below the yield on the bonds. Of course, that trade wouldn't work if bond yields rose, causing bond prices to fall.

However, yields didn't rise. Instead, the 10-year US Treasury bond yield fluctuated around 4.50% from 2001 to 2007. That was a big surprise given that short-term rates were almost certainly going to go up at every FOMC meeting, albeit at an incremental pace, once the Fed commenced its measured rate hikes. Mortgage rates, which tend to move with the 10-year US Treasury yield, also diverged from the steady upward march of the federal funds rate.

That phenomenon in the bond market became known as "Greenspan's conundrum." In his February 16, 2005 semiannual testimony to Congress on monetary policy, the Fed chair said globalization might be expanding productive capacity around the world and moderating inflation. It might also be increasing the size of the global savings pool. He concluded:

> But none of this is new and hence it is difficult to attribute the long-term interest rate declines of the last nine months to glacially increasing globalization. For the moment, the broadly unanticipated behavior of world bond markets remains a conundrum. Bond price movements may be a short-term aberration, but it will be some time before we are able to better judge the forces underlying recent experience.[80]

On March 10, 2005, Fed Governor Ben Bernanke sought to solve the puzzle that Greenspan had presented just three weeks earlier in a speech titled "The Global Savings Glut and the U.S. Current Account Deficit."[81] Bernanke argued that the US bond market during the 2000s was increasingly driven by countries outside of the United States. In his narrative, there was a "global savings glut." The United States was running large trade deficits with the rest of the world, and increasingly with emerging market economies such as China. Chinese and other foreign investors reciprocated by buying our bonds rather than our companies' exported goods, which increasingly were manufactured overseas. Ten years later, in an April 1, 2015 blog post, Bernanke continued to promote this thesis:

> Some years ago I discussed the macroeconomic implications of global flows of saving and investment under the rubric of the "global savings glut". My conclusion was that a global excess of desired saving over desired investment, emanating in large part from China and other Asian emerging market economies and oil producers like Saudi Arabia, was a major reason for low global interest rates. I argued that the flow of global saving into the United States helped to explain the "conundrum" (to use Alan Greenspan's term) of persistently low longer-term interest rates in the mid-2000's while the Fed was raising short-term rates. Strong capital inflows also pushed up the value of the dollar and helped create the very large U.S. trade deficit of the time, nearly 6 percent of U.S. gross domestic product in 2006.[82]

The global savings glut thesis explained Greenspan's conundrum and allowed both Greenspan and Bernanke to blame foreign investors for the easy credit conditions that inflated the US housing bubble. According to their narrative, foreigners purchased lots of mortgage-backed bonds, which kept credit conditions in the housing market too loose despite the Fed's attempts to tighten them.

With the benefit of hindsight, Greenspan's critics blamed the Fed for raising interest rates too gradually, and too predictably. They charged that the resulting reach for yield by investors around the world led to the excesses in the US credit derivatives markets, which fueled the housing bubble.

Keep in mind that the Fed was concerned about deflation at the time, as evidenced by Bernanke's famous 2002 speech on the subject. In addition, the unsettling bursting of the tech bubble at the beginning of the decade and the terrorist attacks of September 11, 2001 likely contributed to the Fed's cautious policy stance.

This stance, the critics contend, resulted in excessive credit demands in the United States that were readily met as investors reached for yield. I tend to agree with the critics, though I also think that there may be some validity to the global savings glut view. After all, in an increasingly globalized world, external forces affect the US credit market too. The Fed isn't totally to blame for creating the credit conditions that led to the housing boom and subsequent bust.

Laissez-Faire

Given his laissez-faire views, Greenspan's Fed wasn't as focused on regulating banks as on managing the economy and monetary policy. As a big champion of deregulation, he argued that it was necessary to allow US banks to compete with big foreign rivals. He also believed that deregulated capital markets would finance more startups and thus increase competition.

In 1996, the Fed allowed banks to derive 25% of their revenue from securities businesses, up from a previous cap of 10%, if they did so through a separate subsidiary. In April 1997, Bankers Trust bought the investment bank Alex. Brown & Co., becoming the first US bank to acquire a securities firm since the 1920s, before the Great Depression. Bankers Trust became a leader in the emerging derivatives business in the early 1990s. In early 1994, the bank suffered an embarrassment when some complex derivative transactions resulted in large losses for major corporate clients.

In August 1997, the Fed's Board of Governors stated that the risks of underwriting had proven to be "manageable" and granted banks the right to acquire securities firms outright. Deutsche Bank acquired Bankers Trust, a major commercial bank, along with Alex. Brown in December 1998. The following year, in March, Bankers Trust pleaded guilty to institutional fraud for failure to turn over to the states' funds from dormant customer accounts and uncashed dividend and interest checks, as required by law.

Under Greenspan, the Fed essentially gutted the Depression-era Glass–Steagall Act of 1933, which had barred commercial banks from the investment banking business. He did that even before Congress provided the final blow with the Gramm–Leach–Bliley Act of 1999. This act, also known as the Financial Services Modernization Act of 1999, was strongly promoted by Senator Phil Gramm (R-TX) and signed into law by President Bill Clinton. It swept away the Glass–Steagall barriers among financial institutions. They now could merge and acquire one another with abandon, becoming instant financial supermarkets. At the time, the popular rationale was that such modernization was necessary so that American banks could compete with Europe's "universal banks."

Greenspan also strongly opposed any regulation of credit derivatives. Greenspan's background as a director of several companies, including JP Morgan for ten years, informed his view of the Fed's role—and its limitations in regulating derivatives. During the Q&A session following his February 17, 2009 speech on regulation before the Economic Club of New York, renowned Goldman Sachs investment strategist Abby Joseph Cohen asked Greenspan for his advice on setting up a new financial regulatory structure.

Greenspan observed that as a member of the JP Morgan board, he had been well informed about the bank's customers and counterparties, whereas at the Fed, "where we regulated these people, we knew very much less than did the Morgan people or indeed any of the other institutions." He suggested that the Fed's reliance on the banks to regulate themselves through "counterparty surveillance as the first line of defense" left no backup defense system. This approach worked just fine "for a goodly long period of time until it cracked in August of 2007."[83] That is, it worked until it didn't. One of the important lessons from the latest financial crisis is that self-regulation is an oxymoron!

So while Greenspan seemed ready, willing, and able to lend a visible hand to the stock market as both a cheerleader and a savior, he was steadfastly hands-off when it came to the credit derivatives markets. The Fed submitted an extraordinary statement to Congress on June 10, 1998 defending Wall Street's right to be left alone when it came to credit derivatives:

> The Board is also dismayed by the prospect that legal uncertainties or unnecessary regulatory burdens could undermine the position of US institutions in what are intensely competitive global markets. We see no social benefits and clear social costs from pushing OTC derivatives activity offshore. . . . Institutional counterparties to privately negotiated contracts also have demonstrated their ability to protect themselves from losses from fraud and counterparty insolvencies. They have insisted that dealers have financial strength sufficient to warrant a credit rating of A or higher. Consequently, dealers are established institutions with substantial assets and significant investments in their reputations.[84]

The Fed warned Congress that any attempt to regulate derivatives would threaten the stability of the financial system. The Fed's position was that our team shouldn't be forced to play by a rule book imposed by the Commodity Futures Trading Commission (CFTC), which was pushing to regulate derivatives, when their competitors abroad were unregulated. In other words, if our competitors are unbound and we're bound, we don't stand a chance.

On July 24, 1998, Greenspan personally reiterated the Fed's position when he testified before a congressional committee on the regulation of OTC derivatives.[85] He stated that he opposed the

CFTC's attempts to regulate this market. He stressed that derivatives are fundamentally different from commodities: It's almost impossible to corner the derivatives market, because most derivatives contracts are settled in cash rather than through the delivery of an underlying commodity. Derivatives prices will vary because contracts in these markets are usually privately negotiated and privately valued. He concluded by stating his confidence in the market professionals to manage their own affairs: "The primary source of regulatory effectiveness has always been private traders being knowledgeable of their counterparties. Government regulation can only act as a backup."

Remarkably, despite the September 1998 collapse of LTCM, which resulted from its huge unregulated positions in derivatives, Greenspan continued to oppose any regulation of the OTC derivatives industry. On February 10, 2000, he once again testified before a congressional committee on this matter.[86] He started out by saying, "These instruments allow users to unbundle risks and allocate them to the investors most willing and able to assume them." He stated, "Imposing government regulation on a market can impair its efficiency." He also warned that Congress had to free derivatives from the threat of regulation or else their markets would move "to foreign jurisdictions that maintain the confidence of global investors without imposing so many regulatory constraints."

With the full support of Greenspan, the Commodity Futures Modernization Act of 2000 was introduced in the House on December 14, 2000. The companion bill was introduced in the Senate on December 15, 2000, right before the Christmas holiday. It was never debated in the Senate. On December 21, 2000, Congress passed it, and President Clinton signed the legislation just before leaving office. The legislation expressly exempted the OTC derivatives market from CFTC oversight. That led directly to the excesses that fueled the housing bubble.

The 2000 Act essentially prohibited the regulation of credit derivatives. Derivatives products were deemed to be neither "futures," requiring regulation under the Commodity Exchange Act of 1936, nor "securities," subject to the federal securities laws. The Act's rationale in exempting them from any specific regulation beyond the general "safety and soundness" standards to which the vendors of these products—banks and securities firms—normally were held by their federal overseers was that OTC derivatives transactions occurred between "sophisticated parties," who presumably knew the risks they were undertaking. Therefore, the parties had no need for government protection; they watched out for themselves and kept each other honest.

Back then, no one who had supported the financial deregulation acts of 1999 and 2000 seemed troubled by the fact that shortly after they were enacted, Enron Corporation—a Houston-based energy, commodities, and services company—blew up. Gramm–Leach–Bliley had exempted from government regulation trades on electronic energy commodity markets, in a provision that later came to be known as the "Enron Loophole." Exploiting this loophole, Enron had created the global market for energy-based derivatives. These customized risk-swapping contracts enabled parties to hedge their exposure to changing energy prices and supply fluctuations. Enron declared bankruptcy on December 2, 2001.

With derivatives free of regulations, Wall Street's investment bankers proceeded to ramp up the assembly lines in their credit derivatives departments that transformed trash into gold. The alchemy was enabled with collateralized debt obligations (CDO) and credit default swaps (CDS), resulting in a huge demand for mortgages that fueled the housing bubble.[87]

Greenspan sent a couple of mixed messages about the exuberance in the housing market. In a speech on February 23, 2004, he said, "Indeed, recent research within the Federal Reserve suggests that many homeowners might have saved tens of thousands of dollars had they held adjustable-rate mortgages rather than fixed-rate mortgages during the past decade, though this would not have been the case, of course, had interest rates trended sharply upward."[88] He was widely criticized for encouraging adjustable-rate borrowing.

In a May 5, 2005 speech, he started to express second thoughts, acknowledging the downside of the deregulation of derivatives. He correctly identified the potential dangers of the rapid growth of the derivatives market and the proliferation of new financial instruments in that market:

> The rapid proliferation of derivatives products inevitably means that some will not have been adequately tested by market stress. Even with sound credit-risk management, a sudden widening of credit spreads could result in unanticipated losses to investors in some of the newer, more complex structured credit products, and those investors could include some leveraged hedge funds. Risk management involves judgment as well as science, and the science is based on the past behavior of markets, which is not an infallible guide to the future.[89]

Nevertheless, he ended his speech on a lame note, saying, "both market participants and policymakers must be aware of the risk-management challenges associated with the use of derivatives to transfer risk, both within the banking system and outside the banking system. And they must take steps to ensure that those challenges are addressed." He clearly continued to believe that market participants would properly manage their business and regulate themselves.

Flaw in His Model

On Greenspan's watch, from August 1987 to January 2006, two asset bubbles inflated. The first was the bubble in the stock market.

The so-called "Buffett Ratio" of the market value of all US equities (excluding foreign issues) to nominal GDP rose from 0.52 during the fourth quarter of 1987 to a then-record high of 1.91 during the first quarter of 2000 (Fig. 15).[90] The second was the bubble in residential real estate. The median price of an existing single-family home soared 161% under Greenspan's watch (Fig. 16). (Arguably, the stage was set for the S&L crisis and real estate bubble of the late 1980s and early 1990s before Greenspan took charge of the Fed. However, they occurred under his watch as well.)

After the housing bubble burst, Greenspan became convinced that it had been inflated by too much available credit because of the global glut of savings. In other words, he solved his conundrum about why bond yields remained low while he was raising the federal funds rate. Foreign investors, not the Fed, caused the bubble. Here is how he explained it in his 2010 testimony before the Financial Crisis Inquiry Commission:

> Whether it was a glut of excess intended saving, or a short-fall of investment intentions, the result was the same: a fall in global real long-term interest rates and their associated capitalization rates. Asset prices, particularly house prices, in nearly two dozen countries accordingly moved dramatically higher. U.S. house price gains were high by historical standards but no more than average compared to other countries. The rate of global housing appreciation was accelerated beginning in late 2003 by the heavy securitization of American subprime and Alt-A mortgages, bonds that found willing buyers at home and abroad, many encouraged by grossly inflated credit ratings.[91]

Nevertheless, the Fed under the leadership of Maestro Greenspan failed to appreciate the magnitude of the financial excesses that were building in the housing finance industry. That was because Greenspan had a blind faith in the unregulated credit derivatives markets. His only concern seemed to be that many of the trades weren't being properly recorded. The Fed's staff continued to write lots of research studies, but virtually none of them focused on what was happening in the credit derivatives market since their boss showed no concern, let alone interest, in the subject. As a result, while Greenspan was heading the Fed, the outstanding amount of home mortgage loans, the "raw material" for most of those derivatives, soared 430% from $1.8 trillion to $9.5 trillion (Fig. 17).

In the movie, *Casablanca* (1942), police Captain Louis Renault walks into the back room of Rick's Café and asserts, "I'm shocked, shocked to find that gambling is going on in here!" As he shuts the place down, the casino manager hands him his recent winnings. Likewise, Alan Greenspan repeatedly professed his shock at what had gone on in the credit casino under his watch, and he lost some of his public admiration when he did so—though Greenspan's shock was a good deal more genuine than Renault's.

In the prepared remarks for his October 23, 2008 testimony before the House Committee on Oversight and Government Reform, at a hearing on the role of federal regulators in the financial crisis, the former Fed chair noted that subprime mortgages were the root of the problem but indicated that the real crisis stemmed from the uncontrolled securitization of those mortgages: "The evidence strongly suggests that without the excess demand from securitizers, subprime mortgage originations (undeniably the original source of crisis) would have been far smaller and defaults accordingly far fewer." He went on: "[S]ubprime mortgages pooled and sold as securities became subject to explosive demand from investors around the world."

Greenspan noted that there had been a surge in global demand for US subprime securities by banks, hedge funds, and pension funds that were supported by "unrealistically positive rating designations by credit agencies." Greenspan continued:

> As I wrote last March: those of us who have looked to the self-interest of lending institutions to protect shareholders' equity (myself especially) are in a state of shocked disbelief. Such counterparty surveillance is a central pillar of our financial markets' state of balance. If it fails, as occurred this year, market stability is undermined.

During his Q&A exchange, he acknowledged the error of his ways: "I made a mistake in presuming that the self-interest of organizations, specifically banks and others, [was] such [that] they were best capable of protecting their own shareholders and their equity in the firms." He concluded:

> So the problem here is something which looked to be a very solid edifice and, indeed, a critical pillar to market competition and free markets did break down. And I think that, as I said, shocked me. I still do not fully understand why it happened and, obviously, to the extent that I figure out where it happened and why, I will change my views. And if the facts change, I will change.

Then he admitted, "I found a flaw in the model that I perceived is the critical functioning structure that defines how the world works, I had been going for 40 years with considerable evidence it was working exceptionally well." In his prepared remarks, Greenspan said that the models used by Wall Street's financial engineers were also flawed:

> In recent decades, a vast risk management and pricing system has evolved, combining the best insights of mathematicians and finance experts supported by major advances in computer and communications technology. A Nobel Prize was awarded for the discovery of the pricing model that underpins much of

the advance in derivatives markets. This modern risk management paradigm held sway for decades. The whole intellectual edifice, however, collapsed in the summer of last year because the data inputted into the risk management models generally covered only the past two decades, a period of euphoria. Had instead the models been fitted more appropriately to historic periods of stress, capital requirements would have been much higher and the financial world would be in far better shape today, in my judgment.

Apparently, he was in so much shock that he offered the committee only one specific recommendation: "As much as I would prefer it otherwise, in this financial environment I see no choice but to require that all securitizers retain a meaningful part of the securities they issue. This will offset in part market deficiencies stemming from the failures of counterparty surveillance." Greenspan's reluctant acknowledgement that securitizers should have skin in their own game certainly was a 180-degree change from his past anti-regulatory bias.[92]

In another one of his post-mortems of the financial crisis provided in a February 17, 2009 speech, Greenspan concluded:

The extraordinary risk management discipline that developed out of the writings of the University of Chicago's Harry Markowitz in the 1950s, produced insights that won several Nobel Prizes in Economics. It was widely embraced not only by academia but also by a large majority of financial professionals and global regulators. But in August 2007, the risk management structure cracked. All the sophisticated mathematics and computer wizardry essentially rested on one central premise: that enlightened self-interest of owners and managers of financial institutions would lead them to maintain a sufficient buffer against insolvency by actively monitoring and managing their firms' capital and risk positions. When in the summer of 2007 that premise failed, I was deeply dismayed. I still believe that self-regulation is an essential tool for market effectiveness—a first line of defense. But, it is clear that the levels of complexity to which market practitioners, at the height of their euphoria, carried risk management techniques and risk-product design were too much for even the most sophisticated market players to handle properly and prudently. Accordingly, I see no alternative to a set of heightened federal regulatory rules for banks and other financial institutions.[93]

Time included Greenspan in its list of "25 People to Blame for the Financial Crisis." Here is why he was chosen:

The Federal Reserve chairman—an economist and a disciple of libertarian icon Ayn Rand—met his first major challenge in office by preventing the 1987 stock-market crash from spiraling into something much worse. Then, in the 1990s, he presided over a long economic and financial-market boom and attained the status of Washington's resident wizard. But the super-low interest rates Greenspan brought in the early 2000s and his long-standing disdain for regulation are now held up as leading causes of the mortgage crisis. The maestro admitted in an October congressional hearing that he had "made a mistake in presuming" that financial firms could regulate themselves.[94]

It is ironic, in my opinion, that Sebastian Mallaby chose to title his informative 2016 biography of Greenspan *The Man Who Knew*.

Chapter 6
Ben Bernanke: The Great Moderator

The Expert on Depressions

Ben Bernanke was Fed chair from February 1, 2006 to January 31, 2014. He is widely renowned as one of the world's top macroeconomists. In other words, he is one of the world's greatest meddlers. On February 20, 2004, when he was a Fed governor, he delivered a remarkable speech, "The Great Moderation," about the extraordinary decline in the variability of both output and inflation. In it, he marveled at what macroeconomists, particularly the ones at the Fed, had accomplished:

> Reduced macroeconomic volatility has numerous benefits. Lower volatility of inflation improves market functioning, makes economic planning easier, and reduces the resources devoted to hedging inflation risks. Lower volatility of output tends to imply more stable employment and a reduction in the extent of economic uncertainty confronting households and firms. The reduction in the volatility of output is also closely associated with the fact that recessions have become less frequent and less severe.[95]

In his low-key fashion, Bernanke bragged: "My view is that improvements in monetary policy, though certainly not the only factor, have probably been an important source of the Great Moderation." Lo and behold, macroeconomists—particularly those running the Fed—had finally found the Holy Grail! Their policies had succeeded in reducing the frequency and depth of recessions while subduing inflation (Fig. 18 and Fig. 19). It was truly a remarkable achievement, according to Bernanke. Macroeconomists had proven that they could deliver us to the Promised Land. Their theories weren't utopian; they weren't impossible dreams—they were pragmatic and successful!

Bernanke had been what I call a "Great Moderator" since the start of his career as a macroeconomist. He was trained to be a Great Moderator. He attended Harvard and graduated in 1975 with a BA in economics summa cum laude, followed by an MA (also from Harvard) and a PhD in economics from the Massachusetts Institute of Technology in 1979. His dissertation was titled *Long-Term Commitments, Dynamic Optimization, and the Business Cycle*, and his thesis adviser was Stanley Fischer, who became Fed vice chair under Janet Yellen during 2014.

After stints teaching at the Stanford Graduate School of Business and NYU, Bernanke became a tenured professor at Princeton. He was chair of the Economics Department for six years before going on public-service leave in 2002 to serve on the Fed's Board of Governors. He resigned from both Princeton and the Fed in the summer of 2005, when President George W. Bush appointed him to chair the CEA. If the CEA post was a test, he passed: Within months, Bush appointed him as chair of the Fed's Board of Governors, succeeding Greenspan, who was retiring after 18 years. Bernanke took the helm on February 1, 2006.

Bernanke was reappointed by President Barack Obama for another four-year term in 2010, but by a Senate vote of 70 to 30—the slimmest margin for a Fed chief ever. There was lots of dissatisfaction on Capitol Hill with the way the Fed had handled the financial crisis of 2008. However, there was widespread agreement that Bernanke had been the right man at the right time to avert a financial meltdown and a depression. I agree with that assessment. We were lucky he was running the show.

After all, Bernanke is one of the leading macroeconomic students of the Great Depression. In academic circles, the Fed has been widely viewed as the main perpetrator of the Great Depression. Milton Friedman and Anna Schwartz blamed the Fed in their 1963 book *A Monetary History of the United States, 1867–1960*.[96]

Before going to Washington, Bernanke spent much of his academic career proving that the Fed was at fault for causing the Great Depression. He published numerous academic journal articles—with lots of econometric analyses of the subject—many of which were compiled into his 2004 book, *Essays on the Great Depression*.[97] In a November 8, 2002 speech at a conference to honor Friedman's 90th birthday, Bernanke, who was still a Fed governor at the time, famously concluded: "Regarding the Great Depression. You're right, we did it. We're very sorry. But thanks to you, we won't do it again." He observed:

> As everyone here knows, in their *Monetary History* Friedman and Schwartz made the case that the economic collapse of 1929–33 was the product of the nation's monetary mechanism gone wrong. Contradicting the received wisdom at the time that they wrote, which held that money was a passive player in the events of the 1930s, Friedman and Schwartz argued that "the contraction is in fact a tragic testimonial to the importance of monetary forces."[98]

I humbly disagree with Friedman, Schwartz, and Bernanke: I am convinced that the Smoot–Hawley Tariff caused the Great Depression. It was enacted on June 17, 1930, triggering massive declines in world trade and commodity prices and an avalanche of bank bankruptcies and debt defaults. The tariff is mentioned only once—in a footnote—in *A Monetary History of the United States*. Bernanke's narrative doesn't even consider the possibility that the tariff could have triggered the global collapse in business, trade, and prices; in fact, the words "Smoot–Hawley Tariff" appear just twice in the whole book. The first occurrence is not until page 266, and the second is in a footnoted reference. In the first spot, Bernanke discounts the "disruptive effect" of "trade restrictions" as a "theoretical possibility" based on weak direct evidence. In the footnote, he refers the reader to an August 1986 NBER working paper by Barry Eichengreen, "The Political Economy of the Smoot–Hawley Tariff."[99]

In any event, Bernanke's findings convinced him that the Fed caused the Great Depression and didn't do enough to end it. He was determined to do whatever he could to ensure the Fed wouldn't make the same mistake again. In his informed opinion, the Fed had failed to provide enough liquidity to stop widespread bank runs during the early 1930s.

On March 20, 2012, in the first of four unusual lectures on the history of the Fed that he delivered at George Washington University, Bernanke referred the students to the 1946 movie *It's a Wonderful Life*, starring Jimmy Stewart, for an example of a bank run. Central banks were invented to stop such financial crises by acting as lenders of last resort, just as Walter Bagehot explained in his 1873 book *Lombard Street: A Description of the Money Market*, Bernanke said. The book is often cited by central bankers during financial crises. Most important is "Bagehot's Dictum," which Bernanke explained as follows:

> And he had a dictum which said that during a panic, central banks should lend freely, to whoever comes to your door as long as they [have] collateral, give them money, this is during a banking panic. Against good assets, to make sure that you get your money back, you need to have collateral and that collateral has to be good or it has to be discounted and they could lend half the value of the collateral, for example, and charge a penalty interest rate so that people don't just take advantage

of the situation but rather they signal that they really need the money because they're willing to pay a slightly higher interest rate. So again, if you follow Bagehot's rule, you can stop financial panics.[100]

In an April 2012 article in *The Atlantic* about him, Bernanke cited Bagehot's *Lombard Street* as his guidebook. "It's beautiful," Bernanke said, once again extolling the 19th-century British essayist for urging central bankers to act decisively to stop financial panics. Defending his own crisis measures, Bernanke said, "Some people don't understand—fulfilling the responsibility as lender of last resort is what the Fed was created to do. This is what central banks have been doing for 300 years."[101]

In his lecture, Bernanke accused the Fed of dereliction of duty at the start of the Great Depression. He didn't say what exactly triggered the downturn, though he implied that it might have been the stock market crash and Treasury Secretary Andrew Mellon's puritanical response to the collapse of the debt-fueled speculative excesses of the Roaring '20s when Mellon heartlessly said, "Liquidate labor, liquidate stocks, liquidate the farmers, liquidate real estate."

In Bernanke's opinion, the Fed failed its first major test, and it was left to President Roosevelt to abandon the gold standard on June 5, 1933, which "allowed monetary policy to be released and allowed the expansion of the money supply." The dollar was devalued by 40% relative to gold in 1933 and 1934. In 1934, the Federal Deposit Insurance Corporation (FDIC) was created to provide deposit insurance, which also put an end to the bank runs.

It is ironic that during 2008, roughly five years after Bernanke's Great Moderation speech, the economy fell into what even he called the "Great Recession." He candidly admitted that he hadn't seen it coming. But he was well prepared to come to the rescue.

In fact, he had presciently outlined his game plan for doing so on November 21, 2002 in one of his first speeches as a Fed governor (the aforementioned "Deflation: Making Sure 'It' Doesn't Happen Here"). The gist of his speech came to be known as "The Bernanke Doctrine." The Great Moderator stated that "the US central bank, in cooperation with other parts of the government as needed, has sufficient policy instruments to ensure that any deflation that might occur would be both mild and brief." He declared, "Sustained deflation can be highly destructive to a modern economy and should be strongly resisted."[102]

In his speech, Bernanke discussed all the ways and means that the Fed could do so. He favored an inflation target of 1.0% to 3.0% to provide enough of a buffer zone for inflation. He called on the Fed to use its "regulatory and supervisory powers to ensure that the financial system will remain resilient if financial conditions change rapidly." If the financial system and economy came unglued nonetheless, the Fed should use all its tools to stabilize them as quickly as possible. He believed in shock-and-awe tactics, with the Fed acting "more preemptively and more aggressively than usual in cutting rates."

In that speech, Bernanke also anticipated new unconventional monetary policy tools. He expressed confidence that even if the federal funds rate were cut to zero ("its practical minimum"), the Fed would have the tools to stop deflation; after all, in a worst-case scenario, the government could always print more money. But he went on to say that such a controversial move wouldn't likely be necessary, as the Fed could accomplish the same result through various asset purchase programs (i.e., what came to be known as "quantitative easing," or "QE" in the US and the asset purchase program, or "APP" in the Eurozone).

Near the end of his speech, Bernanke rhetorically asked why Japan hadn't succeeded in ending deflation and gave his answer:

Political constraints kept the Japanese from doing enough. It was the same conclusion he offered in a widely read paper, "Japanese Monetary Policy: A Case of Self-Induced Paralysis?" delivered in January 2000 when he was a professor at Princeton.[103] Even then, Bernanke was making a list of "nonstandard operations," including QE, that the Bank of Japan (BOJ) could implement to stop deflation. He supported his unconventional policy recommendations by extolling FDR's approach to policymaking:

> But Roosevelt's specific policy actions were, I think, less important than his willingness to be aggressive and to experiment—in short, to do whatever was necessary to get the country moving again. Many of his policies did not work as intended, but in the end FDR deserves great credit for having the courage to abandon failed paradigms and to do what needed to be done.

Said like a true meddler: Even though FDR's policies had unintended consequences, at least FDR had the guts to experiment with the economy, according to Bernanke.

The Great Recession

When it was his turn to run the Fed, Bernanke failed to appreciate the magnitude of the bubble in the housing finance industry, which was well underway by then. Everything started to come unglued during the fourth quarter of 2006 as delinquency rates on subprime mortgages rose, leading to a wave of bankruptcies among subprime lenders. As the name implies, a "subprime mortgage" is a type of loan granted to individuals with poor credit scores, who would not be able to qualify for a conventional mortgage. They proliferated prior to the Great Financial Crisis and set the stage for the debacle. Many of these loans were adjustable-rate mortgages (ARMs) with low and fixed "teaser" rates for a short introductory period, after which they automatically became variable rates. With scheduled rate increases, ARMs were like ticking time bombs set to go off all over the country as more and more subprime borrowers defaulted.

Lots more ARM bombs blew up during 2007. On February 8, 2007, HSBC Holdings, the multinational bank headquartered in London, said it would have to add to loan loss reserves to cover bad debts in the subprime-lending portfolio. On June 20, two hedge funds at Bear Stearns, an investment bank, announced major losses resulting from bad bets on securities backed by subprime loans. On July 30, German bank IKB announced losses linked to US subprime securities. On October 24, Merrill Lynch reported huge losses in its credit derivatives portfolio.

In a May 17, 2007 speech in Chicago titled "The Subprime Mortgage Market," Bernanke recognized the problem in the housing finance industry: "The rise in subprime mortgage lending likely boosted home sales somewhat, and curbs on this lending are expected to be a source of some restraint on home purchases and residential investment in coming quarters." He correctly anticipated that there would be "further increases in delinquencies and foreclosures" through 2008 "as many adjustable-rate loans face interest-rate resets."

However, he provided a relatively sanguine assessment of the situation. He must regret coming to the following premature conclusion:

> All that said, given the fundamental factors in place that should support the demand for housing, we believe the effect of the troubles in the subprime sector on the broader housing market will likely be limited, and we do not expect significant spillovers from the subprime market to the rest of the economy or to the financial system. The vast majority of mortgages, including even subprime mortgages, continue to perform

well. Past gains in house prices have left most homeowners with significant amounts of home equity, and growth in jobs and incomes should help keep the financial obligations of most households manageable.[104]

Bernanke was cautious but not alarmed about the unfolding subprime mortgage crisis during his July 18, 2007 semiannual monetary policy report to Congress. He observed that while "financial markets have remained supportive of economic growth . . . conditions in the subprime mortgage sector have deteriorated significantly, reflecting mounting delinquency rates on adjustable-rate loans." Then he acknowledged that credit quality was deteriorating as yield "spreads on lower-quality corporate debt have widened somewhat, and terms for some leveraged business loans have tightened." But he stuck with his relatively sanguine assessment: "Even after their recent rise, however, credit spreads remain near the low end of their historical ranges, and financing activity in the bond and business loan markets has remained fairly brisk."[105]

In his July congressional testimony, Bernanke observed that the FOMC had maintained the federal funds rate at 5.25% at each of the four meetings since the start of the year. However, the financial crisis worsened during the summer of 2007, so the FOMC cut the federal funds rate by 50 basis points to 4.75% on September 18, and another 25 basis points to 4.50% on October 31, when the FOMC Statement observed that "the pace of economic expansion will likely slow in the near term, partly reflecting the intensification of the housing correction."[106] The federal funds rate was cut yet again at the last meeting of the year, on December 11, 2007, by another 25 basis points to 4.25% (Fig. 20).

The financial crisis intensified dramatically during 2008. Bernanke was starting to dust off his *Lombard Street* manual for dealing with a financial crisis more aggressively. At the start of the year, on January 9, he initiated an unusual special conference call meeting of the FOMC. He was worried about the rapidly deteriorating economic and financial situation. He said:

> I have become increasingly concerned that our policy rate is too high to fully address the downside risks to growth. We have cut 100 basis points since September, and I think that may possibly have roughly offset the credit factors and the housing factors, but I don't think that we can claim that we have done anything in the way of taking out insurance against what I think are some potentially significant downside risks.[107]

Yet no action was taken. However, Bernanke initiated another conference call meeting of the FOMC less than two weeks later, on January 21. This time, the federal funds rate was slashed by an unusually large 75 basis points to 3.50%. In the transcript of that call, William Dudley, the president of the Federal Reserve Bank of New York, sounded the alarm on monoline insurance companies that provide fixed-income investors with financial protection in case of default, thus enhancing the credit rating of the issuers. Their guarantees increase the confidence of investors and enhance market liquidity. Rapidly mounting defaults threatened to overwhelm the monolines and to dry up liquidity in the fixed-income markets, according to Dudley.

Bernanke concluded that a contagion was developing in the credit markets: "There is building in the market a real dynamic of withdrawal from risk, withdrawal from normal credit extension, which I think is very worrisome."[108]

Despite the big rate cut at the beginning of the year, the credit crunch spread quickly over the rest of the year. On March 16, the Fed convinced JP Morgan to buy Bear Stearns, but only after the Fed agreed to acquire up to $30 billion of Bear's distressed assets, putting them on the Fed's balance sheet in a vehicle called

"Maiden Lane LLC." On March 19, the government lowered the capital requirements on Fannie Mae and Freddie Mac—the housing-related government-sponsored enterprises (GSEs)—to provide liquidity to the mortgage market. On July 11, the FDIC assumed control of IndyMac, a California bank that had been one of the leading lenders making home loans to borrowers without proof of income. On July 13, the Fed authorized Fannie and Freddie to borrow from the discount window for emergency funding. On September 6, both were placed in conservatorship, with life support provided by the US Treasury.

The January 21 rate cut was quickly followed up with a 50-basis-point reduction to 3.00% following the scheduled meeting of the FOMC on January 29–30 because financial markets remained "under considerable stress, and credit had tightened further . . ." according to the FOMC statement. At the next meeting of the FOMC, on March 18, another 75-basis-points cut brought the federal funds rate down to 2.25%. It was lowered again by 25 basis points to 2.00% on April 30. None of those actions stopped the crisis, yet the federal funds rate remained at 2.00% during the next three scheduled meetings of the FOMC, in June, August, and September.

The financial crisis turned into a full-blown contagion on Monday, September 15. That day, while Bank of America was agreeing to acquire Merrill Lynch, Lehman Brothers filed for bankruptcy due to losses resulting from holding on to large positions in subprime and other lower-rated tranches of securitized mortgages. Investors went into a full panic when the Fed did nothing to rescue Lehman.

On Thursday, September 16, AIG imploded following the failure of its Financial Products unit. *The Financial Crisis Inquiry Commission Report* (2011) concluded in January 2011 that "AIG failed and was rescued by the government primarily because its

enormous sales of credit default swaps were made without putting up the initial collateral, setting aside capital reserves, or hedging its exposure."[109]

Bernanke subsequently claimed that the Fed didn't have the
legal authority to bail out Lehman. Yet on Sunday, September 21,
the Fed announced that Goldman Sachs and Morgan Stanley, the
last two independent investment banks, would become bank-hold-
ing companies, subjecting them to new regulation and supervision. The move also signaled that the Fed wouldn't let them fail,
because it gave them access to the Fed's borrowing window. Why
the same courtesy wasn't extended to Lehman Brothers remains a
mystery. The *Financial Crisis Inquiry Commission Report* (2011) fault-
ed the Fed for failing to rescue Lehman after having done so for
Bear Stearns and the GSEs and immediately before rescuing AIG.
(See Appendix 4, Bernanke's Fed and the Lehman Bankruptcy.)

The Fed chair undoubtedly recognized when Lehman and
AIG collapsed that the US was facing a financial and economic
disaster potentially even worse than the Great Depression. The
FOMC lowered the federal funds rate by 50 basis points to 1.50%
on yet another emergency conference call on October 7. That
was followed up with another 50-basis-point cut to 1.00% at the
October 28–29 FOMC meeting. At the December 16 meeting, it was
lowered to a range of 0.00% to 0.25%.

The zero lower bound had been reached.

Bernanke teamed up with Treasury Secretary Hank Paulson to
press Congress to enact the Troubled Asset Relief Program (TARP).
Congress did so on October 3. TARP was supposed to spend $700
billion to purchase toxic assets and equity from financial institutions. Instead, it mostly bolstered the capital of the major money
center banks, which is why it is commonly called the "bank bailout of 2008," consistent with the Bagehot Doctrine's emphasis on
stopping bank runs.

After Lehman hit the fan and as the federal funds rate was rapidly cut to zero, it was also time to implement the Bernanke Doctrine. The Fed chair dusted off his 2002 speech and started methodically to implement his list of crisis management measures. In late 2008, the Fed set up several emergency credit facilities and implemented unconventional monetary policy tools to pump liquidity into the financial markets, consistent with the Bernanke Doctrine's emphasis on doing whatever it takes to avoid deflation and depression.

Reinventing the Fed's Tool Kit

Under Bernanke's leadership, the Fed was remarkably effective at creating numerous emergency credit facilities and new policy tools that helped to contain the crisis so that it wouldn't turn into a full-blown contagion and collapse of the financial system. As the crisis popped up in various parts of the financial system, Bernanke masterfully played whack-a-mole using three sets of tools:

- **Liquidity facilities for financial institutions.** The first set was closely tied to the central bank's traditional role as the lender of last resort for financial institutions. In addition to the Fed's discount window, the traditional borrowing facility for distressed banks, these facilities included the Term Auction Facility, Primary Dealer Credit Facility, and Term Securities Lending Facility. Credit swap agreements were approved on a bilateral basis with several foreign central banks to relieve liquidity problems arising in global bank-funding markets.

- **Liquidity facilities for borrowers and investors.** A second set of tools, targeting distressed borrowers and investors in key credit markets, included the Commercial Paper Funding Facility, the Asset-Backed Commercial Paper Money Market Mutual Fund Liquidity Facility, the Money Market Investor Funding

Facility, and the Term Asset-Backed Securities Loan Facility.[110] Collectively, the Fed's emergency loans rose from $391 billion during the first week of September 2008 to peak at $1.7 trillion during the week of December 10.

- **Quantitative easing programs.** In addition to these targeted facilities, the Fed greatly expanded its traditional tools related to open-market operations. On November 25, 2008, the Fed announced the first round of a program of QE. There were three rounds all told (Fig. 21 and Fig. 22).

    QE1 from November 25, 2008 to March 31, 2010. The first round entailed the purchase of the direct obligations of housing-related GSEs—Fannie Mae, Freddie Mac, and the Federal Home Loan Banks—and mortgage-backed securities (MBS) backed by Fannie Mae, Freddie Mac, and Ginnie Mae. Over the next several quarters, the Fed would purchase up to $100 billion in GSE direct obligations and up to $500 billion in MBS. The program was expanded on March 16, 2009 to include purchases of $300 billion in US Treasuries. Under QE1, the Fed purchased $1.5 trillion in bonds, including $1.2 trillion in US Agency debt and MBS and $300 billion in US Treasuries.

    QE2 from November 3, 2010 to June 30, 2011. The second round started seven months after QE1 was terminated. It entailed the purchase of $600 billion of longer-term Treasury securities by the end of the second quarter of 2011, a pace of about $75 billion per month. Under the program, the Fed purchased $826 billion in US Treasuries, while its holdings of US Agency debt and MBS declined $246 billion as securities matured.

    QE3 from September 13, 2012 to October 29, 2014. The third round was open-ended, with the FOMC committing to purchase $40 billion per month in Agency MBS. No total was announced, nor was a termination date. On December 12, 2012, the program was expanded to include $45 billion per month in "longer term" Treasuries. On December 18, 2013, QE3 was tapered to $35 billion per month in MBS and $40 billion per month in Treasuries. It was terminated on October 29, 2014 after the Fed purchased $832 billion in MBSs and $808 billion in Treasuries.[111]

Ben Bernanke had transformed the Fed into "Feddie," supplementing and shoring up Fannie and Freddie. Because of the three rounds of QE from November 25, 2008 through October 29, 2014, the Fed's holdings of MBS increased from zero to $1.8 trillion, and the Fed's holdings of Treasuries increased from $476 billion to $2.5 trillion. By the way, the Fed officially prefers the term large-scale asset purchases (LSAP) rather than QE.[112]

I wasn't surprised by QE1, because Bernanke previously had revealed his game plan in response to such alarming circumstances. Furthermore, I had noted in my commentaries of October and early November 2008 that mortgage interest rates hadn't dropped along with government bond yields, as the federal funds rate was cut to zero. I predicted that the Fed would address this problem. The Fed did so with QE1.

The S&P 500 bottomed at 666 on March 9, 2009 on an intraday basis. It bottomed on a closing basis at 676 on March 9. I turned bullish on March 16 partly because that same day, the Fed announced that its QE1 bond-buying program would be expanded.

While I was all for QE1, I was not a fan of QE2. Apparently, the Fed's staff ran the in-house econometric model and concluded around mid-2010 that QE1 hadn't done enough to keep the economic recovery going on its own. The model showed that a negative federal funds rate somewhere around -0.50% to -0.75% would be required to do so. But since no major central bank had crossed the zero lower bound with negative interest rates back then, Bernanke must have asked the Fed staff to estimate how much in

QE2 purchases would be required to have the same stimulative effect as the negative federal funds rate called for by the model.

Bernanke first suggested the need for more QE in his Jackson Hole speech on August 27, 2010. He said, "Notwithstanding the fact that the policy rate is near its zero lower bound, the Federal Reserve retains a number of tools and strategies for providing additional stimulus." First and foremost, he mentioned additional purchases of bonds: "I believe that additional purchases of longer-term securities, should the FOMC choose to undertake them, would be effective in further easing financial conditions."[113]

William Dudley, the president of the Federal Reserve Bank of New York, gave a speech on October 1, 2010 favoring another round of QE with specific numbers: "[S]ome simple calculations based on recent experience suggest that $500 billion of purchases would provide about as much stimulus as a reduction in the federal funds rate of between half a point and three quarters of a point." His basic argument was that despite the downside of additional QE, it was the only tool the Fed had left to meet its congressional mandate to lower the unemployment rate. Indeed, the speech was titled "The Outlook, Policy Choices and Our Mandate." The word "mandate" appeared 17 times in the speech, including the title.[114]

At the time, I argued that if the Fed's econometric model was calling for a negative official policy rate, then either there was something wrong with the model or the Fed was trying to fix economic problems that could not be fixed with monetary policy. In my opinion, when the federal funds rate was lowered to zero, Fed officials should have said that that was all they could do. While I expected and endorsed QE1, I was not convinced that QE2 and the subsequent QE3 were necessary. But there I go again, critiquing monetary policy.

Bernanke kept me focused on doing my job by explaining why he believed that his job was to implement QE2. One day after he did so, he defended the Fed's decision in a highly unusual op-ed article for the November 4, 2010 issue of *The Washington Post* pointedly titled "What the Fed Did and Why: Supporting the Recovery and Sustaining Price Stability."[115] In brief, the Fed wanted to drive up the prices of bonds and stocks:

> Lower corporate bond rates will encourage investment. And higher stock prices will boost consumer wealth and help increase confidence, which can also spur spending. Increased spending will lead to higher incomes and profits that, in a virtuous circle, will further support economic expansion.

Bernanke made my job easier. All I had to do was remain bullish on bonds and stocks, which I could do with confidence knowing that the Fed chair said that QE2 was aimed at driving up their prices. While QE2 and subsequently QE3 didn't seem to be doing much to stimulate the economy and revive price inflation, they fueled asset inflation, which was one of the reasons I remained bullish on stocks and bonds.

The global financial markets became dependent on the Fed's ultra-easy monetary policies, as evidenced by their "taper tantrum" during May and June 2013. On May 21, in congressional testimony, Bernanke first suggested that the Fed may start phasing out its asset purchases in a "few meetings." That sent bond yields higher, stock prices lower, and depressed foreign currencies, especially in emerging economies, which are very sensitive to Fed policy actions.

At his press conference following the June 18–19 meeting of the FOMC, Bernanke unveiled a set of revised economic projections that were slightly more optimistic than its previous estimates. Bernanke said that if those projections panned out, the Fed would "ease the pressure on the accelerator." He added that if the unemployment rate fell to 7% by mid-2014, the Fed would terminate QE3. The stock market sold off on the news, with the S&P 500 down 1.4%, even though Bernanke stressed that the Fed's actions could change if the economy changed.[116]

Bernanke repeatedly stated that, even after tapering started, the Fed would not allow US monetary conditions to tighten and would keep short-term interest rates near zero for a long period, at least until 2015 and quite possibly beyond. The phrase "considerable time" was used in more than two years of FOMC statements to describe how long monetary policy would remain accommodative—from the September 13, 2012 statement through the December 17, 2014 statement—a year past the end of Bernanke's stay as Fed chair. Nevertheless, the financial markets were noticeably relieved when the September 18, 2013 FOMC statement noted that the Fed's asset purchases were not on a "preset course," which appeared in every subsequent statement through the September 17, 2014 statement. QE3 was terminated at the end of the following month.[117]

No one has been as committed to moderating the business cycle with monetary policy as former Fed Chair Ben Bernanke. He reiterated this view in an October 4, 2015 *The Wall Street Journal* op-ed, "How the Fed Saved the Economy," timed to coincide with the release of his memoir, *The Courage to Act: A Memoir of a Crisis and Its Aftermath*:[118]

> What the Fed can do is two things: First, by mitigating recessions, monetary policy can try to ensure that the economy makes full use of its resources, especially the workforce. High unemployment is a tragedy for the jobless, but it is also costly for taxpayers, investors and anyone interested in the health of the economy. Second, by keeping inflation low and stable, the Fed can help the market-based system function better and make it easier for people to plan for the future. Considering the economic risks posed by deflation, as well as the probability

that interest rates will approach zero when inflation is very low, the Fed sets an inflation target of 2%, similar to that of most other central banks around the world.[119]

When Bernanke kindly gave me permission to quote from his op-ed, he informed me that he hadn't selected the title; the headline writers at *The Wall Street Journal* titled it.

In his book, Bernanke did acknowledge that the "experience of the Great Moderation had led both banks and regulators to underestimate the probabilities of a large economic or financial shock." In my opinion, attempts by the central banks to moderate the business cycle can have unintended consequences that make the economy more vulnerable to financial instability and deeper recessions.

In an interview with television host Charlie Rose conducted on Sunday, June 16, 2013 and aired on Monday, President Barack Obama said that Bernanke "has already stayed a lot longer than he wanted or he was supposed to." On Tuesday, stock prices rose on a widely reported story that Ben Bernanke most likely would leave the Fed when his term as chair expired on January 31, 2014. Why was that bullish for stocks? Because Bernanke would most likely be replaced by Fed Vice Chair Janet Yellen. She tended to be at least as dovish as Bernanke and had explicitly said that she favored keeping the federal funds rate near zero until the jobless rate fell to 6.5%.

Chapter 7
Janet Yellen:
The Gradual Normalizer

Monetary Policy for Yalies

On February 3, 2014, Janet Yellen became the 15th chair of the Fed and its first female chair; she served her four-year term until February 3, 2018. She had been vice chair since October 4, 2010. Prior to joining the Federal Reserve Board in Washington, D.C., she had served as the president of the Federal Reserve Bank of San Francisco since June 14, 2004. She had started her government service as the 18th chair of the CEA, from February 18, 1997 to August 3, 1999. In some ways, I found her easier to read than her three predecessors. Perhaps that was because we're both Yalies.

On April 16, 1999, CEA Chair Yellen gave a speech at a reunion of the Yale graduate economics department. She declared that the liberal Keynesian orthodoxy preached by Yale's Professor James Tobin had conquered Washington. Tobin was one of the major disciples of John Maynard Keynes in the United States. According to Yellen, who is Tobin's foremost disciple, everyone in the room shared the same goal—they all wanted to be do-gooders: "I suspect that many of us here tonight were attracted to economics and to policy positions in government because we believed in its potential for improving economic welfare."

She said Tobin had suggested that the title of her speech be "Yale Economics in Washington." She readily obliged, saying, "I will try to make the case that the lessons that we learned here at

Yale remain the right and relevant ones for improving economic performance, that Yale-trained economists in Washington are succeeding in making their voices heard, and, where Yale economics has been applied, it is working."

Then Yellen claimed that while most economists "appreciate the role of markets and incentives," only Yalies can see when they aren't working properly and know how to fix them: "I have noticed that Yalies often have a sharper eye for identifying market failures and greater concern for policies to remedy them than economists from institutions I will leave nameless." Her comments made me wonder whether at any time in her professional life Yellen considered the possibility that government policies can cause markets to fail, requiring more government policies to fix the failure that the government caused in the first place. At Yale, there were no courses in the unintended negative consequences of well-intentioned macroeconomic policies.

The original sin for macroeconomists, in my opinion, was the passage of the Employment Act of 1946, which established the CEA. As Yellen noted—favorably, of course—the Act mandated that the federal government should moderate the business cycle, thus "promoting balanced and noninflationary economic growth, and fostering low unemployment." The law has certainly been a full employment act for macroeconomists working for the federal government.

Yellen, like Bernanke, was a Great Moderator. She extolled the "Yale macroeconomic paradigm." She said that "as I have taught and hopefully practiced it," the model "combines a Keynesian understanding of economic fluctuations with a neoclassical perspective on long-run growth. . . . The IS-LM and aggregate demand/ aggregate supply models, hopefully still staples in Yale's classes, provide the simplest description of the short run paradigm." She believed in this model more than ever as a result of her experience in Washington.

Like a true-blue Yalie Keynesian, she claimed that a capitalist economy can't maintain full employment without the help of Yalie macroeconomists:

> The Yale macroeconomic paradigm provides clear answers to key questions dividing macroeconomists along with policy prescriptions. Will capitalist economies operate at full employment in the absence of routine intervention? Certainly not. Are deviations from full employment a social problem? Obviously.

Rhetorically asking whether "policymakers have the knowledge and ability to improve macroeconomic outcomes rather than make matters worse," she replied to herself with an unequivocal, "Yes."

Near the end of her speech, Yellen raised one cautionary flag: "Decades ago, economists recognized an unfortunate implication of the IS-LM model: that the simultaneous attainment of financial market openness, monetary policy independence, and exchange rate stability—three desirable macroeconomic goals—was simply impossible! Countries would have to forego at least one or risk financial crisis." Less than a year after her pep rally at Yale, the US economy fell into a recession when the technology bubble in the stock market, inflated by Greenspan's Fed, popped.[120]

As the new Fed chair, Janet Yellen made her first rookie's mistake during her first press conference on March 19, 2014, when she defined the "considerable time" mentioned in the latest FOMC statement to mean "something on the order of around six months or that type of thing."[121] That was widely interpreted as suggesting that the Fed might start raising the federal funds rate six months after QE was terminated. The termination was generally expected to happen by the end of 2014 and did occur that year in late

October. However, the first hike in the federal funds rate after QE was terminated didn't occur until the end of the following year.

Yellen seemed to back away from her prediction in an extraordinarily impassioned and personal speech on Monday, March 31, 2014 in Chicago, when she said that the Fed remained committed "to do what is necessary to help our nation recover from the Great Recession."[122] In her speech, she briefly described the struggle of three workers in the Windy City, implying that she intended to maintain ultra-easy monetary policy until they and people like them had good jobs.

The next day, Jon Hilsenrath reported in *The Wall Street Journal* that one of the three persons named by Yellen "had a two-decade-old theft conviction," while another one "had a past drug conviction." Hilsenrath deadpanned: "Academic research suggests people with criminal backgrounds face unique obstacles to employment." He added that a "Fed spokeswoman said Tuesday that Ms. Yellen knew of the people's criminal backgrounds and that they were 'very forthright' about it in conversations with the chairwoman before the speech. In her remarks, she said they exemplified the trends she was discussing, such as downward pressure on wages or the challenge of finding a job for the long-term unemployed."[123]

The July 21, 2014 issue of *The New Yorker* included a lengthy article about Yellen. It confirmed that she is an impassioned liberal:

> Yellen is notable not only for being the first female Fed chair but also for being the most liberal since Marriner Eccles, who held the job during the Roosevelt and Truman Administrations. Ordinarily, the Fed's role is to engender a sense of calm in the eternally jittery financial markets, not to crusade against urban poverty.

Yellen intended "to help American families who are struggling in the aftermath of the Great Recession." She and her husband George Akerlof have published numerous papers on why labor markets don't automatically work to maintain full employment.[124] The government can do the job better: "I come from an intellectual tradition where public policy is important, it can make a positive contribution, it's our social obligation to do this. We can help to make the world a better place."[125]

After she became Fed chair in early 2014, the FOMC finally terminated the QE program on October 29 of that year. There was lots of chatter among Fed watchers about rate hikes coming in 2015. Based on my assessment of Yellen, I concluded that she would be very slow and cautious in raising rates. Indeed, during September 2014, I predicted a "one and done" rate hike in the coming year.

Yellen finally delivered that rate increase of 25 basis points at the last FOMC meeting of 2015, raising the federal funds rate range to 0.25%–0.50% (Fig. 23). At the end of that year, I again predicted one-and-done for 2016. Much to my chagrin, Fed Vice Chair Stanley Fischer rattled financial markets around the world at the beginning of 2016, warning that they hadn't fully discounted the possibility of four rate hikes in 2016.

Adding to the commotion at the beginning of the year was John Williams, who was president of the San Francisco Fed at the time. On January 4, he also predicted that the FOMC would be raising the federal funds rate four to five times during 2016. A week and a half later, on January 15, he said that a slowdown in China spilling over to the US is keeping him up at night. On January 29, he told reporters: "Standard monetary policy strategy says a little less inflation, maybe a little less growth . . . argue for just a smidgen slower process of normalizing rates."[126]

I stuck with my forecast, and the next rate hike occurred at the last FOMC meeting of 2016. The federal funds rate range was raised to 0.50%–0.75%. There were three more rate hikes during 2017 at the March, June, and December meetings of the FOMC, bringing the range up to 1.25%–1.50%.

Yellen had succeeded in gradually normalizing monetary policy without any major incident. The S&P 500 rose 55% while she headed the Fed from February 3, 2014 through February 3, 2018.

'The Fairy Godmother of the Bull Market'

Early on when Yellen became Fed chair (and even when she was vice chair), I noticed that the stock market often would rise after she gave a speech on the economy and monetary policy. She was among the most dovish members of the FOMC, and she now ruled the aviary, which also included a few hawks. So I remained bullish on the outlook for stocks, anticipating that under her leadership, the FOMC would normalize monetary policy at a gradual pace. Indeed, I often referred to Yellen as the "Fairy Godmother of the Bull Market."

On September 29, 2016 in a video conference with bankers in Kansas City, Yellen crossed the line, in my opinion, when she suggested that the Fed should be authorized by Congress to buy corporate bonds and stocks. Yellen and I both learned from Professor Tobin about the "Portfolio-Balance Model."[127] The idea is that assets are substitutable for each other. So if the Fed buys government bonds, reducing their supply, that will drive more demand into other bonds as well as equities. The resulting increase in wealth should stimulate spending. In her video talk, Yellen said:

> Now because Treasury securities and, say, corporate securities and equities are substitutes in the portfolios of the public, when we push down yields—let's say on Treasuries—there's often and typically spillover to corporate bonds and to equities as well [such] that those rates fall or that equity prices rise, stimulating investment. But we are restricted from investing

> in that wider range of assets. And if we found—I think as oth-
> er countries did—that [we] had reached the limits in terms of
> purchasing safe assets like longer-term government bonds, it
> could be useful to be able to intervene directly in assets where
> the prices have a more direct link to spending decisions.

Got that? If the Fed runs out of Treasuries, "it could be useful" to buy corporate bonds and stocks. Spoken like a true-blue meddler. She strongly suggested that she was all for adding that option to the Fed's toolkit just in case the other tools used to tinker with the economy didn't work. She was very blunt about her willingness to distort US capital markets because they clearly weren't working well enough on their own to achieve the Fed's goals, in her opinion. (See Appendix 5, Yellen on Fed Purchasing Corporate Bonds and Stocks.)

Yellen noted that the BOJ had been buying corporate bonds and stocks for a while, and the European Central Bank (ECB) had been buying corporate bonds since June of that year. That's true, but there was no evidence that these purchases were boosting growth or reviving capitalism's animal spirits in either Japan or the Eurozone. Both have relatively inferior capital markets compared to the vibrant ones in the United States. They still depend too much on their banks for financial intermediation. Their banks have been broken for a long time, and the flat yield curve and negative interest-rate policies of the BOJ and ECB surely weren't helping their banks.

Yellen concluded her response by saying, "But while it's a good thing to think about, it's not something that is a pressing issue now, and I should emphasize that while there could be benefits to, say, the ability to buy either equities or corporate bonds, there would also be costs as well that would have to be carefully considered in deciding if it's a good idea."

In my opinion, the costs are considerable. Intervening so broadly in the capital markets would disrupt the process of creative destruction that is integral to capitalism. It would keep zombie companies in business, which would be deflationary and reduce profitability for well-run competitors. Investors wouldn't get to determine the economy's winners and losers if the Fed buys simply to prop up stock prices. Depending on the circumstances, such an overreaching "Yellen Put" would result in a huge speculative bubble for sure.

In short, Fed intervention in the corporate bond and equity markets is a bad idea.

Limits of Macroeconomists

On October 14, 2016, Yellen gave a speech at a conference sponsored by the Boston Fed and attended by Fed and academic economists. The topic of discussion: "The Elusive 'Great' Recovery: Causes and Implications for Future Business Cycle Dynamics." Her talk was titled "Macroeconomic Research After the Crisis."[128] It was a remarkable speech that should have been titled "Macroeconomic Research in Crisis." The unemployment rate had dropped from a peak of 10.0% during October 2009 to 4.9% in August 2016. The Fed had hiked once at the end of 2015 and was going to do it again at the end of 2016. Yellen explained why such gradual normalization of monetary policy made sense.

She talked about "hysteresis," the idea that persistent shortfalls in aggregate demand could adversely affect the supply side of the economy. Then she rhetorically asked: "If we assume that hysteresis is in fact present to some degree after deep recessions, the natural next question is to ask whether it might be possible to reverse these adverse supply-side effects by temporarily running a 'high-pressure economy,' with robust aggregate demand and a tight labor market." My commentary on her speech was titled "Some Like It Hot." I concluded that Yellen was in no hurry to rush the pace of rate hikes.

What I found unusual about her speech was that she admitted there might be "limits in economists' understanding of the economy." Then she proceeded to list several questions that she hoped "the profession will try to answer." Apparently, on-the-job experiences had moderated the confidence she had expressed at the Yalie reunion. She suggested that perhaps macroeconomists need to do more work using "disaggregated data and models." In other words, they should be microeconomists! Admittedly, I may be putting words in her mouth.

She got into some real meaning-of-life questions for macroeconomists. For example: "How does the financial sector interact with the broader economy?" Now get this one: "What determines inflation?" Remember, this is coming from the Fed chair who, in a sense, wrote the book on macroeconomics, or at least the Tobin notes!

During Yellen's term as Fed chair, she and other Fed officials were baffled that inflation remained below their 2.0% target, particularly when the unemployment rate suggested that the labor market was close to full employment during 2017. On numerous occasions, Yellen had expressed her faith in the Phillips curve model—which posits that there is a tradeoff between unemployment and inflation—and used it to predict that wage inflation would move higher. I suggested that Fed officials needed to order from Amazon to understand one of the forces keeping inflation down. In a September 26, 2017 speech, Yellen for the first time conceded the point in public, saying, "The growing importance of online shopping, by increasing the competitiveness of the U.S. retail sector, may have reduced price margins and restrained the ability of firms to raise prices in response to rising demand." In a speech on

October 15, 2017, Yellen candidly stated, "The biggest surprise in the U.S. economy this year has been inflation. . . . Inflation readings over the past several months have been surprisingly soft."

Yellen's speech suggested that she was coming around to my strongly held view that economists need to go out and talk to real people instead of tweaking their models and having heated debates with one another over theories that are divorced from reality. As a wise man once said: "In theory, there is no difference between theory and practice, but in practice, there is."

To be fair, the Fed does attempt to get grassroots perspectives on the economy in several ways. Its *Beige Book* is one; the Fed's website explains:

> Each Federal Reserve Bank gathers anecdotal information on current economic conditions in its District through reports from Bank and Branch directors and interviews with key business contacts, economists, market experts, and other sources. The Beige Book summarizes this information by District and sector. An overall summary of the twelve district reports is prepared by a designated Federal Reserve Bank on a rotating basis.[129]

In addition, several of the Fed district banks conduct monthly surveys of business conditions in their regions. I've found that the average of the general business indexes for five of the districts (Dallas, Kansas City, New York, Philadelphia, and Richmond) is highly correlated with the national manufacturing purchasing managers' index.[130] The Fed also surveys senior loan officers of up to 80 large domestic banks and 24 US branches and agencies of foreign banks on a quarterly basis.[131] That doesn't sound very folksy, but at least the Fed is trying to get some feedback on regional economies from the local folks.

Near the end of her term as Fed chair, Yellen faced a challenge launched by a few congressional Republicans to force the FOMC to follow a rules-based approach to setting monetary policy. The concept was originally pushed by Milton Friedman, who believed that the Fed should stick to a set growth rate in the money supply.

The Fed's July 7, 2017 *Monetary Policy Report*, which accompanied Yellen's congressional testimony, included a section titled "Monetary Policy Rules and Their Role in the Federal Reserve's Policy Process."[132] The basic message was that the FOMC does pay attention to simple models such as the Taylor Rule, which prescribes the level of the federal funds rate based on two gaps: (1) the one between actual and targeted inflation and (2) the one between actual and potential real GDP.

However, the Fed's policymakers believe that these models ignore too many "considerations" that require their judgment when setting the federal funds rate. In the "rules versus discretion" debate, they clearly favor the latter approach. For Fed watchers like myself, discretion, rather than rules, in the formulation of monetary policymaking means that we will continue to find gainful employment as profilers of Fed officials.

President Donald Trump did not reappoint Yellen for a second term to chair the Fed. He considered John Taylor, who devised the Taylor Rule, for the post. Instead, he chose Fed Governor Jerome Powell on November 2, 2017. I think Yellen did a good job of managing the gradual normalization of monetary policy and solidifying Bernanke's achievement in reviving the economy. Under both, bond and stock investors enjoyed significant bull markets. Now, let's move on to Yellen's successor and the current Fed head as of this writing.

Chapter 8

Jerome Powell:
The Pragmatic Pivoter

Following the Script

Jerome Powell's term as Fed chair started on February 5, 2018. Trump could have appointed Yellen to another term as Fed chair. It didn't take long for the President to regret his choice of Powell instead.

Powell has a law degree from Georgetown University. He also had lots of experience on Wall Street. He became a Fed governor on May 25, 2012. I had expected when Powell took over the Fed that he would continue pursuing Yellen's gradual normalization of monetary policy; I've had to adjust that view because Powell has adjusted his.

In his debut congressional testimony, Powell signaled that his leadership would not differ much from Yellen's. He emphasized in that semiannual testimony on monetary policy—delivered to the House of Representatives on February 27 and the Senate on March 1—that the change in Fed leadership wouldn't significantly alter the course of monetary policy.[133] He said that he would continue the "gradual" pace of normalization unless the incoming data suggested doing otherwise. That was widely interpreted to mean that the three or four 25-basis-point rate hikes that the FOMC projected at the December 2017 meeting (under Yellen) remained the likely scenario for 2018 (under Powell). Initially, this was all very reassuring to financial markets eager to understand what the regime change would mean in terms of interest rates.

His testimony was upbeat on the prospects for the economy: "While many factors shape the economic outlook, some of the headwinds the U.S. economy faced in previous years have turned into tailwinds," he said. "In particular, fiscal policy has become more stimulative and foreign demand for U.S. exports is on a firmer trajectory. Despite the recent volatility, financial conditions remain accommodative."

On inflation, Powell told Congress: "We continue to view some of the shortfall in inflation last year as likely reflecting transitory influences that we do not expect will repeat." But he explained: "In this environment, we anticipate that inflation on a 12-month basis will move up this year and stabilize around the FOMC's 2 percent objective over the medium term."

Powell came across as a straight-shooter—willing to admit to uncertainty and dropping the often-ambiguous verbiage of his predecessors. In response to a question about whether unemployment could drop further if sidelined workers decided to rejoin the labor force, he honestly answered: "The only way to know is to . . . find out."

Powell was pragmatic too. He was asked about the discrepancy in the actual federal funds rate and the substantially higher one suggested by the widely followed Taylor Rule.[134] Powell responded that such rules can be helpful, but the targets they produce can't be viewed in a vacuum. His views on the subject were consistent with Yellen's: "Personally, I find these rule prescriptions helpful. Careful judgments are required about the measurement of the variables used, as well as about the implications of the many issues these rules do not take into account."

Powell's first press conference as Fed head, on March 21, was a non-event.[135] He told investors merely what they had learned from his congressional testimony: that he would remain on the gradual policy path that his predecessor set out before him. His outlook for the US economy remained upbeat with the headwinds-turned-to-tailwinds sentiment expressed in his testimony, though that specific metaphor wasn't reused in the press conference. But as in the testimony, Powell repeated the word "gradual" to describe the pace of federal funds rate increases several times.

Powell was trained as a lawyer rather than as an economist. So he is much less infatuated with economic models and theories than his three predecessors who have PhDs in economics. That's a good thing, in my opinion, since central bankers have been too dependent on unobservable theoretical measures of economic "slack" such as the NAIRU and potential output.

His matter-of-factness regarding models and theories was evident during his first press conference. Powell observed that "the relationship between changes in slack and inflation is not tight," which puts it simply! When asked about the shape of the yield curve, Powell observed that an inverted yield curve might not signal a recession as it had consistently in the past when "inflation was allowed to get out of control." So "the Fed had to tighten . . . and put the economy into a recession." He concluded, "That's really not the situation we're in now."

I agreed with his assessment.

Powell remained on course to gradually normalize monetary policy through the end of 2018. Recall that the federal funds rate range had been fixed at 0.00%–0.25% from December 15, 2008 through December 15, 2015. Under Yellen, the federal funds rate was raised to 0.25%–0.50% on December 16, 2015 and again to 0.50%–0.75% on December 14, 2016. During 2017, still under Yellen's watch, the federal funds rate was raised by three additional quarter-point increments at the FOMC meetings during March (0.75%–1.00%), June (1.00%–1.25%), and December (1.25%–1.50%).

Powell followed Yellen's playbook during his first FOMC meeting as the chair of the committee. The federal funds rate range was raised to 1.50%–1.75% in March (Fig. 24). He followed that up with hikes during June (1.75%–2.00%), September (2.00%–2.25%), and December (2.25%–2.50%).

It was all going according to plan until it wasn't.

The financial markets tested Powell during the fall of 2018, much as they had tested Greenspan during October 1987, Bernanke during May and June of 2013, and Yellen during March 2014.

Without much fanfare, the stage was set for the upcoming drama at Powell's first meeting as chair of the FOMC. The March 21, 2018 dot plot showed the committee's median forecast for the federal funds rate in 2020 had been raised from 3.10% at the previous meeting to 3.40%, further above the "longer run" forecast of 2.90%, which had also been raised from 2.80%. (See Appendix 6, FOMC Projections for the Federal Funds Rate, 2017–2022.)

By then, the markets were starting to focus more on the outlook for monetary policy in 2019 and 2020. The FOMC's June and September dot plots continued to project federal funds rates of 3.10% in 2019 and 3.40% in 2020. If the US economy continued to perform as well as the Fed expected, the federal funds rate would be raised to 3.25%–3.50% during 2020. That would have been two 25-basis-point hikes above the SEP's longer-run projection of 3.00% for the federal funds rate.

Suddenly, changed language in the September 26 FOMC statement drew more attention to the dot plot projections for 2020. The passage "The stance of monetary policy remains accommodative"—which had appeared in every FOMC statement since December 16, 2015, when the Fed's latest rate-hiking program began—had been removed for the September 26 statement.

At his September 26 press conference, Powell said that the language simply had "outlived its useful life," so the Fed would continue its gradual rate increases toward a neutral stance. Nevertheless, some Fed watchers interpreted the deletion to mean that the Fed was setting up for more aggressive rate increases despite Powell's reassurances to the contrary. The markets were starting to fear that the Fed might be turning from accommodative to neutral to outright restrictive, given the strength of the economy. Stock prices began to fall.

During the Q&A of his September 26 press conference, Powell was asked whether the Fed might end the tightening cycle in a "restrictive posture," as Fed Governor Lael Brainard had suggested in a September 12 speech. Powell responded: "It's very possible." He added: "Maybe we will keep our neutral rate here [i.e., at 3.00%], and then go one or two rate increases beyond it." In her speech, Brainard explained:

> In the latest FOMC SEP median path, by the end of next year, the federal funds rate is projected to rise to a level that exceeds the longer-run federal funds rate during a time when real GDP growth is projected to exceed its longer-run pace and unemployment continues to fall. The shift from headwinds to tailwinds may be expected to push the shorter-run neutral rate above its longer-run trend in the next year or two, just as it fell below the longer-run equilibrium rate following the financial crisis.[136]

Investors' fears were further confirmed by the release of the September FOMC meeting minutes on October 17. The word "restrictive" appeared for the first time during the current economic expansion. And it did so twice (emphasis mine):

> Participants offered their views about how much additional policy firming would likely be required for the Committee to sustainably achieve its objectives of maximum employment and 2 percent inflation. A few participants expected that policy would need to become modestly **restrictive** for a time and

a number judged that it would be necessary to temporarily raise the federal funds rate above their assessments of its longer-run level in order to reduce the risk of a sustained overshooting of the Committee's 2 percent inflation objective or the risk posed by significant financial imbalances. A couple of participants indicated that they would not favor adopting a **restrictive** policy stance in the absence of clear signs of an overheating economy and rising inflation.[137]

It increasingly seemed that monetary policy and fiscal policy were on a collision course, as the former was tapping on the economy's brakes while the latter was keeping the pedal to the metal. President Trump and Larry Kudlow, the director of the National Economic Council, publicly chastised the Fed for raising interest rates. They firmly believed that their supply-side policies of deregulation and tax cuts would boost productivity-led economic growth without heating up inflation, as long as monetary policy didn't get in the way.

That conflicting mix of fiscal and monetary policies sent stock prices plunging 19.8% from September 20 through December 24, but Powell got most of the blame (Fig. 25). Some off-the-cuff comments he made in an October 3 interview with Judy Woodruff heightened investors' anxiety about the Fed's policy course:

> So interest rates are still accommodative, but we're gradually moving to a place where they will be neutral, not that they'll be a restraint on the economy. We may go past neutral, but we're a long way from neutral at this point, probably.[138]

That contradicted the deletion of the accommodative language from the latest FOMC statement, and implied that the Fed would be raising interest rates through 2020 as outlined in the dot plot. More confusion ensued. On October 25, in his first public speech as Fed vice chair, Richard H. Clarida echoed Powell, saying,

"However, even after our September decision, I believe U.S. monetary policy remains accommodative." To say so was a rookie's mistake by Clarida, but Powell should have known better.

Clarida walked his October 25 statement back for himself, and maybe for Powell too, on Friday, November 16, saying in a CNBC interview: "As you move in the range of policy that by some estimates is close to neutral, then with the economy doing well it's appropriate to sort of shift the emphasis toward being more data dependent." He was seconding Atlanta Fed President Raphael Bostic. The day before, on November 15, he said the Fed is "not too far" from reaching a "neutral" rate. But the investment community was left scratching their heads: There's a big difference between Clarida's "close to" and Bostic's "not too far from" on one hand and Powell's "a long way off from" on the other.

Powell's Pivot

In my commentaries and in a few press interviews, I called on the Fed to pause its rate hiking. On October 29, I wrote: "What's the rush to raise interest rates? Why not pause the rate hikes and assess how the economy is responding to them so far? . . . In my opinion, the plunge in stock prices, especially the ones of cyclical companies, suggests that the economy may not be as strong as the Fed perceives and that inflationary risks remain low." CNBC's Jim Cramer was saying the same, along with the White House.

In a November 14 Q&A discussion led by Dallas Fed President Robert Kaplan, Powell turned more dovishly cautious, comparing monetary policy to walking through a room full of furniture when the lights go out. "What do you do? You slow down. You stop, probably, and feel your way," he said. "It's not different with policy." He also warned against relying too much on data that are revised frequently. He said, "You pick things up sooner talking to business people because they start to feel it, and then it shows up in the data."[139]

My November 19 *Morning Briefing* was "On Your Mark, Get Set, Pause." I wrote:

> President Donald Trump and Larry Kudlow, his economic adviser, have been calling for Fed officials to pause their inter-est-rate hiking. So has CNBC's Jim Cramer. And so have I. Fed Chair Jerome Powell and his colleagues may be starting to get the message and act accordingly.

The Tuesday November 27 issue of *The Wall Street Journal* included an article by Nick Timiraos titled "Fed Shifts to a Less Predictable Approach to Policy Making."[140] It was based on interviews with Fed officials who "will be deciding whether and when to raise interest rates more on the basis of the latest signs of economic vigor—such as in inflation, unemployment and growth—and less on forecasts of how the economy is expected to perform in the months and years to come." They were admitting that they are more uncertain about the level of the neutral interest rate and were "looking for clues in markets and economic data that might sug-gest whether this point might be higher or lower."

The very same day, in a November 27 speech, Clarida reiter-ated that both the neutral rate of interest and the unemployment rate that is consistent with stable inflation are unmeasurable. So needing to get a fix on them "supports the case for gradual policy normalization, as it will allow the Fed to accumulate more infor-mation from the data about the ultimate destination for the policy rate." That also supported the case for longer pauses in between rate hikes, in my opinion.[141]

In a speech at The Economics Club of New York on Wednesday, November 28, Powell confirmed my assessment when he said, "Interest rates are still low by historical standards, and they remain just below the broad range of estimates of the level that would be neutral for the economy—that is, neither speeding up nor slowing down growth."[142] Stock investors jumped for joy upon hearing Powell's "just below" comment.

The next day, on November 29, the minutes of the November 7–8 FOMC meeting came out.[143] The word "restrictive" had been dropped. In my November 29 commentary, I exuberantly wrote:

> The Fed's critics will say that now we have a fourth Fed chair in a row providing the stock market with a put, i.e., the Powell Put. Maybe so. However, if Janet Yellen was the "Fairy Godmother of the Bull Market," as we often fondly called her, then Powell for now is the bull market's Santa. The Santa Claus rally that started on Monday should drive the S&P 500 back to retest its 9/20 record high around 2900 by the end of this year.

My optimism was about a month too early. The Fed's message remained confusing. Indeed, Powell inadvertently freaked the markets out again at his December 19 press conference when he responded to a question on monetary policy as follows: "So we thought carefully about this, on how to normalize policy, and came to the view that we would effectively have the balance sheet runoff on automatic pilot and use monetary policy, rate policy, to adjust to incoming data."[144]

The Fed's message became clearer and increasingly dovish at the start of the new year. On Friday, January 4, 2019, along with a blowout employment report, dovish remarks from Powell sent the DJIA soaring 746 points and the S&P 500 jumping 8.4%. Speaking on a panel with former Fed chairs Ben Bernanke and Janet Yellen at the annual meeting of the American Economic Association and Allied Social Science Association in Atlanta, Powell emphasized that the monetary policy path was not on autopilot.[145]

Powell said that the Fed is willing to be "patient." He noted that to keep the US economic expansion on track, "there is no preset path for policy." He stated: "We will be prepared to adjust policy quickly and flexibly and use all of our tools to support the economy should that be appropriate." Powell used the example of early 2016, when the Fed expected to raise rates four times but did so only once as the economy weakened. Later, the gradual path of rate hikes resumed during 2017 and 2018. "No one knows whether this year will be more like 2016," he said. "But what I do know is that we will be prepared to adjust policy quickly and flexibly."

In the past, Powell was wary of the models that drove policy for his predecessors. Powell specifically questioned the relationship between wages and broader inflation. Confirming this view, he said on the panel that the "link between . . . wage inflation and price inflation is pretty weak." He added: "Wages going up isn't necessarily inflation."

Equity markets suddenly seemed to matter a lot more to Powell. He even said that the Fed was starting to give more weight to the markets, and so might pause rate hiking for a while. Markets are "obviously well ahead of the data," but "we're listening very carefully," Powell said. I concluded in my January 7 commentary that "[t]he Dow Vigilantes may have gotten their Powell Put!"

The Fed's balance-sheet reduction was not an "important part of the story," according to Powell. But "if we reached a different conclusion, we wouldn't hesitate to make a change." For perspective, the Fed's QE programs following the 2008 recession led the Fed to grow its balance sheet to more than $4.5 trillion. The Fed had been rolling off $50 billion per month of that since October 2017. Some viewed this as quantitative tightening. So Powell's statement that the Fed is flexible (and not on "automatic pilot," as he had said during his December 19 press conference) came as a relief to investors. Interestingly, Powell read his initial remarks from a script, presumably to avoid another off-the-cuff gaffe.

Powell's January 30, 2019 press conference marked what came to be known as the "Powell Pivot."[146] He confirmed that he was becoming more patient and flexible regarding rate hiking in 2019, consistent with the FOMC consensus stance apparently emerging. His opening remarks included lots of reasons to pause interest-rate increases, notwithstanding December's signs of economic strength. The press conference, especially the Q&A session, seemed to be more scripted than his prior ones.

Powell's take on the stance of monetary policy shifted from a "gradual" tightening approach in December 2018 to "a patient, wait-and-see approach" in January 2019. Consider the following points on which Powell pivoted:

- **Appropriate.** In December, "two interest rate increases over the course of next year" was his expectation. In January's press conference, he called the current policy stance "appropriate" several times. "[T]he case for raising rates has weakened somewhat," he said. Citing "growing evidence of cross-currents," Powell said that "common sense risk management suggests patiently awaiting greater clarity." He added, "We think there's no pressing need to change our policy stance and no need to rush to judgment."

- **Near neutral.** December's press conference found Powell implying there was room to raise interest rates, as he said they'd reached the "bottom end" of what might be considered a "neutral" range (i.e., where rates would neither accelerate nor slow the economy). He also mentioned the possibility of "circumstances in which it would be appropriate" for the Fed to raise rates "past neutral." In January's press conference, he said: "[O]ur policy rate is now in the range of the Committee's estimates of neutral." No intention of moving toward a restrictive stance was indicated as it was in December.

- **Cross-currents.** In December, Powell dismissed the economy's emerging downside risks, or "cross-currents"—including financial market volatility and tightening financial condition. They didn't fundamentally alter the outlook, he said. At the January press conference, however, Powell changed his tune, saying that cross-currents could result in a "less favorable outlook." Slow growth in Europe and China, Brexit, ongoing trade negotiations between the US and China, and the effects from the partial government shutdown coupled with weakness in surveys of businesses and consumer sentiment gave "reasons for caution," he said. He also suggested that the upside risks to the economic outlook, including the "risk of too-high inflation," had diminished.

- **No decisions.** In December, Powell said that he "would effectively have the balance sheet runoff on automatic pilot," adding "I don't see us changing that." That changed in January, when he stated that "we will not hesitate to make changes" to balance-sheet policy. He added that "no decisions have been made" on the plan for balance-sheet normalization and that there are a lot of moving "pieces."

- **Patient.** During his January press conference, Powell mentioned the words "patient" or "patience" a total of eight times, four times in his opening remarks and four times during the Q&A. This compares with only once during the Q&A of the December press conference.

In a February 6 interview on CNBC, former Fed Chair Yellen said interest rates could go up or down. "It's not out of the question that the Fed may need to raise rates again," she said. But then she added: "If global growth really weakens and that spills over to the United States, or if financial conditions tighten more and we do see a weakening in the US economy, it's certainly possible the next move is a cut, but both outcomes are possible."[147] Echoing Powell's January 4 comments, she also recalled the unexpected policy shifts of 2016 to emphasize the importance of maintaining policy flexibility.

Powell gave his semiannual testimony on the economy before the Senate Banking, Housing and Urban Affairs Committee on February 26.[148] If his goal was to make it as boring as possible so as not to disturb markets, he succeeded. That's a compliment because Powell's previous off-the-cuff style caused a lot of market havoc. Powell seemed to have quickly learned during his short tenure as Fed chair that credible messaging is key. So his basic message to Congress, and financial markets, was that the Fed will be patient with rates, cautious and flexible with the balance sheet, and mindful of global risks.

Powell's Pirouette

Stock prices soared during the first few months of 2019 as Powell's Pivot morphed into Powell's Pirouette. The Fed chair was still talking about normalization in a March 8, 2019 speech titled "Monetary Policy: Normalization and the Road Ahead."[149] Powell had the following to say about the normalization of monetary policy:

> Delivering on the FOMC's intention to ultimately normalize policy continues to be a major priority at the Fed. Normalization is far along, and, considering the unprecedented nature of the exercise, it is proceeding smoothly. I am confident that we can effectively manage the remaining stages.

The words "normal" or "normalization" appeared 27 times in his speech.

For the first time, Powell specified the expected endpoint for the wind-down of the Fed's balance sheet. Until now, various Fed officials had said that the Fed would likely return the balance sheet to a level higher than it was before the recession (i.e., a new normal). Total assets on the Fed's balance sheet increased by $3.6 trillion from $0.9 trillion at the start of 2008 to a peak of $4.5 trillion during February 2016. Since then, assets had fallen by $0.6 trillion to $3.9 trillion at the time of Powell's March speech.

Powell said that "something in the ballpark of the [fourth-quarter 2019] projected values may be the new normal. The normalized balance sheet may be smaller or larger than that estimate and will grow gradually over time as demand for currency rises with the economy. In all plausible cases, the balance sheet will be considerably larger than before the crisis." As for the normality of the federal funds rate, Powell reiterated that the "federal funds rate is now within the broad range of estimates of the neutral rate—the interest rate that tends neither to stimulate nor to restrain the economy."

In the March 8 speech, Powell did his best to convince Fed watchers and other onlookers to pay less attention to the FOMC's dot plot. Don't look too closely at the Fed's dot plot or you might miss the larger monetary policy picture, warned Powell. To make his point, he showed two unusual images: an unrecognizable close-up of a bouquet of flowers from impressionist painter Georges Seurat's "A Sunday Afternoon on the Island of La Grande Jatte" and a very recognizable image of the full painting. He warned that monetary impressionists may not be seeing the forest for the trees, to mix up the metaphor.[150]

This was not the first time that a Fed chair had provided Fed watchers with an art class on interpreting the Fed's dot-based pictures of monetary policy. In his speech, Powell reviewed two previous instances. In 2014, the dots caused "collateral confusion," according to then-Fed Chair Janet Yellen, when the markets misread the Fed's intentions. She stated that what matters more than the dots is what is said in the FOMC statement released after each meeting. Similarly, former Fed Chair Ben Bernanke once said that the "dots" are merely inputs to the Fed's policy decision making; they don't account for "all the risks, the uncertainties, all the things that inform our collective judgement."

Powell's Pirouette occurred on June 4, in his opening remarks at a conference in Chicago.[151] He got to the point in the second paragraph of his written remarks:

> I'd like first to say a word about recent developments involving trade negotiations and other matters. We do not know how or when these issues will be resolved. We are closely monitoring the implications of these developments for the U.S. economic outlook and, as always, we will act as appropriate to sustain the expansion, with a strong labor market and inflation near our symmetric 2 percent objective.

Fed watchers immediately concluded that the next move by the Fed might be to lower the federal funds rate rather than to raise it, sending the S&P 500 to another record new high.

Interestingly, the rest of his speech suggested that Powell and his colleagues had become totally obsessed with the "effective lower bound" (ELB) for the federal funds rate. Indeed, the abbreviation "ELB" appeared 26 times in his speech. Powell never explicitly defined ELB, however. In the past, Fed officials were more explicit, calling it the "zero lower bound" (ZLB). In his March 8 speech, Powell stated: "Just over 10 years ago, the Federal Open Market Committee . . . lowered the federal funds rate close to zero, which we refer to as the effective lower bound, or ELB. Unable to lower rates further, the Committee turned to two novel tools to promote the recovery."[152]

In his latest speech, Powell was concerned that the federal funds rate was too close to the ELB. He was also worried about what the Fed can do when the federal funds rate falls to the ELB:

> The next time policy rates hit the ELB—and there will be a next time—it will not be a surprise. We are now well aware of the challenges the ELB presents, and we have the painful experience of the Global Financial Crisis and its aftermath to guide us. Our obligation to the public we serve is to take those measures now that will put us in the best position [to] deal with our next encounter with the ELB.

Leaving no doubt about his concern, Powell said: "In short, the proximity of interest rates to the ELB has become the preeminent monetary policy challenge of our time, tainting all manner of issues with ELB risk and imbuing many old challenges with greater significance." In a matter of only a few months, Powell had turned from talking about raising interest rates to worrying about what the Fed would do once the federal funds rate was back down to zero!

Powell reiterated the Fed's standing-by-to-ease status at his June 19 press conference, stating, "In light of increased uncertainties and muted inflation pressures, we now emphasize that the Committee will closely monitor the implications of incoming information for the economic outlook and will act as appropriate to sustain the expansion, with a strong labor market and inflation near its 2 percent objective."[153] In the June FOMC statement, the "appropriate" phrase replaced the "patient" phrase.[154]

Powell also omitted another word from his June press conference that had made headlines following his May press conference. In May, he argued that recent low inflation readings were likely "transient." But during his June press conference, he didn't mention it again.

During the June FOMC meeting, Powell encountered his first dissenting vote since becoming Fed chair, from James Bullard, the loquacious president of the Federal Reserve Bank of St. Louis, who argued for a rate cut at that meeting. What's more, eight Fed officials were now forecasting a rate cut in the coming year, according to the SEP.

On Wednesday, July 10 and Thursday, July 11, 2019, Powell presented the Fed's semiannual testimony on monetary policy to two congressional committees.[155] On Wednesday, he implied that he was ready to cut the federal funds rate at the next FOMC meeting at the end of the month. He was more emphatic about it on Thursday during his Q&A before a Senate committee.

In his prepared remarks on Wednesday, Powell emphasized his concern that uncertainty about trade negotiations between the US and China might be depressing the global economy and weighing on the US economic outlook. He mentioned the trade issue no less than eight times. Here's one example: "However, inflation has been running below the Federal Open Market Committee's (FOMC) symmetric 2 percent objective, and crosscurrents, such as trade tensions and concerns about global growth, have been weighing on economic activity and the outlook."

On Thursday, Powell told the Senate Banking Committee, "The relationship between unemployment and inflation became weak" about 20 years ago, and "[i]t's become weaker and weaker and weaker." He also told the senators that the so-called "neutral rate," or policy rate that keeps the economy on an even keel, is lower than past estimates have put it—meaning monetary policy had been too restrictive. "We're learning that interest rates—that the neutral interest rate—is lower than we had thought, and I think we're learning that the natural rate of unemployment is lower than we thought," he said. "So monetary policy hasn't been as accommodative as we had thought."

In a July 16 speech, at a conference organized by the Banque de France, Powell stated: "Many FOMC participants judged at the time of our most recent meeting in June that the combination of these factors strengthens the case for a somewhat more accommodative stance of policy."[156]

Two days later, on July 18, two of Powell's colleagues weighed in with comments that seemed to telegraph increased odds of a federal funds rate cut at the next FOMC meeting at the end of July—Federal Reserve Bank of New York President John Williams and Federal Reserve Vice Chairman Richard Clarida.

In a speech titled "Living Life Near the ZLB," Williams argued that monetary policy should be eased more preemptively and aggressively the closer that the federal funds rate is to the ZLB. He said that, based on simulation models, "monetary policy can mitigate the effects of the ZLB."[157] He mentioned three ways it can do so:

> The first: don't keep your powder dry—that is, move more quickly to add monetary stimulus than you otherwise might. When the ZLB is nowhere in view, one can afford to move slowly and take a "wait and see" approach to gain additional clarity about potentially adverse economic developments. But not when interest rates are in the vicinity of the ZLB. In that case, you want to do the opposite, and vaccinate against further ills. When you only have so much stimulus at your disposal, it pays to act quickly to lower rates at the first sign of economic distress.

His second recommendation was "to keep interest rates lower for longer" to lower bond yields, resulting in "more favorable financial conditions overall," which "will allow the stimulus to pick up steam, support economic growth over the medium term, and allow inflation to rise." Finally, he promoted "policies that promise temporarily higher inflation following ZLB episodes." He observed, "In model simulations, these 'make-up' strategies can mitigate nearly all of the adverse effects of the ZLB."

Williams ended his speech by saying that the actions he recommended "should vaccinate the economy and protect it from the more insidious disease of too low inflation." In my opinion, comparing near-zero inflation to an insidious disease is bizarre.

Williams' public relations department rushed to set the record straight with *The Wall Street Journal*, which reported after the market's close on July 18:

> New York Fed President John Williams didn't intend to suggest Thursday that the central bank might make a large interest rate cut this month, a spokesman said Thursday. In the speech, presented at an academic conference in New York, Mr. Williams said policy makers needed to confront potential weaknesses more quickly given the prospect that a historically low interest rate could fall to zero sooner, leaving less room to stimulate growth in a downturn.

That same day, July 18, in a Fox Business Network interview, Clarida said that the economy is in a "good place." Yet he alluded to "uncertainties" that might weaken the economy. He concluded, "You don't need to wait until things get so bad to have a dramatic series of rate cuts." He added, "We need to make a decision based on where we think the economy may be heading and, importantly, where the risks to the economy are lined up."[158]

By the way, in his speech in Paris, Powell lamented that being a central banker is tougher than it was during Greenspan's days at the Fed:

> It is challenging, because we are operating in a changing macroeconomic environment with tools that, while no longer new,

remain less familiar to the public. Moreover, our audience has become more varied, more attuned to our actions, and less trusting of public institutions. Gone are the days when the Federal Reserve Chair could joke, as my predecessor Alan Greenspan did, "If I turn out to be particularly clear, you've probably misunderstood what I said." Central banks must speak to Main Street, as well as Wall Street, in ways we have not in the past, and Main Street is listening and engaged.[159]

Getting Trumped

Even though Trump appointed Powell, the two have had a testy relationship. The July 11, 2019 issue of my daily commentary was titled "Powell Gets Trumped!" I wrote that President Trump wants the Fed to lower interest rates, while Fed Chair Powell insists that the Fed is independent and won't bow to political pressure. Yet Trump figured out the way to force the Fed to lower interest rates. I noted that in his July 10 congressional testimony, Powell mentioned the trade issue *eight times* in his prepared remarks. All Trump had to do was keep creating uncertainty about US trade policy.

At the July 31 meeting, the FOMC voted to lower the federal funds rate's target range from 2.25%–2.50% to 2.00%–2.25%, the first rate cut since 2008. In addition, the FOMC decided to terminate quantitative tightening (QT) ahead of schedule: "The Committee will conclude the reduction of its aggregate securities holdings in the System Open Market Account in August, two months earlier than previously indicated." From October 1, 2017 through July 31, 2019, the Fed's balance sheet was pared from $4.4 trillion to $3.7 trillion.

The Wednesday, July 31 FOMC statement attributed this decision to "the implications of global developments for the economic outlook as well as muted inflation pressures."[160] Also, the word "uncertainties" was used regarding the economic outlook—the first time this word had appeared in an FOMC meeting statement since March 18, 2003. Back then, the concern was about "geopolitical uncertainties," specifically the imminent war with Iraq. This time, uncertainties were similarly geopolitical, centering around Trump's escalating trade wars.

Despite the rate cut, the S&P 500 fell 1.1% on Wednesday. That's because in his press conference following the FOMC meeting, Powell characterized the move as a "midcycle adjustment."[161] He mentioned the phrase three times in his Q&A with reporters, implying that another rate cut at the September meeting was not a foregone conclusion.

On Wednesday afternoon, Trump was quick to attack the Fed's decision. He tweeted:

> What the Market wanted to hear from Jay Powell and the Federal Reserve was that this was the beginning of a lengthy and aggressive rate-cutting cycle which would keep pace with China, The European Union and other countries around the world. . . . As usual, Powell let us down, but at least he is ending quantitative tightening, which shouldn't have started in the first place—no inflation. We are winning anyway, but I am certainly not getting much help from the Federal Reserve!

The next day, Trump said that the US will impose a 10% tariff on an additional $300 billion worth of Chinese imports during September. The new tariff would be on top of the 25% levy that Trump had already imposed on $250 billion worth of Chinese imports—so the US would be taxing nearly everything China sends to the US. Trump added that the tariffs could be raised to 25% or higher if the talks continued to drag on without any significant progress, but he allowed that alternatively they could be removed if a deal is struck.

An August 1, 2019 Bloomberg post observed that Trump's escalation of the trade war with China the very day after he was disappointed by the Fed's lame decision was not coincidental: "[A]fter the Fed chairman said his rate cut was justified by trade tensions, it makes sense the president would be tempted to create more of them."

How did the President's dissatisfaction with Powell get so bad? Let's retrace the steps.

The President made his first critical remark about the Fed on July 19, 2018, saying in a CNBC interview, "I'm not thrilled" the central bank is raising borrowing costs and potentially slowing the economy. "I don't like all of this work that we're putting into the economy and then I see rates going up."

On October 19, 2018, he slammed the Fed, complaining "they're so tight. I think the Fed has gone crazy."

He took direct aim at the Fed chair on November 27, 2018, telling *The Washington Post* that he was "not even a little bit happy with my selection of Jay." He added, "I think the Fed is a much bigger problem than China" for the US economy.[162]

On September 11, 2019, Trump escalated his war against the Fed. In a series of tweets, he said, "The Federal Reserve should get our interest rates down to ZERO, or less, and we should then start to refinance our debt," adding that "the USA should always be paying the lowest rate." He continued to criticize his handpicked Fed chair, saying, "It is only the naïveté of Jay Powell and the Federal Reserve that doesn't allow us to do what other countries are already doing." He concluded, "A once in a lifetime opportunity that we are missing because of 'Boneheads.'"[163]

The President had gone from calling for a moderate rate cut at the beginning of the year to urging the Fed to adopt the negative-interest-rate policies (NIRP) of the ECB and the BOJ! In my commentary, I observed that the President has "NIRP envy."

Alan Blinder, a former vice chair of the Fed, defended Powell in a September 18, 2019 *Wall Street Journal* op-ed titled, "When Presidents Pummel the Fed." He observed that the Fed had been bashed during previous administrations, particularly when Lyndon Johnson, Ronald Reagan, and George H.W. Bush occupied the White House. The Fed enjoyed a period of tranquility, or at least a reprieve from Fed bashers at the White House, when Bill Clinton, George W. Bush, and Barack Obama were Presidents. Then came Trump, who had criticized Yellen for keeping monetary policy too loose and threatened to fire Powell for raising interest rates in 2018, and then again for not cutting them fast enough during 2019. Blinder concluded that Trump was "setting up Mr. Powell and the Fed as scapegoats if the U.S. economy falters."[164]

Data Dependent

While Powell's "midcycle adjustment" comment threw a damp rag on investors' hopes of a series of rate cuts, the FOMC statement still promised that the Fed "will act as appropriate to sustain the expansion." That became the new boilerplate clause in the June 2019 FOMC statement, implying that the Fed was ready to lower interest rates, which it did in July.

The midcycle adjustment continued when the federal funds rate was cut again by 25 basis points on September 18 to a range of 1.75%–2.00%. The move was widely expected by then. Powell was becoming so intent on not upsetting the financial markets by this point that he brought scripted answers even to his post-meeting press conference, which required anticipating the questions in advance! No more off-the-cuff replies for him. He succeeded in saying nothing to rock the boat.

If I were in Powell's shoes (there I go again!), I would keep the press conferences short. In the preliminary prepared remarks,

I'd review what the FOMC had decided to do at the latest meeting of the committee and why. Then, I'd say: "As always, the future course of monetary policy will remain data dependent." During the Q&A, I would repeat this mantra whenever asked about the future course of monetary policy.

In his September 18 press conference, Powell seemed to be reading from my suggested script. The word "data" was mentioned 17 times in the context of messaging that the Fed is data dependent, 11 times by him and six by reporters. During his prior presser, in July, Powell used the word in that context five times, fewer than reporters' six times. So Powell accounted for the majority of the mentions, or 65% of them, up from 45% at July's press conference.

His emphasis on data dependence reflected the Fed's greater uncertainty about the future. The words "uncertain" or "uncertainty" appeared 21 times, 13 of those times by Powell, up from nine times in July, when all mentions were Powell's. In both press conferences, he mentioned the words four times during his prepared preliminary remarks.

So the Fed was uncertain about the future course of the economy—all the more reason to be data dependent. That was the gist of his September 2019 press conference, and the financial markets were fine with that.

In the first three FOMC statements of 2019 (January, March, and May), the key boilerplate clause had been: "[T]he Committee will be patient as it determines what future adjustments to the target range for the federal funds rate may be appropriate to support these outcomes." That implied that the Fed wasn't rushing to raise or to lower interest rates.

Powell had pivoted from calling for more rate hikes during October 2018 to waiting and seeing patiently whether incoming data warranted hikes early in 2019, to possibly cutting the federal funds rate if that was deemed appropriate, to cutting it during July and September. At the end of October, the FOMC lowered the federal funds rate again to a range of 1.50%–1.75%.

During his October 30 press conference, Powell said, "So I think we would need to see a really significant move up in inflation that's persistent before we would consider raising rates to address inflation concerns." If so, then the Fed is likely to remain on hold through the 2020 presidential election.

I concluded that Powell's renewed patient stance for monetary policy, after the Fed lowered the federal funds rate three times, was bullish for equities. That forecast was confirmed by the stock market's meltup following his October 30 press conference. It was only a year before, on October 3, 2018, that Powell had triggered a meltdown in the stock market. The S&P 500 was back at an all-time high by the end of November and making more new record highs during December 2019.

Powell is a pragmatist and knows how to pivot. As such, his policy decisions will remain data dependent.

Two Credit Crunches

During his September 2019 press conference, Powell briefly spoke about the inversion of the yield curve and the curve's so-called "long end" (i.e., the 10-year US Treasury bond yield). It was music to my ears, because his views happened to coincide with mine on both subjects. He opined, as I have, that an inverted yield curve may not be as good a predictor of recessions as in the past because the long bond yield has been pulled down by negative bond yields in Europe and Japan, which have been brought down by the negative interest-rate policies of the ECB and BOJ.

Powell said that the "yield curve is something that we follow carefully." He observed that "there's this large quantity of negative yielding and very low yielding sovereign debt around the world, and inevitably, that's exerting downward pressure on U.S. sovereign rates without really necessarily having an independent signal." Starting during the late summer of 2018, I had observed frequently that US bond yields have been tethered to German and Japanese bond yields.[165]

By the way, in a July 2019 study titled "The Yield Curve: What Is It Really Predicting?," my colleague Melissa Tagg and I argued that the Fed should pay more attention to the curve—raising interest rates during the yield curve's positively sloped ascensions, pausing when it is flat, and cutting rates during negatively sloped inversions. In other words, the flattening of the yield curve during the first half of 2019 supported the Fed's decision to pause rate hiking earlier that year. The inversion of the yield curve during the spring and summer of 2019 supported the Fed's easing decisions made at the July, September, and October meetings.[166]

In our study, we observed that the yield curve has a good track record of calling recessions because it has often accurately anticipated the credit crunches that have caused recessions (Fig. 26). There were a few signs of a credit crunch in late 2018, particularly in global corporate bond markets. In the United States, during December through early January, there were 40 days without a high-yield bond sale, the longest stretch in data going back to 1995, according to Dealogic.[167] But the capital markets rebounded in early 2019 after Powell signaled a pause in US rate hikes. The yield curve spread between the federal funds rate and the 10-year US Treasury bond yield briefly turned negative during the spring and summer of 2019. But it rebounded into positive territory during November and December in response to the Fed's three rate cuts from July through October. The Fed chair deserves credit for his flexibility.

During September 16 and 17, 2019, there was a brief credit crunch in the repo market. Here is how the Bank for International Settlements explains the market:

> A repo transaction is a short-term (usually overnight) collateralised loan, in which the borrower (of cash) sells a security (typically government bonds as collateral) to the lender, with a commitment to buy it back later at the same price plus interest. Repo markets redistribute liquidity between financial institutions: not only banks (as is the case with the federal funds market), but also insurance companies, asset managers, money market funds and other institutional investors. In so doing, they help other financial markets to function smoothly. Thus, any sustained disruption in this market, with daily turnover in the US market of about $1 trillion, could quickly ripple through the financial system. The freezing-up of repo markets in late 2008 was one of the most damaging aspects of the Great Financial Crisis (GFC).[168]

Here is how Powell described the problem in an October 8 speech:

> In mid-September, an important channel in the transmission process—wholesale funding markets—exhibited unexpectedly intense volatility. Payments to meet corporate tax obligations and to purchase Treasury securities triggered notable liquidity pressures in money markets. Overnight interest rates spiked, and the effective federal funds rate briefly moved above the FOMC's target range. To counter these pressures, we began conducting temporary open market operations. These operations have kept the federal funds rate in the target range and alleviated money market strains more generally.[169]

Short-term rates spiked from about 2% to 10%. The federal funds rate rose five basis points above the Fed's target range. Powell observed that the supply of bank reserves provided by the Fed must grow over time along with the economy. He recounted that

the Fed's March press release on balance-sheet normalization stated that at some point, the FOMC would begin increasing the Fed's
securities holdings to maintain an appropriate level of reserves.[170]
Then he said, "That time is now upon us."

In an October 11, 2019 press release, the Fed announced that
beginning on October 15 it "will purchase Treasury bills at least
into the second quarter of next year in order to maintain over time
ample reserve balances at or above the level that prevailed in early
September 2019."[171] More details were provided in a separate New
York Fed statement (and accompanying FAQs).[172] The initial pace
of these "reserve management" (RM) purchases would be approx-
imately $60 billion per month and would be in addition to ongoing
purchases of Treasuries related to the reinvestment of principal
payments from the Fed's maturing holdings of agency debt and
agency mortgage-backed securities. As the new holdings matured,
the principal payments would be reinvested into Treasury bills.

Many Fed watchers concluded that these purchases were yet
another round of QE. After all, the Fed was once again expanding its balance sheet sizably. However, in his October 8 speech,
Powell insisted that this operation is not the same as QE: "I want
to emphasize that growth of our balance sheet for reserve management purposes should in no way be confused with the large-
scale asset purchase programs that we deployed after the financial
crisis." Take your pick: RM, QE, or LSAP. Whatever it's called, the
Fed's balance sheet was expanding again.

Chapter 9

Forward Guidance: Heads Up

The Fed's Wordsmith

The Fed chairs and their colleagues have tended to communicate their policy intentions by repeating certain keywords, like "gradual," "patient," and "appropriate." This word game has been going on for quite some time. Indeed, I sometimes suspect that the Fed has a wordsmith on staff. If so, this position was most likely created by Fed Chair Alan Greenspan. The role of the wordsmith is to come up with one word or a short phrase that best describes and communicates both the current stance and the future course of monetary policy. That word or phrase is then repeated in the FOMC statements and minutes, and by the Fed chair and other Fed officials regularly in their speeches and interviews. It is their monetary policy mantra.

The FOMC officially views this "forward guidance" as one of their policy tools. Fed Chair Bernanke explained how it fits into the Fed's toolkit in a November 19, 2013 speech titled "Communication and Monetary Policy," at the National Economics Club's annual dinner. He observed: "The public's expectations about future monetary policy actions matter today because those expectations have important effects on current financial conditions, which in turn affect output, employment, and inflation over time." He stressed that "expectations matter so much that a central bank may be able to help make policy more effective by working to shape those expectations."[173]

Here, I recap how some of the FOMC's mantra words and phrases have been used over the years to provide forward guidance (Fig. 27):

- **'Measured.'** Beginning with the May 4, 2004 FOMC statement under Fed Chair Alan Greenspan, the FOMC used the following phrase: "[T]he Committee believes that policy accommodation can be removed at a pace that is likely to be measured."[174] Those exact words remained in the statements through November 1, 2005. Over this 18-month period, the federal funds rate was raised 12 times, from 1.00% to 4.00%, in "measured" increments of 25 basis points at each FOMC meeting, with the first on June 30, 2004.

  The language around the keyword was tweaked in the December 12, 2005 statement as follows: "The Committee judges that some further measured policy firming is likely to be needed to keep the risks to the attainment of both sustainable economic growth and price stability roughly in balance."[175] The statement also announced that the federal funds rate was raised to 4.25%.

- **'Firming may be needed.'** The word "measured" was eliminated from the FOMC's vocabulary after that statement, but nearly the exact language around it was maintained for an additional two statements (i.e., the January 31, 2006 and March 28, 2006 statements): "The Committee judges that some further policy firming may be needed to keep the risks to the attainment of both sustainable economic growth and price stability roughly in balance." The federal funds rate was raised to 4.50% at the January meeting and to 4.75% at the March meeting.[176] That also happened to be the first FOMC decision under Fed Chair Ben Bernanke.

The May 10, 2006 statement raised the federal funds rate to 5.00% and similarly noted: "The Committee judges that some further policy firming may yet be needed to address inflation risks but emphasizes that the extent and timing of any such firming will depend importantly on the evolution of the economic outlook as implied by incoming information."[177] The federal funds rate was increased again on June 29, 2006 to a peak of 5.25%, where it remained until the September 18, 2007 meeting, when it was lowered to 4.75%.

The FOMC included variations of the same wording in the June 29, 2006 through January 31, 2007 statements: "The extent and timing of any additional firming that may be needed to address these risks will depend on the evolution of the outlook for both inflation and economic growth, as implied by incoming information."[178]

From the March 21, 2007 to the August 7, 2007 meetings, the Fed was no longer in firming mode but more balanced, as suggested by the following phrase used: "Future policy adjustments will depend on the evolution of the outlook for both inflation and economic growth." The federal funds rate remained at 5.25%.

- **'Will act as needed.'** There were two unscheduled statements during August 2007, in which the Fed expressed concern about the disorderly functioning of financial markets. On September 18, 2007, the FOMC voted to cut the federal funds rate by 50 basis points, from 5.25% to 4.75%. The statement noted that developments in financial markets "have increased the uncertainty surrounding the economic outlook" and that the Committee "will act as needed to foster price stability and sustainable economic growth."[179] The federal funds rate was cut again to 4.50% on October 31, 2007. That language remained in the statements through December 11, 2007, when the committee announced that it was lowering the federal funds rate from 4.50% to 4.25%.

On January 21, 2008 in an unscheduled conference call, the FOMC voted to cut the federal funds rate by 75 basis points to 3.75%.[180] A sense of urgency to ease policy was added to the statement, which was released the next day: "Appreciable downside risks to growth remain. The Committee will continue to assess the effects of financial and other developments on economic prospects and will act in a timely manner as needed to address those risks."[181] "Timely manner" made it into a total of three FOMC statements through March 18, 2008.

"Timely manner" was dropped, and "will act as needed" remained, in the April 30, 2008 statement.[182] By then, the Fed had lowered the federal funds rate from 3.50% to 2.00%. The FOMC took rates down further, to 1.00% on October 29, 2008, just before the Fed changed its phrasing again.

- **'Exceptionally low levels.'** In the December 16, 2008 statement, the Fed had established a historically low target range for the federal funds rate of 0.00%–0.25%.[183] The economic situation had turned more desperate, as evidenced by the following language in the statement: "The Federal Reserve will employ all available tools to promote the resumption of sustainable economic growth and to preserve price stability. In particular, the Committee anticipates that weak economic conditions are likely to warrant exceptionally low levels of the federal funds rate for some time."

  "[A]ll available tools" was changed to "a wide range of tools" in the September 23, 2009 statement, and dropped from the December 16, 2009 statement.[184]

The "exceptionally low levels" phrase was attached to time frames of "for an extended period" in the June 22, 2011 statement; "at least through mid-2013" was in the August 9, 2011 statement; "at least through late 2014" was in the January 25, 2012 statement; and "at least through mid-2015" was in the September 13, 2012 statement.[185] The time frame then was extended to "as long as the unemployment rate remains above 6-1/2 percent" in the statement of December 12, 2012.[186]

In the January 25, 2012 statement, the phrase "highly accommodative" joined "exceptionally low levels" to describe the policy stance.[187] The committee stated: "To support a stronger economic recovery and to help ensure that inflation, over time, is at levels consistent with the dual mandate, the Committee expects to maintain a highly accommodative stance for monetary policy." In other words, the Fed saw the US economy as improving but still fragile. The new phrase appeared 34 times in the statements, often twice, over roughly 32 months through September 17, 2014.

- **'Balanced approach.'** In the January 30, 2013 statement, the Fed eliminated the use of "exceptionally low levels."[188] In the December 12, 2012 statement just before that, "balanced approach" was added to go along with "highly accommodative." The use of "balanced" was intended to communicate that the committee at some point would consider slowly removing policy accommodation. The statement noted: "When the Committee decides to begin to remove policy accommodation, it will take a balanced approach consistent with its longer-run goals of maximum employment and inflation of 2 percent."

The Fed abandoned "highly accommodative" in the October 29, 2014 statement.[189] It was axed under Fed Chair Janet Yellen, whose first FOMC decision as Fed chair was several months earlier on March 19, 2014. However, "balanced approach" hung around through the October 28, 2015 statement.[190]

- **'Considerable time.'** As previously noted, under both Bernanke and Yellen, the phrase "considerable time" was used to describe how long monetary policy would remain accommodative from the September 13, 2012 statement through the December 17, 2014 statement, though QE3 was terminated at the end of October 2014.

- **'Gradual.'** In the December 16, 2015 statement, the FOMC lifted the federal funds rate to a range of 0.25%–0.50% after nearly seven years near zero.[191] At the same time, the FOMC adopted "gradual" to describe the likely path of future policy moves, specifically: "The Committee currently expects that, with gradual adjustments in the stance of monetary policy, economic activity will continue to expand at a moderate pace and labor market indicators will continue to strengthen."

    "Gradual" was Yellen's last keyword as Fed chair. Under her leadership, the federal funds rate was raised some more on December 14, 2016 to 0.50%–0.75%. During 2017, it was raised three times on March 15 to 0.75%–1.00%, on June 14 to 1.00%–1.25%, and on December 13 to 1.25%–1.50%. The gradual approach was passed on to Powell, who voted for the first time in his new position as Fed chair on March 21, 2018 to raise the rate to 1.50%–1.75%.

- **'Patient.'** In early 2019, "patient" became the FOMC's new keyword in the January 30, 2019 statement.[192] At that point, the FOMC had raised the federal funds rate range a total of four times under Powell to 2.25%–2.50%. The FOMC had become increasingly concerned about persistently low inflation as well as possible further slack in the labor market and geopolitical risks, especially the US-China trade dispute. Considering this, the FOMC opted for a wait-and-see approach before making future adjustments to rates up or down. The statement noted: "In light of global economic and financial developments and muted inflation pressures, the Committee will be patient as it determines what future adjustments to the target range for the federal funds rate may be appropriate to support these outcomes." Ironically, the word "patient" didn't last long.

- **'Appropriate.'** In the June 19, 2019 statement, the FOMC deleted the word "patient" and emphasized "appropriate."[193] The statement noted: "In light of these uncertainties [to the outlook] and muted inflation pressures, the Committee will closely monitor the implications of incoming information for the economic outlook and will act as appropriate to sustain the expansion, with a strong labor market and inflation near its symmetric 2 percent objective."[194]

In his 2013 speech cited above, Bernanke proceeded to distinguish between qualitative, date-based, and data-dependent forward guidance for the likely course of the federal funds rate. For example, when the FOMC cut the rate to zero at the end of 2008, the statement said it would stay there "for some time." In March 2009, that was changed to "an extended period." In August 2011, the FOMC got more specific, stating that the rate would likely remain near zero at least through mid-2013. Then at the end of 2012, the FOMC said that the federal funds rate wouldn't be increased as long as the unemployment rate exceeded 6.5%. Bernanke emphasized that such data-dependent conditions are "thresholds" rather than "triggers" for policy action.

This is head-spinning stuff!

The Fed's word games are intended to communicate its monetary policy stance to the financial markets as simply as possible. Yet it can also create plenty of confusion and uncertainty. It might be better if the FOMC would just avoid ambiguous one-word characterizations of its stance altogether and save markets the head-scratching. Instead, statements could just repeat *this* mantra—suitable for every occasion—over and over: "Monetary policy will continue to be data dependent."

Chapter 10

Mario Draghi and Haruhiko Kuroda: The Deflation Fighters

Whatever It Takes in the Eurozone

Like the Fed, the other major central banks responded to the Great Financial Crisis by adopting unconventional monetary policies that have become all too conventional. The ECB, the BOJ, and the People's Bank of China (PBOC) have been struggling with many of the same problems that have been confronting the Fed. They've also had to respond to some unique problems. Let's start with the ECB.

In 2010, the Eurozone confronted yet another financial crisis. Many people had started to question the stability and even the viability of the European Monetary Union (EMU) causing much angst in many quarters. The EMU had been adopted by the 19 countries that compose the Eurozone back on January 1, 1999, when they all agreed to scrap their own currencies and use only the euro from that day forward. Igniting the intense fears about the potential disintegration of the decade-old Eurozone were a chronic budget crisis and financial turmoil in Greece. Suddenly, investors around the world were alerted that not all bonds issued by Eurozone governments might be as sound as Germany's high-quality credits.

The yield spreads between the government bonds of the other Eurozone nations and Germany and France had narrowed dramatically from 1995 through 1998 in anticipation of the formation of the Eurozone at the start of 1999 (Fig. 28). The spreads were close to zero across the region from 1999 through mid-2008. They started to widen as a result of the Great Financial Crisis. The Greek debt crisis, which began in late 2009, caused yields to soar on the government bonds issued by the so-called peripheral Eurozone countries—Portugal, Ireland, Italy, Greece, and Spain—from 2010 through 2012 (Fig. 29). Collectively, they were dubbed the "PIIGS." Their spreads widened dramatically relative to the yields of the core Eurozone countries—France, Germany, and the Netherlands.

Under Jean-Claude Trichet, who served as president of the ECB from November 1, 2003 through October 31, 2011, the central bank responded to the initial Greek debt crisis with its securities market programme (SMP) during May 2010. The ECB purchased sovereign bonds issued by distressed Eurozone member states in the secondary market. Those purchases were offset by auctioning fixed-term deposits at the ECB. As a result, SMP amounted to sterilized debt monetization in that it increased liquidity in the bond market without having an inflationary effect. In addition, the ECB increased its loans to Eurozone credit institutions from €0.4 trillion in early 2011 to €1.3 trillion by mid-2012 (Fig. 30). These efforts didn't work, as yield spreads continued to widen or remained elevated.

Mario Draghi succeeded Trichet as head of the ECB on November 1, 2011. He earned a PhD in economics from the Massachusetts Institute of Technology in 1976. He worked at Goldman Sachs from 2002 until 2005 before becoming the governor of the Bank of Italy in December 2005, where he served until October 2011.

"Whatever it takes" was famously uttered by the ECB's president in an important, yet unscripted speech at the Global Investment Conference in London on July 26, 2012. Draghi started his July 2012 speech by saying that the "euro is like a bumblebee."

He explained, "This is a mystery of nature because it shouldn't fly but instead it does." Near the end of his stream of consciousness, he suggested that the bee might need some help to keep flying, and he was ready to provide just that: "Within our mandate, the ECB is ready to do whatever it takes to preserve the euro. And believe me, it will be enough."[195]

Draghi's whatever-it-takes speech seemingly worked wonders. The yield spreads of the PIIGS narrowed significantly relative to those of both France and Germany. That's because Draghi followed his July speech by announcing at his August 2 press conference that the ECB "may undertake outright open market operations of a size adequate to reach its objective."[196] On September 6, outright monetary transactions (OMT) replaced the SMP, which was terminated. Under OMT, sovereign bonds were purchased in the secondary market, with the liquidity created through these transactions fully sterilized.[197] Not only did yield spreads narrow in the Eurozone, interest rates fell across the board. That allowed the ECB, near the end of 2014, to reduce its loans to credit institutions back down close to the early 2011 level.

However, economic growth remained lackluster, and inflation fell below 1.0% during early 2014. Fearing deflation could be next, the ECB broke through the ZLB, adopting a NIRP. On June 5, 2014, the ECB announced that its official deposit facility rate, which banks earn on their overnight deposits at the ECB, would be lowered to –0.10% (Fig. 31).[198] It was subsequently lowered four more times, as of this writing, to –0.50% on September 12, 2019.

On June 5, 2014, the ECB announced the first of a series of Targeted Longer-Term Refinancing Operations (TLTROs), a second series (TLTRO II) on March 10, 2016, and a third series (TLTRO III) on March 7, 2019.[199] The TLTROs were designed so that the amount that banks can borrow from the ECB was linked to their loans. In both TLTRO II and III, the more loans participating banks made to nonfinancial corporations and households (except mortgages), the lower was the interest rate on the borrowed funds. In fact, as long as banks lent the money to the real economy, they could get cash back (rather than pay interest on it) based on the ECB's negative deposit rate.[200]

In addition, on January 22, 2015, the ECB adopted a quantitative easing program by expanding its asset purchase program (APP), which had been introduced in 2009. When the expanded program was announced, headline inflation had been below 1.0% for over a year and had turned negative the previous month. The ECB added sovereign bonds to its existing private-sector APP.[201] On June 2, 2016, the APP was expanded to include corporate bond purchases.[202] The ECB's holdings of the securities of Eurozone residents in euros for monetary purposes soared by €2.3 trillion from €0.6 trillion at the start of 2015 to €2.9 trillion by the end of 2018 (Fig. 32).[203] Most of that represented bonds issued by Eurozone governments. But there were no offsetting transactions that effectively sterilized APP purchases as was done for SMP purchases. So the APP amounted to outright monetization of government debt.

Conservative critics of the APP claimed that it was illegal. On its website, the ECB responded that "[i]t pursues its mandate of price stability with the instruments defined in the Treaties. Outright purchases of marketable instruments are explicitly mentioned as a monetary policy instrument (in Article 18.1 of the Statute of the ESCB [European System of Central Banks])." Furthermore, the ECB can purchase "government bonds, as long as they are bought on the secondary market from investors and not on the primary market, i.e., directly from Member States."[204] So it was legal based on the technicality that the bonds were bought in the secondary market rather than directly from issuing governments.

Monthly purchases under the APP were €60 billion from March 2015 until March 2016, €80 billion from April 2016 until

March 2017, €60 billion from April 2017 to December 2017, €30 billion from January 2018 to September 2018, and €15 billion from October 2018 to December 2018. The program was terminated at the end of 2018.[205]

By 2018, Draghi and his colleagues started to phase out their unconventional monetary policies. It would be a significant accomplishment for Draghi if the ECB's monetary policies could at least begin to be normalized by the time his term expired near year-end 2019. At the beginning of 2018, APP monthly purchases were cut in half from €60 billion to €30 billion. At his April 26, 2018, press conference, Draghi confirmed that APP would continue at a pace of €30 billion until the end of September 2018, "or beyond, if necessary." Regarding interest rates, he said, "We continue to expect them to remain at their present levels for an extended period of time, and well past the horizon of our net asset purchases."[206]

At his June 14, 2018 press conference, he announced that the pace of APP purchases would be cut to €15 billion per month from October to December 2018, then would stop. Reinvesting the principal payments from maturing securities purchased under APP would continue for the foreseeable future. He was more specific about interest rates at this press conference, saying that the ECB's interest rates would remain unchanged "at least" through the summer of 2019 and longer if necessary.[207]

At his December 13 press conference, Draghi confirmed that APP would be terminated by the end of the year and reiterated that "we intend to continue reinvesting, in full, the principal payments from maturing securities purchased under the APP for an extended period of time past the date when we start raising the key ECB interest rates."[208] Again, he stated that rates would remain unchanged at least through the summer of 2019.

Despite all the ECB's efforts, inflation remained well below the central bank's 2.0% target, and economic growth slowed

significantly in early 2019. So at his March 7, 2019 press conference, Draghi said that interest rates would remain unchanged "at
least through the end of 2019." He also unveiled a new batch of
cheap long-term loans for banks.[209]

At his June 6, 2019 press conference, Draghi said that interest
rates would remain unchanged "at least though the first half of
2020." He also strongly suggested that the next rate move would
be a cut rather than a hike, and that the APP might be reactivated.
Also, he said banks would be allowed to borrow from the ECB
at a rate just 10 basis points above its –0.40% deposit rate if they
exceeded the ECB's lending benchmarks in a new TLTRO. In the
Q&A session after his June 6 press conference, Draghi said several
members of the Governing Council had raised the possibility of
rate cuts in the meeting, while others mentioned restarting asset
purchases.[210]

The minutes of that June 6 meeting, released on July 11, 2019,
confirmed that there was broad support for these actions. Officials
noted that they should be ready to use all policy tools, including
interest-rate cuts and fresh bond purchases, "in the light of the
heightened uncertainty which was likely to extend further into the
future."[211]

In a June 18, 2019 speech in Sintra, Portugal, Draghi refreshed
his whatever-it-takes approach to central banking by saying,
"In the absence of improvement, such that the sustained return
of inflation to our aim is threatened, additional stimulus will be
required." He declared:

> The (European) Treaty requires that our actions are both nec-
> essary and proportionate to fulfil our mandate and achieve
> our objective, which implies that the limits we establish on
> our tools are specific to the contingencies we face. If the crisis
> has shown anything, it is that we will use all the flexibility

within our mandate to fulfil our mandate—and we will do so
again to answer any challenges to price stability in the future.

He also said, "We remain able to enhance our forward guidance
by adjusting its bias and its conditionality to account for variations in the adjustment path of inflation. This applies to all instruments of our monetary policy stance." He added: "Further cuts in
policy interest rates and mitigating measures to contain any side
effects remain part of our tools. And the APP still has considerable
headroom."[212]

In his July 25, 2019 press conference, Draghi again suggested
that more stimulus was on the way. Released on August 22, the
minutes of the July 24–25 meeting of the ECB's Governing Council
noted that officials had discussed a broad stimulus "package,"
which would be more effective than a series of actions.[213]

During his September 12, 2019 press conference, Draghi
announced his extremely dovish final actions, solidifying his leg-
acy as the ECB president who tried to do "whatever it takes" to
support the Eurozone economy. "You remember me saying . . . that
all instruments were on the table . . . ready to be used, well today
we did it," Draghi proclaimed.[214]

The key interest rate was lowered further into negative territory, the APP was reintroduced, and banks were provided with
support to sustain the transmission of monetary policy to the
real economy. The ECB's latest APP would add to the €4.7 trillion
already carried on the central bank's massive balance sheet, which
increased by €2.3 trillion since Draghi presided over the ECB in
late 2011.

The ECB lowered its deposit facility rate 10 basis points to
–0.50%. The interest rate on the main refinancing operations and
the rate on the marginal lending facility were kept at 0.00% and
0.25%, respectively. Draghi explained that the central bank should

hold these rates "at their present or lower levels until we have seen the inflation outlook robustly converge to a level sufficiently close to, but below, 2% within our projection horizon, and such convergence has been consistently reflected in underlying infla- tion dynamics." Headline CPI inflation had remained well below the ECB's 2.0% target since early 2013, while core CPI inflation had persisted significantly below target since around 2009.

The APP was reintroduced at €20 billion per month starting on November 1, 2019. The projected amount of monthly purchases was sizable, but nowhere near the €80 billion per month seen at the height of the ECB's asset purchases from April 2016 to March 2017. Draghi said during his press conference that at the newly intro- duced pace there is "headroom to go on for quite a long time." To speed the pace of asset purchases, the ECB would have had to significantly broaden its scope of assets eligible for purchase.

Surprisingly, no estimated end date was set for terminating this second round of the expanded APP. Forward guidance for rates instead had been tied to inflation, and the asset purchas- es would continue for "as long as necessary" up until "shortly before" the ECB started raising its key interest rates—meaning that the APP, too, was tied to inflation. So if inflation remained stubbornly low, the ECB's ultra-easy policy could go on forever, or at least for a long time. If all the purchases were of Eurozone gov- ernment bonds, the APP would monetize €240 billion of that debt every year for the foreseeable future!

Mario Draghi's eight-year term as ECB president ended on November 1, 2019. He was succeeded by Christine Lagarde. While not an economist, Lagarde, like Powell, has lots of learning-by-do- ing experience in finance. She served as France's Minister of the Economy, Finance and Industry from 2007 through 2011. She then headed the IMF from July 5, 2011 until she resigned to preside over the ECB.

On September 4, 2019, she addressed European Union lawmakers in Brussels at her confirmation hearing. She strongly suggested that she was likely to stick with Draghi's ultra-easy monetary policies. She defended them, saying that "the crisis would have been a lot worse" without such measures and agreed with the ECB's view that the economy would need monetary support "for an extended period of time." She praised the "agility" of the ECB under Draghi to come up with new tools to confront the Eurozone's chronic financial crisis. However, to mollify some of the ECB's conservative critics in Germany, she pledged to review the ECB's negative-interest-rate and asset-purchasing policies.

Lagarde suggested that there are limits to what the ECB can effectively do to stimulate the economy, calling on Eurozone governments to step up structural reforms and fiscal spending. "I'm not a fairy," she told European Parliament during her nomination hearing. "I was present when Draghi actually said 'We will do whatever it takes,'" she said, referring to Draghi's 2012 pledge to defend the EMU. She added, "I hope I will never have to say something like that, I really do, because if I had it would mean that the other economic policy makers are not doing what they had to do."[215]

Lagarde may not be Tinker Bell, but she might have to be an escape artist like Harry Houdini. According to unnamed sources mentioned in the September 12, 2019 issue of *The Wall Street Journal*, "at least five officials on the ECB's 25-member rate-setting committee opposed the decision to restart QE." They included the governors of the Dutch, French, and German central banks and two members of the ECB's executive board.[216]

On November 22, 2019, Lagarde delivered her first speech as ECB president, "The future of the euro area economy." Remarkably, she spoke about monetary policy almost in passing, in just one paragraph in fact. Instead, she presented a case for fiscal policy to focus on more public investments in infrastructure, R&D, and education. She also said she wanted to see more economic integration in the EMU.[217] She is one of the first major central bankers to acknowledge that monetary policy may have lost its effectiveness.

Neverland in Japan

Following the Great Financial Crisis, the BOJ also joined the shock-and-awe campaigns of the major central banks. In a political comeback, Shinzō Abe was elected Japan's Prime Minister on December 26, 2012, having resigned from that position in 2007 for health reasons. He pledged to revive the Japanese economy by focusing on stimulative fiscal and monetary policies as well as deregulation, his so-called "three arrows." In January 2013, the BOJ set a 2% inflation target and released a joint statement with the government on the price target and structural reforms.

During February 2013, BOJ Governor Masaaki Shirakawa announced his intention to resign in March, a month before his term ended. He was from the old school of central banking. Shirakawa studied at the University of Chicago steeped in Milton Friedman's conservative principles for monetary policy.

Abe picked Asian Development Bank President Haruhiko Kuroda to be the new head of the BOJ. Kuroda has a master's degree in economics from Oxford University. He had been an advocate of looser monetary policy in Japan. He agreed with the views of US economist Irving Fisher, who warned about the dangers of deflation. "During the Great Depression, Fisher argued that the most serious problem of deflation is to make real debt mushroom and damage the whole economy," Kuroda said in an interview just before his BOJ nomination. "So I have long advocated aggressive monetary easing to eradicate deflation in Japan."[218]

Kuroda moved rapidly. The BOJ implemented its new quantitative and qualitative monetary easing program (QQE) on April 4, 2013. The press release announced that the BOJ would "enter a new phase of monetary easing both in terms of quantity and quality. It will double the monetary base and the amounts outstanding of Japanese government bonds (JGBs) as well as exchange-traded funds (ETFs) in two years, and more than double the average remaining maturity of JGB purchases." The press release promised that as a result of these policies: "The Bank will achieve the price stability target of 2 percent in terms of the year-on-year rate of change in the consumer price index (CPI) at the earliest possible time, with a time horizon of about two years."

More specifically, the monetary base would be increased at an annual pace of ¥60 trillion to ¥70 trillion, from ¥138 trillion at the end of 2012 to ¥200 trillion at the end of 2013 and ¥270 trillion at the end of 2014 (Fig. 33). The bank's Governing Council voted unanimously to significantly increase its purchases of JGBs and extend the average maturity of the bonds it purchased from three years to seven years. Kuroda, like Draghi, said that he would do "whatever it takes" to drive growth. Sure enough, the bank added that it would also buy relatively riskier capital market assets such as ETFs and real estate trust funds![219]

The BOJ expanded and extended the QQE program with its so-called "QQEE" program announced on October 31, 2014. According to the bank's press release, it aimed to triple the pace of its stock and property funds purchases, extend the average maturity of its bondholding by three years to 10 years, and raise the ceiling of its annual JGB purchases by ¥30 trillion to ¥80 trillion. In a separate announcement, Japan's huge public pension fund promised to invest more in stocks.[220] Japan's monetary base rose to ¥519 trillion by November 2019, up 274% since the start of QQE.

How did all that work out?

The yen plunged 38% from late 2012 through mid-2015. That was great for the stock market, as the Nikkei rose 127% over the same period (Fig. 34). However, exports didn't get the big boost that was widely expected. Inflation was still stuck near zero. Economic growth remained lackluster.

In his opening remarks at a conference in Tokyo on June 4, 2015, Kuroda said, "I trust that many of you are familiar with the story of Peter Pan, in which it says, 'The moment you doubt whether you can fly, you cease forever to be able to do it.'" *The Wall Street Journal* observed: "Japan's central bank chief invoked the boy who can fly to emphasize the need for global central bankers to believe in their ability to solve a range of vexing issues, whether stubbornly sluggish growth or entrenched expectations of price declines." According to the *Journal*, Kuroda added, "Yes, what we need is a positive attitude and conviction."[221]

On January 21, 2016, Kuroda emphatically ruled out negative interest rates: "We are not considering a cut in interest on bank reserves," he told the Japanese Parliament. The BOJ feared that negative rates would make banks reluctant to sell their JGBs, thus undermining its QQEE. A mere eight days later, on January 29, the BOJ unexpectedly lowered the official rate on new bank reserve deposits into negative territory (i.e., –0.10%). Japan's mischievous Peter Pan surprised everyone.

Later that same year, on September 21, the BOJ announced a yield curve control program. It was more "aw-shucks" than shock-and-awe. The guidelines reiterated that the "short-term policy interest rate" would be the same as the bank deposit rate (–0.10%), and that the BOJ would purchase government bonds "so that 10-year JGB yields will remain more or less at the current level (around zero percent)."[222] At the same time, the BOJ also introduced an "inflation-overshooting" commitment to expand the monetary base until the year-on-year rate of increase in the observed CPI exceeded 2.0% and stayed above the target in a stable manner.

In a December 7, 2017 speech, Kuroda conceded that the BOJ still had "a long way to go to achieve the price stability target of 2 percent."[223] By mid-June 2019, the BOJ had postponed the timing for hitting its 2.0% inflation target six times since it was established in 2013.[224]

In a November 18, 2019 Reuters interview, Kuroda said the BOJ has room to deepen negative interest rates, but he signaled there were limits to how far it can cut rates or ramp up stimulus.

According to Reuters, "Kuroda also said there was still enough Japanese government bonds (JGB) left in the market for the BOJ to buy, playing down concerns its huge purchases have drained market liquidity. After years of heavy purchases to flood markets with cash, the BOJ now owns nearly half of the JGB market."

The BOJ's QE program, which started during April 2013, was likely to be continued through 2020. Bank reserve balances at the BOJ rose to a record high of ¥352 trillion during November 2019, up 740% since the start of the program.

Despite his best efforts, Peter Pan couldn't fix the biggest problem facing Japan's economy: a shrinking population. Japan's fertility rate has fallen below the population replacement rate. The number of deaths has increasingly exceeded the number of live births since 2007. This may be the main reason why inflation remains close to zero in Japan despite the BOJ's ultra-easy policies.

Credit Binge in China

Meanwhile, the shockingly awesome program of central bank liquidity pumping was continuing in China without much fanfare. Since the Great Financial Crisis, the PBOC has presided over one of the greatest expansions of credit in human history. All that liquidity seems to have lost its stimulative impact, as evidenced by slowing economic growth in China. Yet the PBOC continued to pump it into the financial system, mostly by cutting the required reserve requirement ratio to encourage the banks to lend more and more.

During China's economic boom years, the required reserve ratio was raised dramatically from a low of 6.0% during September 2003 to a high of 17.5% during June 2008 (Fig. 35). The Global Financial Crisis led to the creation of two separate required reserve ratios: one for small- and medium-sized banks and one for large banks. Both were reduced in late 2008 to lows of 13.5% and 15.5%, respectively.

China's economy rebounded smartly during 2010 through 2011, and both ratios were raised to record highs of 19.5% and 21.5%. But in 2012 economic growth began to slow, and the PBOC responded by lowering the required reserve ratios numerous times. By September 2019, the ratio for smaller banks was down to 11.0% and 13.0% for large banks.

The result of all this monetary easing has been a massive increase in bank lending, yet China's economic growth continued to slow. From December 2008 through November 2019, Chinese bank loans quintupled from 30.3 trillion yuan to 152.0 trillion yuan. In dollars, they soared $17.3 trillion, also quintupling from $4.4 trillion to $21.7 trillion over this period (Fig. 36).

China may be the epicenter of the world's next financial bubble. The October 2019 *Global Financial Stability Report,* produced by the IMF, warned:

> In China, overall corporate debt is very high, and the size of speculative-grade debt is economically significant. This is mainly because of large firms, including state-owned enterprises. In addition, the debt-at-risk in China is found to be very sensitive to deteriorations in growth and funding conditions

(because of a large share of speculative-grade debt) and it surpasses postcrisis crests in the adverse scenario presented in this chapter. The assessment of the potential systemic impact of corporate vulnerabilities is complicated by the implicit government guarantees and the lack of granular data on corporate sector exposures of different segments of the large, opaque, and interconnected financial system in China.[225]

On the other hand, China's risk is mitigated because, like Japan, it owes its debt to its own people. That's confirmed by the rapid increase in the M2 money supply, which has outpaced bank loans for many years. The Chinese have a high saving rate, which is why bank deposit growth remains so strong.

Despite the flood of bank loans, China's inflation-adjusted GDP has been growing at a slower and slower pace since early 2009. On a year-over-year basis, it fell from 12.2% during the first quarter of 2010 to 6.0% during the third quarter of 2019. Similarly, inflation-adjusted retail sales growth fell from a record high of 17.0% during July 2009 to 5.6% during October 2019 (also on a year-over-year basis using the 12-month average).

As in Japan, much of the slowdown can be attributed to China's rapidly aging demographic profile. China's fertility rate has been below the population replacement rate of roughly 2.1 since 1994. That's been happening in most countries around the world as a result of urbanization. In rural agricultural economies, children have an important economic value helping with the crops and the herds. In urban environments, children provide no economic benefit and are much more costly to raise. The demographic situation was exacerbated significantly in China by the government's one-child policy that was imposed from 1979 through 2015.

There is nothing that monetary policy can do to deal with demographic challenges. That doesn't mean that the central bank hasn't tried to do just that by stimulating economic growth with lots of easy credit. However, the bang-per-yuan of credit clearly has been diminishing. To see this, I like to track the ratio of China's industrial production to bank loans (Fig. 37). It has dropped by 52% from a peak of 106.6 during December 2007 to only 50.9 during December 2019.

Band of Bankers

So far, the major central banks have succeeded in averting both deflation and another financial crisis. They can also take credit for lowering unemployment significantly since the Great Recession.

However, inflation remains below their target of 2.0% notwithstanding all the liquidity that they provided. Moreover, their unconventional policies seem to be losing their effectiveness, which raises the question of whether they will have enough ammo left to fight the next recession. Another concern is that their untested policies may have unintended negative consequences, including undermining financial stability in unexpected ways, as I discuss in the next chapter.

Clearly, Fed watching has evolved into a global pursuit of watching all the major central banks because their policies have global repercussions. For example, Fed officials started to normalize monetary policy during 2015. They had to reverse course during 2019. Their best-laid plans were frustrated in part because the ECB and BOJ maintained their ultra-easy polices. These policy divergences contributed to the strengthening of the US dollar, which weighed on US inflation and weakened US exports.

Here is another important example of the interaction of monetary policies around the world: China's central bank has enabled an unprecedented credit binge that has been providing life support to lots of unprofitable zombie companies that should be out of business. However, easy credit conditions allow them to stay in business, exacerbating global deflationary pressures, which are frustrating the efforts of the other central bankers to achieve their inflation mandates.

Chapter 11
Central Monetary Planners: All Planned Out

Target Practice

In its first-ever "longer-run goals and policy strategy" statement, the FOMC, on January 25, 2012, announced a specific target for inflation of 2.0%. Ben Bernanke, who was the Fed chair then, had been pushing for this for some time. This brought the Fed in line with many of the world's other major central banks that already had adopted a formal inflation target.

During the 1990s, the inflation-targeting approach was adopted by several pioneering central banks, including the Reserve Bank of New Zealand, the Bank of Canada, the Bank of England, Sweden's Riksbank, and the Reserve Bank of Australia. During the following decade, the adopters included both advanced and emerging economies such as Brazil, Chile, Israel, Mexico, the Philippines, South Africa, South Korea, and Thailand. They were followed by the Czech Republic, Hungary, and Poland.

In 1998, the Bank of England's Monetary Policy Committee started setting interest rates to target the Retail Prices Index (RPI) inflation rate at 2.5%. The target was lowered to 2.0% in December 2003, when the CPI replaced the RPI as the UK Treasury's inflation index. If inflation overshoots or undershoots the target by more than 1.0 percentage point, the governor of the Bank of England is required to write a letter to the Chancellor of the Exchequer explaining why and what he intends to do about it.

During October 1998, prior to the introduction of the euro in January 1999, the Governing Council of the ECB defined price stability as "a year-on-year increase in the Harmonised Index of Consumer Prices (HICP) for the euro area of below 2%," adding that price stability "was to be maintained over the medium term." In May 2003, following a thorough evaluation of the ECB's monetary policy strategy, the Governing Council reiterated that "in the pursuit of price stability, it aims to maintain inflation rates below, but close to, 2% over the medium term."[226]

Japan's Prime Minister Shinzō Abe declared a "monetary regime change" on January 22, 2013 as the central bank bowed to government pressure, setting a 2.0% inflation target aimed at helping the country emerge from its prolonged bout of deflation. "This opens a passageway toward bold monetary easing," Abe told reporters after the BOJ and the government jointly announced the inflation target and plans for "open-ended" central bank asset purchases, like the strategy followed by the Fed to keep market interest rates low.[227]

Prior to 2000, the Fed had focused on the CPI inflation rate, particularly the core rate excluding food and energy. This core concept was originated by Fed Chair Arthur Burns in the early 1970s to allow for an easier monetary policy in the face of rapidly rising oil and food prices, which he deemed to be transitory.

A footnote in the FOMC's February 2000 *Monetary Policy Report* to Congress explained why the committee had decided to switch to the inflation rate based on the personal consumption expenditures deflator (PCED):

> The chain-type price index for PCE draws extensively on data from the consumer price index but, while not entirely free of measurement problems, has several advantages relative to the CPI. The PCE chain-type index is constructed from a formula that reflects the changing composition of spending

and thereby avoids some of the upward bias associated with the fixed-weight nature of the CPI. In addition, the weights are based on a more comprehensive measure of expenditures. Finally, historical data used in the PCE price index can be revised to account for newly available information and for improvements in measurement techniques, including those that affect source data from the CPI; the result is a more consistent series over time.[228]

Nevertheless, Fed Chair Alan Greenspan refused to consider setting an official inflation target. In an October 11, 2001 speech, he shot down the idea promoted by some of his colleagues and a few academics. He said that "a specific numerical inflation target would represent an unhelpful and false precision. Rather, price stability is best thought of as an environment in which inflation is so low and stable over time that it does not materially enter into the decisions of households and firms."[229]

Soon after Ben Bernanke replaced Greenspan as head of the Fed on February 1, 2006, he started setting the stage for an official inflation target. Bernanke literally wrote the book on this subject. When he was an academic economist focusing his research on monetary policy, he became intrigued by inflation targeting and went on to co-author a book titled *Inflation Targeting: Lessons from the International Experience* (1999), as well as to write several articles about this approach.[230]

As I discussed in Chapter 1, the FOMC's quarterly SEP includes the consensus projections for the headline and core PCED inflation rates for the current year and next two years, as well as a longer-run projection for the headline rate. Before 2012, many Fed officials had in mind an informal "comfort zone" of 1.0% to 2.0% for the longer-run inflation rate. But the Fed never commented officially on this zone and didn't formalize it until early 2012.[231]

It was on January 25, 2012 that the FOMC issued a statement formally targeting the longer-run projection at 2.0%. The statement presented the case for targeting inflation within its dual mandate as follows:

> The inflation rate over the longer run is primarily determined by monetary policy, and hence the Committee has the ability to specify a longer-run goal for inflation. The Committee judges that inflation at the rate of 2 percent, as measured by the annual change in the price index for personal consumption expenditures, is most consistent over the longer run with the Federal Reserve's statutory mandate.[232]

The FOMC's statement capped a long crusade by Bernanke to make monetary policy more transparent and accountable—less opaque and secretive than it had been under Greenspan. The statement noted:

> Communicating this inflation goal clearly to the public helps keep longer-term inflation expectations firmly anchored, thereby fostering price stability and moderate long-term interest rates and enhancing the committee's ability to promote maximum employment in the face of significant economic disturbances.

Why 2.0%? That was deemed to be the rate compatible with price stability. Fed officials feared that targeting inflation closer to zero would increase the risk of deflation. Other central banks also target 2.0% for the same reason.

How well have they been doing at hitting this inflation target? Let's just say they could use some target practice: Since the Great Financial Crisis through 2019, inflation has remained stubbornly below 2.0% in the United States, the Eurozone, and Japan.

The failure of their ultra-easy monetary policies to boost inflation and stimulate faster economic growth has perplexed the macroeconomists running the major central banks. Their grad-school professors had taught them that easy money should push both economic growth and inflation higher. The output gap model posits that when actual output is above (below) potential output, inflation tends to rise (fall). To boost inflation, the mostly Keynesian-trained central bankers learned that low interest rates and plentiful credit would heat up consumer spending and business capital outlays, pushing actual output above potential. More demand for goods and services would increase the demand for labor, pushing up wages, which would get marked up into higher prices, as predicted by the Phillips curve.

The monetarist model also has failed miserably at predicting inflation. While Milton Friedman had his fans and his critics, virtually every student of economics learned and agreed with his mantra: "Inflation is always and everywhere a monetary phenomenon."

Is it really?

Central banks since the Great Financial Crisis have pumped oceans of liquidity into their banking systems, causing the monetary base (i.e., the sum of currency and bank reserves provided by the central banks or "high-powered money") to soar exponentially. However, the money multiplier (i.e., the ratio of the money supply to the monetary base) collapsed after the Great Financial Crisis, so the growth rates of the broad measures of the money supply, such as M2, remained in the low single digits. The velocity of money, which is the ratio of nominal GDP to M2, also collapsed after the financial crisis, especially using high-powered money in the denominator rather than M2.

Considering all this, let's go back to the Fed's inflation-targeting statement and pull out this key line: "The inflation rate over the longer run is primarily determined by monetary policy, and hence the Committee has the ability to specify a longer-run goal for inflation." I believe the reason that inflation hasn't responded to the ultra-easy monetary policies adopted by the major central banks since the Great Financial Crisis is that it *isn't primarily determined by monetary policy*. I'm not saying that monetary policy doesn't matter, just that it isn't the sole or even primary determinant of inflation; there are other drivers playing major but under-appreciated deflationary roles and operating beyond the scope of monetary policy.

That's why it has been so hard to get inflation back up to a measly 2.0% on a sustainable basis following the Great Financial Crisis, especially in Japan and the Eurozone, at least through the end of 2019 (Fig. 38 and Fig. 39). In the United States, both the headline and the core PCED inflation rates also have remained stubbornly below 2.0% post-crisis through the end of 2019—which flies in the face of traditional economic doctrine (Fig. 40).

The December 2, 2019 issue of the *Financial Times* reported that the Fed is seriously considering a "make up" strategy for targeting inflation. The article was titled "US Federal Reserve considers letting inflation run above target." Here is the gist of the plan: "The Fed's year-long review of its monetary policy tools is due to conclude next year and, according to interviews with current and former policymakers, the central bank is considering a promise that when it misses its inflation target, it will then temporarily raise that target."[233]

With all due respect, that's hilarious! Why do Fed officials want to embarrass themselves by targeting inflation over 2.0% when they haven't been able to move it up to 2.0% since officially targeting that level in January 2012? Since then through late 2019, the headline PCED has been tracking an annual trendline with a constant 1.3% growth rate (Fig. 41). As a result, during November 2019, the PCED was 4.7% below where it should have been if it had been tracking 2.0%. To get back to the steeper trendline by the end of 2022, the PCED would have to increase by about 12.0%, or 4.0% per year! A longer workout period would moderate the needed inflation make-up. However, the open question remains: How will they boost inflation above 2.0% at all if they haven't been able to get there since 2012?

Fed Governor Lael Brainard, speaking to reporters on November 26, 2019, said that a strict make-up rule would be too hard to explain to the public. She said so following a speech she gave advocating a more flexible approach, such as targeting an inflation range of 2.0% to 2.5% after a period of below-target results.[234] Good luck with that.

The Great Inflation Delusion

In my opinion, the central bankers, with their ultra-easy monetary policies, are fighting four very powerful forces of deflation: Détente, Disruption, Demography, and Debt. I call them the deflationary "4Ds." Let me explain:

- **Détente.** Détente occurs following wars. Such periods of peacetime lead to globalization with freer trade, which means more competitive global markets for labor, capital, goods, and services. The latest period of détente started when the Cold War ended during 1989. There have been many previous periods of détente following wars. The resulting globalization resulted in deflation, along with growing and proliferating prosperity.

  History shows that prices tend to rise rapidly during wartimes and then fall during peacetimes. War is inflationary; peace is deflationary.

  We can clearly see this phenomenon in the CPI for the US, which is available since 1800 on an annual basis (Fig. 42). It spiked sharply during the War of 1812, the Civil War, World War I, and World War II through the end of the Cold War. During peacetimes, prices fell sharply for many years following all the wars listed above, except for the peace so far since the end of the Cold War. Prices still are rising in the United States, though at a significantly slower pace than when the Cold War was most intense. (Of course, there have been local wars since then, and all too many terrorist attacks, but none that has substantially disrupted global commerce.)

Wars, in effect, are trade barriers that restrict global competition. During wars, countries don't trade with their enemies. Wars disrupt commerce among allies facing military obstacles to trading with one another. Markets are fragmented.

During wars, power shifts from markets to governments as economic activity is focused on military victory. The economy's resources are marshaled for the war effort. Commodity prices tend to soar as the combatants scramble to obtain raw materials. There is a shortage of workers, as a significant portion of the labor force is drafted to fight in the trenches. Material and industrial resources shift to the defense industries. Entrepreneurs, engineers, and scientists are recruited by the government to win the war by designing more effective and lethal weapons. As a result, there are shortages of consumer goods. The upward pressure on labor costs and prices often is met with government-imposed wage and price controls that rarely work.

Peacetimes tend to be deflationary because freer trade in an expanding global marketplace increases competition among producers. Domestic producers no longer are protected by wartime restrictions on both domestic and foreign competitors. There are fewer geographic limits to trade and no serious military impediments. Power shifts back from the government to global markets. Economists mostly agree that the fewer restrictions on trade and the bigger the market, the lower the prices paid by consumers and the better the quality of the goods and services offered by producers. These beneficial results occur thanks to the powerful forces unleashed by global competition during peacetimes.

As more consumers become accessible around the world, more producers around the world seek them out by offering them competitively priced goods and services of better and better quality. Entrepreneurs have a greater incentive to research and develop new technologies in big markets than in small ones. The engineers and scientists who were employed in the war industry are hired by companies scrambling to meet the demand of peacetime economies around the world. Big markets permit a greater division of labor and more specialization, which is conducive to technological innovation and productivity.

My war-and-peace model of inflation simply globalizes the model of perfect competition found in the microeconomic textbooks. At the market's equilibrium price, aggregate demand equals total supply. Both consumers and producers are "price takers." No one has enough clout in the market to dictate the price that everyone must pay or receive. No one firm or group of firms can set the price.

In competitive markets, there are no barriers to entry. Anyone with the right resources can start a business in any industry. In addition, there's no protection from failure. Unprofitable firms restructure their operations, get sold, or go out of business. There are few if any zombies (i.e., living-dead firms that continue to produce even though they are bleeding cash). They should go out of business and be buried. These firms can only survive if they are kept on life support by government subsidies, usually because of political cronyism.

An increase in demand would raise the market price, stimulating more production among current competitors and attracting new market entrants. If demand drops such that losses are incurred, competitors will cut production, with some possibly shutting down if the decline in demand is permanent. New entrants certainly won't be attracted.

Profits are reduced to the lowest level that provides just enough incentive for enough suppliers to stay in business to satisfy demand at the going market price. Consumer welfare is maximized. Obviously, there can't be excessive returns to producers in a competitive market. If there are, those returns will be eliminated as new firms flood into the excessively profitable market. Firms that try to increase their profits by raising prices simply will lose market share to firms that adhere to the market price. That's a good way to go out of business.

Competition is inherently deflationary. No one can raise their price in a competitive market because it is capped by the intersection of aggregate supply and demand. However, anyone can lower their price if they can cut their costs by boosting productivity.

- **Disruption.** The best way to cut costs and boost productivity is with technological innovations. Companies that can innovate on a regular basis ahead of their competitors can cut their prices, gain market share, and be sustainably more profitable than their competitors. Firms that do so gain a competitive advantage that allows them to have a higher profit margin for a while. That's especially true if their advantage is sufficiently significant to put competitors out of business. However, some of their competitors undoubtedly will innovate as well, and there always seem to be new entrants arriving on the scene with innovations that pose unexpected challenges to the established players.

  In other words, technology is inherently disruptive and deflationary since there is a tremendous incentive to use it to lower costs across a wide range of businesses.

The technology industry is itself prone to deflationary pressures because it is so competitive. Tech companies spend enormous sums of money on research and development, so they must sell as many units of their new products as possible before the next "new, new thing" inevitably comes along. The industry is so competitive that it must eat its young to survive. The result is that tech companies tend to offer more fire power at lower prices with the introduction of each new generation of their offerings. In other words, the technology industry provides the perfect example of what economist Joseph Schumpeter called "creative destruction."[235]

The Fed hasn't paid enough attention to the impact of technology on the economy. Until 2019, I don't recall seeing any significant studies by the Fed's staff on this important subject. That may be changing, finally. The Federal Reserve Bank of Dallas hosted a conference on May 22–23, 2019, on "Technology-Enabled Disruption: Implications for Business, Labor Markets and Monetary Policy."[236] The topics covered all the obvious bases, focusing on how technological innovation is disrupting business models, keeping a lid on price inflation, impacting the labor market, and stimulating merger-and-acquisition activity. The overview description of the conference succinctly summarized the disinflationary impact of technology as follows:

> Technology-enabled disruption means that workers are increasingly being replaced by technology. It also means that existing business models are being supplanted by new models, often technology-enabled, that bring more efficiency to the sale or distribution of goods and services. As part of this phenomenon, consumers are increasingly able to use technology to shop for goods and services at lower prices with greater convenience—which has the impact of reducing the pricing power of businesses. This reduced pricing power, in

turn, causes businesses to further intensify their focus on creating greater operational efficiencies. These trends appear to
be accelerating.[237]

- **Demography.** One of the greatest success stories in the history of technological innovation has been in agriculture. Thomas
Robert Malthus never saw it coming. Between 1798 and 1826, he
published six editions of his widely read treatise *An Essay on the
Principle of Population.* He rejected the notions about mankind's
future advancements that were popular at the time, believing
instead that poverty cannot be eradicated but is a permanent
fixture in the economic firmament. He explained this supposed
principle by arguing that population growth generally expanded too fast in times and regions of plenty, until the size of the
population relative to the primary resources, particularly food,
caused distress. Famines and diseases were nature's way of
keeping population growth from outpacing the food supply:

> That the increase of population is necessarily limited by the
> means of subsistence, that population does invariably increase
> when the means of subsistence increase, and, that the superior
> power of population is repressed, and the actual population
> kept equal to the means of subsistence, by misery and vice.

Malthus was the original "dismal scientist." His pessimistic
outlook was probably the most spectacularly wrong economic
forecast of all times, and a classic for contrarian thinkers. Grain
production soared during the 1800s thanks to new technologies,
more acreage, and rising yields. During the first half of the century, chemical fertilizers revived the fertility of European soil,
and the milling process was automated using steam engines.
During the second half of the century, vast new farmlands were
opened in the United States under the Homestead Act of 1862,
and agriculture's productivity soared with the proliferation of

mechanical sowers, reapers, and threshers. Tremendous progress in agriculture continued during the 20th century, particularly during the Green Revolution of the 1950s and 1960s.

The huge productivity gains in agriculture forced farm workers to move to the cities to find work. The resulting urbanization of populations around the world led to a sharp drop in fertility rates. In recent years, they have dropped below population replacement everywhere but in India and Africa. As a result of widespread urbanization, children no longer provide the benefit of labor in rural economies. Instead, they are a significant cost in urban settings. Malthus never saw that coming either.

Demographic profiles are turning increasingly geriatric around the world. People are living longer. They are having fewer children. Economies with aging demographic trends are likely to grow more slowly and have less inflation.

Older people tend to be more frugal than younger ones. That's partly because they know that they are likely to live longer than previous generations, but don't know how much longer. Old people tend to downsize. Younger people today tend to be minimalists compared to the Baby Boom generation. Many of them are burdened with student debt. Many prefer to rent apartments in cities and use ride-sharing services rather than buy cars. They are getting married later in life, if at all, and having fewer children. These demographic trends suggest slow growth in consumption and add to deflationary pressures.

China's one-child policy from 1979 to 2015 exacerbated the plunge in the country's fertility rate below the population replacement level. The policy reflected the government's Malthusian fear that without such a policy, population growth would outstrip the food supply, resulting in widespread famine. By some estimates, the often-brutal policy prevented 300 million to 500 million births. As a result, China is rapidly turning into the world's largest nursing home. Young adults who are only children must support their elderly parents financially in a country without a comprehensive, nationwide social security system. A young married couple with no siblings has four senior parents to support. That financial burden alone is discouraging couples from having more than one child even though the government now is encouraging them to do so.

- **Debt.** Aging demographic trends are causing governments to spend more on social security and health care. Since the elderly dependency ratios (i.e., the number of working-age adults to the numbers of seniors) are falling globally, governments are forced to borrow more to support more seniors; tax revenues alone can't keep up with seniors' needs. Debt accumulated for this purpose is likely to weigh on economic growth rather than to stimulate it.

The forces of deflation that had been mounting since the end of the Cold War were held back by rapid credit expansion around the world. Central banks were lulled by the decline in inflation and the proliferation of prosperity following the end of the Cold War into believing that they had moderated the business cycle. Indeed, they attributed this achievement to their policies rather than to globalization, and they dubbed it the "Great Moderation"—which presumably started during the mid-1980s but ended abruptly with the Great Recession. Along the way, and especially after the Great Recession, they kept the punch bowl full, providing lots of cheap credit, enabling lots of borrowing by households, businesses, and governments.

The central bankers simply ignored the implications of soaring debt. Their macroeconomic models didn't give much, if any, weight to measures of debt. Predictably, their easy monetary policies reduced the burden of servicing previous debts, which could be refinanced at lower rates, allowing borrowers to borrow more. By declaring that they had moderated the business cycle, the central bankers encouraged both borrowers and lenders to be less cautious about the potential dangers of too much leverage.

Central banks have facilitated an extraordinary borrowing binge on a global basis for many years. Debt-to-GDP ratios, debt-to-income ratios, and debt-to-profits ratios all have soared the world over. Governments borrowed like there was no tomorrow. In the United States, buyers bought homes with no money down and "liar's loans," where credit was granted without a formal credit check. In the Eurozone, banks lent to borrowers in the so-called PIIGS—Portugal, Ireland, Italy, Greece, and Spain—as though they had the same credit ratings as German borrowers. That turned out to be a bad assumption.

Some of these credit excesses hit the fan in 2008, and the consequences were clearly deflationary. The Great Moderation turned into the Great Recession. To avert another Great Depression, the central banks of the major industrial economies scrambled to flood the financial markets with even more credit. China's debt binge has been unprecedented since the Great Financial Crisis. Emerging market economies likewise could borrow on favorable terms despite their often-spotty credit histories.

So far, the ultra-easy monetary policies of the central banks have succeeded in offsetting the natural, peacetime forces of deflation. Of course, central banks existed in the past when deflation prevailed, but monetary theory and operating procedures were primitive. Today's central bankers claim that this all proves they are better than ever at managing the economy with monetary policy. I hope they're right, but I have my doubts.

Could it be that many borrowers are mostly maxed out on their lines of credit and credit cards, or have concluded on their own that they are tapped out? As an empirical observation, we can see that easy credit has lost its effectiveness in stimulating demand because it has been too easy for too long.

On the other hand, easy money may be boosting supply. In the past, an important barrier to entry in many industries was a lack of financing. Technology is especially dependent on venture capital. Low interest rates and booming stock markets around the world since the early 1990s provided plenty of cheap capital to fund new technologies that have been both disruptive and deflationary.

Furthermore, easy money has been propping up lots of unprofitable businesses that have lots of debt and are adding excess capacity. These zombies should be shut down, or at least restructured. Instead, they are contributing to deflationary forces.

The bottom line is that easy money isn't always inflationary and stimulative. It may be again in the future, but over the past few years since the Great Financial Crisis, other deflationary forces have come into play, and monetary policy may have contributed to them via its unexpected and unintended consequences. In other words, with all due respect to Milton Friedman, easy money can be deflationary!

The 4Ds combined tend to weigh on economic growth and are inherently deflationary. This explains why unconventional ultra-easy monetary policies have become conventional over the past 11 years. The central bankers are doing more of the same and getting the same disappointing result. As in the ancient Greek myth of Sisyphus, every time they push the boulder up the hill, it comes rolling back down.

Central bankers tend to be macroeconomists who were taught in graduate school that inflation is a monetary phenomenon. They were also taught to hate deflation as much as inflation. That's why the major central banks have all pegged 2.0% as their Goldilocks inflation target, not too hotly inflationary or frigidly deflationary.

But surely, they must have learned over the past 11 years since the Great Financial Crisis that inflation isn't a monetary phenomenon after all. They must realize that the four powerful forces of deflation are microeconomic in nature. Occasionally, they acknowledge these forces, demonstrating that they aren't completely clueless. Nevertheless, they go blithely about their business, inexplicably confident in the power of their policy tools to overcome these poorly understood forces somehow or other.

In a July 16, 2019 speech in Paris, Fed Chair Powell acknowledged in passing that inflation may not be solely a monetary phenomenon: "Many factors are contributing to these changes— well-anchored inflation expectations in the context of improved monetary policy, demographics, globalization, slower productivity growth, greater demand for safe assets, and weaker links between unemployment and inflation. And these factors seem likely to persist."[238] He also acknowledged that these factors collectively may continue to keep the "neutral rate of interest low" (i.e., too close to zero), which is the dreaded ELB. He concluded: "This proximity to the lower bound poses new complications for central banks and calls for new ideas."

The problem is that the central bankers have run out of new ideas (and policy tools), so they keep trying the same old ones. Their delusion is that doing more of the same (i.e., providing ultra-easy monetary conditions) should eventually boost inflation to 2.0%.

Where has all this liquidity been going?

Arguably, some of it has averted outright deflation so far. Quite a bit of it seems to have flowed into global bond and stock markets, and real estate too. There has been inflation in asset prices rather than in the prices of goods and services. If the central bankers persist in the delusions that fuel their ultra-easy monetary policies, the outcome may continue to be asset-price inflation.

That's fine, until it isn't, as I discuss in the next chapter on financial stability and instability.

Monetary Utopia or Myopia?

The 10-year period from 2008 through 2018 was widely perceived to be the "Age of the Central Bankers." They undoubtedly view it as a Golden Age, in which they proved that they had the will and the means to stop the Great Financial Crisis from turning into a totally disastrous financial meltdown, and the Great Recession from turning into another Great Depression. However, looking back, they must take some of the blame for having set the stage for the latest world financial crisis by enabling too much credit expansion in the first place. Furthermore, looking ahead, there might still be severe unintended consequences of their unprecedented experiments with ultra-easy monetary policies.

As I've said before and will say again: I'm an investment strategist, not a preacher. I don't do right or wrong; I do bullish or bearish. While I have had many reasons to be critical of monetary policymaking in the United States and overseas, my job is to predict how long those policies will be bullish and when they might turn bearish. Nevertheless, I do have a few questions and opinions on monetary policymaking.

For starters, how much longer must inflation remain subdued for central bankers to consider the possibility that inflation may not be a monetary phenomenon, or at least not solely a monetary phenomenon? Their central conceit is that they can control the economy thanks to the quantity theory of money:

$$M \bullet V = P \bullet Y$$

This assumes that they can determine the money supply (M) and that the velocity of money (V) is constant or at least predictable. If so, then they can drive nominal GDP (i.e., P times Y) and raise the price level (P) once real GDP (Y) is equal to or exceeds its noninflationary potential.

By the way, they also need to have a constant or predictable money multiplier model:

$$M = m \bullet H$$

The multiplier (m) is the ratio of the broad money supply (M) to high-powered money (H), which is mostly bank reserves under the control of the central bank. Neither the money multiplier nor the velocity of money has been constant, or even predictable, for a long time, and even less so since the Great Financial Crisis (Fig. 43 and Fig. 44). Since then, high-powered money has soared thanks to the central banks' various QE programs, yet the growth rates in broad measures of the money supply have remained subdued as the money multiplier has plunged. Exacerbating the control problem for the central banks is that the velocity of money fell at the same time.

While the central bankers can take some credit for reviving economic growth, I think that's what economies naturally do. In the United States, Fed officials have been mystified that the tightening of the labor market hasn't boosted wages, which would then bring inflation closer to their target. When might they consider the possibility that the forces subduing price inflation are keeping a lid on wage inflation?

When might the central bankers abandon concepts such as the NAIRU and the natural real rate of interest (r*), which—while interesting as intellectual exercises—cannot be measured? Attempts to estimate them have strongly suggested that they aren't constants. As I noted in Chapter 8, Fed officials including Powell and Clarida have acknowledged that these variables are unmeasurable, yet they still run their models to measure them!

For central bankers, utopia would be a world where m, V, NAIRU, and r* are all constant—or at least measurable and predictable. By the way, the word "utopia" comes from the fictional society in Sir Thomas More's 1516 book *Utopia*. He created the name from the ancient Greek words for "no" and "place."

I find contrarian perspectives intellectually refreshing, especially if they come from important central bankers. That gives me a hint that the consensus views they tend to share may be changing.

I particularly enjoyed an October 4, 2017 speech by Daniel Tarullo, who served as a Fed governor from January 2009 through April 2017: "Monetary Policy Without a Working Theory of Inflation."[239] Tarullo provided an insider's view on what has and hasn't been "useful for policymaking." He had become increasingly skeptical about the Fed's focus on unobservable variables such as the ones I just described. He then discussed why the Phillips curve model, which posits that there is a tradeoff between unemployment and inflation, is useless. One of his main conclusions is that "monetary policy will need to confront the likelihood that we may be in for an indefinite period in which no Phillips curve or other model will be a workable guide to policy."

Another interesting speech by a central banker was delivered on September 22, 2017 by Claudio Borio, the head of the Monetary and Economic Department of the Bank for International Settlements.[240] It was titled "Through the Looking Glass." I appreciated it because we are likeminded about the groupthink of central bankers. Regarding inflation, he said, "Yet the behavior of inflation is becoming increasingly difficult to understand. If one is completely honest, it is hard to avoid the question: how much do we really know about the inflation process?"

He followed up with two seemingly rhetorical questions: "Could it be that we know less than we think? Might we have overestimated our ability to control inflation, or at least what it would take to do so?" The rest of the speech essentially answers "yes" to both questions. Borio, a master of rhetorical questions, then asked:

> Is it reasonable to believe that the inflation process should have remained immune to the entry into the global economy of the former Soviet bloc and China and to the opening-up of other emerging market economies? This added something like 1.6 billion people to the effective labour force, drastically shrinking the share of advanced economies, and cut that share by about half by 2015.

Borio deduced that measures of domestic slack are insufficient gauges of inflationary or disinflationary pressures. Furthermore, there must be more global slack given "the entry of lower-cost producers and of cheaper labour into the global economy." That must "have put persistent downward pressure on inflation, especially in advanced economies and at least until costs converge." Borio explains that technological innovation might also have rendered the Phillips curve model comatose or dead, by reducing "incumbent firms' pricing power—through cheaper products, as they cut costs; through newer products, as they make older ones obsolete; and through more transparent prices, as they make shopping around easier." He concluded:

> No doubt, globalisation has been the big shock since the 1990s. But technology threatens to take over in future. Indeed, its imprint in the past may well have been underestimated and may sometimes be hard to distinguish from that of globalisation.

He added a final zinger, arguing that the impact of real factors on inflation has been underestimated and that the impact of monetary policy on the real interest rate has been underestimated too.

These points go to the heart of what I've been puzzling out over my past 40-plus years on Wall Street: The true causal relationships among economic forces, irrespective of commonly accepted assumptions and age-old dogma.

Chapter 12

Financial Stability:
The Third Mandate

Negative Rates and Consequences

Following the Great Financial Crisis, the most unconventional monetary policy tool ever used by the central banks was used for the first time: negative interest rates. The goal of permitting interest rates to sink below zero is to gin up economic growth and inflation. Yet it's not hard to imagine how a policy of negative interest rates might backfire, catalyzing undesirable effects and leading to the opposite of the intended results. Negative interest rates could reduce inflationary expectations by signaling that deflation is a viable concern. They are also bound to cause investors to reach for any remaining positive yields from bonds and stocks of companies, even those with poor credit ratings. That can easily set the stage for a financial crisis, resulting in a recession.

On July 2, 2009, Sweden's Riksbank, the world's oldest central bank, was the first one to implement a negative interest rate when it pushed its overnight lending rate to –0.25%. Denmark's central bank followed, lowering its policy rate to –0.20% during July 2012. As noted in Chapter 10, the BOJ and the ECB first lowered their official interest rates into negative territory on June 5, 2014 and January 29, 2016, respectively. Government bond yields turned negative in Europe and Japan as well. Even some corporate bonds had negative yields. On August 5, 2019, Denmark's third-largest bank announced that it would offer 10-year mortgages at a rate of −0.50%.

The May 20, 2019 issue of *The Wall Street Journal* included an article titled "Negative Rates, Designed as a Short-Term Jolt, Have Become an Addiction." It focused on the failure of negative interest rates to revive European economies:

> The negative-rate policy's ineffectualness is a sign of just how weak Europe's economic engines are, and how vulnerable. The policy threatens pensions, creates the risk of real-estate bubbles and doesn't fully quell the specter of deflation. European banks struggle with weak interest income and thin margins on loans, putting them behind American peers in profitability and making it harder for them to finance the economy.[241]

During his July 25, 2019 press conference, ECB President Mario Draghi was asked whether business spending might be depressed by managements assuming that interest rates will stay very low "forever basically." Draghi responded that construction spending was doing well. He did not mention the weakness in capital spending but did acknowledge: "Certainly we have to ask ourselves: are all these instruments going to be effective forever?"

Even when he asked that question, there was plenty of evidence that the Eurozone's economy was slowing significantly. The region's real GDP rose just 1.2% year over year during the third quarter of 2019. The ECB's ultra-easy monetary policies, including negative interest rates, were already less effective. Yet Draghi defended his policies as follows:

> We believe they are effective. Are there decreasing returns? Maybe there are as well, but would that exempt monetary policy from doing what is necessary or what we believe necessary based on the current information? The answer is no.[242]

In an August 26, 2019 article titled "Negative Interest Rates and Inflation Expectations in Japan," two economists at the Federal Reserve Bank of San Francisco reviewed Japan's experience with negative interest rates. They examined movements in yields on inflation-indexed and deflation-protected JGBs "to gauge changes in the market's inflation expectations from the BOJ moving to negative policy rates." They found that "this movement resulted in decreased, rather than increased, immediate and medium-term expected inflation." Their conclusion: "This therefore suggests using caution when considering the efficacy of negative rates as expansionary policy tools under well-anchored inflation expectations."[243]

After its foray into negative rates at the start of 2016, the BOJ was warned by a Japanese lawmaker: "You have sent a message to the people that they had better watch out because Japan's economy is in trouble."[244]

Negative interest rates paid by a central bank on commercial banks' excess reserves are supposed to encourage the banks to lend more. However, a study dated July 30, 2019, based on data for 6,558 banks from 33 OECD countries from 2012 through 2016, found that bank lending was *weaker* in countries that had adopted negative interest rates.[245] A follow-up study found that bank margins and profits fell in countries with negative interest rates compared to countries that did not adopt this policy.[246] A summary of these two studies observed:

> Negative interest rates are supposed to stimulate the domestic economy by facilitating an increase in the demand for bank loans. In theory this could increase new capital investment by firms and domestic consumption, via credit creation. But the research showed bank margins were being squeezed, curbing loan growth and damaging banking profits.[247]

What are the odds that the Fed will go negative? They are probably low, but not insignificant. I noted in Chapter 7 that during 2010, the Fed's econometric model was calling for the FOMC to cut the federal funds rate below zero to stimulate economic growth and boost inflation back up closer to 2.0%. However, Bernanke must have recognized that doing so would have been too radical and highly controversial. He chose QE2 purchases of $600 billion in bonds, which the model predicted would have the equivalent stimulative impact as a negative federal funds rate of –0.75%.

Bernanke first suggested the need for more quantitative easing (i.e., QE2) in his Jackson Hole speech on August 27, 2010. Fed officials viewed that as an alternative to dropping the ELB below zero. In an October 1 speech that year, William Dudley, the president of the Federal Reserve Bank of New York, explained that QE2 "would provide about as much stimulus as a reduction in the federal funds rate of between half a point and three quarters of a point." He argued that was the only tool the Fed had left to meet its congressional mandate to lower the unemployment rate.

As I noted in Chapter 7, it was my expressed opinion back then that if the Fed's econometric model was calling for a negative official policy rate, then either there was something wrong with the model or the Fed was trying to fix economic problems that could not be fixed with monetary policy. When the federal funds rate was lowered to zero in late 2008, Fed officials should have said that that was all they could do. If the federal funds rate falls to zero again in the future, I hope that they will resist going negative, especially given that the ECB and BOJ have done so without any success.

The issue of the ELB was thoroughly discussed at the July 30–31, 2019 FOMC meeting. ELB was mentioned 15 times, up from no mention in the June meeting's minutes.[248] While the presumption seemingly remained that the federal funds rate wouldn't be lowered below zero, the minutes hinted that Fed officials might be thinking that if they must lower the federal funds rate to zero, it's a slippery slope from there to considering going negative.

All the ELB references were in a special section at the beginning of the July minutes titled "Review of Monetary Policy Strategy, Tools, and Communication Practices." Ten months earlier, in a November 15, 2018 press release, the Fed announced that it would "review the strategies, tools, and communication practices it uses to pursue its congressionally-assigned mandate of maximum employment and price stability."[249] As a result, there was likely to be an ongoing discussion of the ELB and other monetary policy issues in future FOMC meetings as well.

Oddly, in my opinion, there were lots of high-fives in the review section, as committee participants congratulated one another for lowering the federal funds rate to zero at the end of 2008, and then supplementing this ELB with QE programs. The only regret that Fed officials expressed during their discussion of this subject was that they hadn't implemented more unconventional policy measures after they hit the ELB:

> In particular, a number of participants commented that, as many of the potential costs of the Committee's asset purchases had failed to materialize, the Federal Reserve might have been able to make use of balance sheet tools even more aggressively over the past decade in providing appropriate levels of accommodation.

Here's what might happen the next time the federal funds rate falls to the ELB, which Fed officials apparently believed remained a distinct possibility:

> If policymakers are not able to provide sufficient accommodation at the ELB through the use of forward guidance or balance sheet actions, the constraints posed by the ELB could

be an impediment to the attainment of the Federal Reserve's dual-mandate objectives over time and put at risk the anchoring of inflation expectations at the Committee's longer-run inflation objective. Participants looked forward to a detailed discussion over coming meetings of alternative strategies for monetary policy.

The question is: what's left to consider that hasn't already been tried but negative interest rates?

Yet at his September 18, 2019 press conference, Powell declared that negative interest rates aren't likely on his watch. During the Q&A, he said, "I do not think we'd be looking at using negative rates, I just don't think those will be at the top of our list." Did that mean it was still on the list, but at the bottom? Powell added, "If we were to find ourselves at some future date again at the ELB, again not something we are expecting, then I think we would look at using large scale asset purchases and forward guidance." He stated, "We feel that they worked fairly well," and concluded, "We did not use negative rates."[250]

It's unsettling that Fed officials concluded that because their unconventional policies didn't have "adverse implications for financial stability," as previously noted, they should be even more aggressive with their ultra-easy policies next time. In effect, the FOMC defined "success" as avoiding blowing up the financial system with its policies.

On December 19, 2019, Sweden's central bankers raised the Riksbank's key interest rate (the repo) for the first time since early 2015, from −0.25% to 0.00%, after a meeting at which they said that inflation had been close to its 2.0% target since the start of 2017. However, the bank said it expected the interest rate to remain at zero "in the coming years."

The Riksbank warned that if negative rates continued for too long "the behaviour of economic agents may change and negative effects may arise."[251] More specifically, the bank's December 2019 *Monetary Policy Report* observed "that low interest rates can create incentives for excessive risk-taking in the economy. Assets may become overvalued, risk may be incorrectly priced and the indebtedness of various agents may increase in an unsustainable manner."[252]

Watching Financial Stability and Instability

Several data series in the *Financial Accounts of the United States* provided early warnings about the speculative extravaganza in the housing market in the early years of the new millennium before the housing bubble burst in 2007. They included the rapidly increasing quarterly series tracking home mortgages and home equity loans, as well as corporate bonds and commercial paper issued by asset-backed security issuers. The problem is that no one at the Fed paid much, if any, attention to them, even though the data are compiled by the Fed![253]

It may be hard to believe, but the reality is that the Fed's economists didn't spend much time analyzing credit market developments. I've skimmed through the titles of all the Fed staff's working papers posted on the Fed's website between 2005 and 2008; few seem to be about credit issues and even fewer about credit derivatives, which greatly exacerbated the financial crisis. Many of these instruments were designed to generate higher yields than were provided by the credit market's plain vanilla securities, mostly because the Greenspan Fed raised the federal funds rate too slowly (i.e., "at a measured pace") during the early 2000s. The resulting demand for securities offering higher yields was met with a deluge of credit derivatives that turned out to be much riskier than the credit-rating agencies and investors recognized.

To end the Great Financial Crisis, the major central banks loosened credit all over again. They lowered money market interest rates to historical lows, fueling unprecedented demand for higher yields in the bond and stock markets (Fig. 45 and Fig. 46). During the bull market in stocks that began March 2009, I increasingly generalized Marty Zweig's famous dictum about not fighting the Fed to "Don't fight the central banks." I noted that the Fed, the ECB, the BOJ, and the PBOC have an unlimited supply of dollars, euros, pounds, yen, and yuan that they can pour into the financial markets. They certainly demonstrated their willingness and ability to adopt unconventional, ultra-easy monetary policies during and after the Great Financial Crisis. The central bankers were like Walter Bagehot on steroids.

The major central bankers also have maintained—either stating explicitly or suggesting implicitly—that the transmission mechanism of their ultra-easy monetary policies works by boosting asset prices, with the resulting wealth effects stimulating their economies. Higher stock prices are expected to boost consumer spending. Low mortgage rates should stimulate housing activity and push home prices higher. Low bond yields are expected to stimulate business borrowing for capital spending. If some of the corporate borrowing is used to buy back shares, that's okay because it boosts stock prices.[254]

This process has been great for stock and bond investors. However, the transmission mechanism hasn't worked as well as the central bankers expected. They have continued to struggle to avert deflation while economic growth has remained subpar, with secular stagnation plaguing the Eurozone and Japan. So they have persisted with their ultra-easy policies, which have driven stock prices to record highs and bond yields to record lows.

During the latest bull market in stocks, many a vocal bearish prognosticator has warned that the stock market was on a "sugar high" from all the liquidity injected by the central banks into the financial markets. My response: "So what's your point?" Their point was often simply that "this will all end badly." I've responded, "All the more reason to make lots of money before that happens." The pessimists in turn have countered that the central banks were just "kicking the can down the road." My reply has been: "That might be better than doing nothing." The doomsayers have said that it was all heading toward a widely dreaded end-game in a repeat of 2008 or worse. I've countered with arguments suggesting there might be no end to this game. Japan comes to mind as a country that has maintained ultra-easy monetary and fiscal policies to combat the 4Ds since the early 1990s without calamity, so far.

Nevertheless, I can understand investors' unease about the extreme measures that the major central banks have been taking to avoid another financial crisis. They were indeed extreme, and without precedent. From time to time, I too was shocked by the central bankers' latest maneuvers and accused them of being "central monetary planners." I objected to their conceit that monetary policy could solve all our problems. The central bankers occasionally admitted that they didn't really believe that but had no choice other than doing whatever it took to save the day, since fiscal policymakers seemed incapable of taking appropriate action.

The risk in all this is that the unconventional policies of the central banks have become all too conventional. They were designed to avoid another financial crisis, but they could very well set the stage for the next one. Ultra-easy monetary policies with interest rates set so low by the central banks once again have caused a desperate reach for yield by investors. That increases the likelihood that dodgy borrowers will have access to too much credit. The result could very well be financial instability and another financial crisis.

This time, Fed officials at least are aware of that risk, as a result of the Great Financial Crisis. They started formally to monitor financial stability at the end of 2018. That was 10 years after the crisis—but, hey, better late than never. They issued their first-ever *Financial Stability Report* on November 11, 2018.[255] The stated purpose of this semi-annual report is "to promote public understanding and increase transparency and accountability for the Federal Reserve's views on this topic."

The report explained that the adverse events that occurred during the Great Financial Crisis were dramatically worsened by an unstable financial system. More generally, it observed:

> A stable financial system, when hit by adverse events, or "shocks," continues to meet the demands of households and businesses for financial services, such as credit provision and payment services. In contrast, in an unstable system, these same shocks are likely to have much larger effects, disrupting the flow of credit and leading to declines in employment and economic activity.
>
> Consistent with this view of financial stability, the Federal Reserve Board's monitoring framework distinguishes between shocks to and vulnerabilities of the financial system. Shocks, such as sudden changes to financial or economic conditions, are typically surprises and are inherently difficult to predict. Vulnerabilities tend to build up over time and are the aspects of the financial system that are most expected to cause widespread problems in times of stress.

The Fed's framework for monitoring financial stability therefore focuses primarily on assessing vulnerabilities in four broad categories, described as follows in the report:

> **Elevated valuation pressures are signaled by asset prices that are high relative to economic fundamentals or historical norms and are often driven by an increased willingness**

of investors to take on risk. As such, elevated valuation pressures imply a greater possibility of outsized drops in asset prices.

Excessive borrowing by businesses and households leaves them vulnerable to distress if their incomes decline or the assets they own fall in value. In the event of such shocks, businesses and households with high debt burdens may need to cut back spending sharply, affecting the overall level of economic activity. Moreover, when businesses and households cannot make payments on their loans, financial institutions and investors incur losses.

Excessive leverage within the financial sector increases the risk that financial institutions will not have the ability to absorb even modest losses when hit by adverse shocks. In those situations, institutions will be forced to cut back lending, sell their assets, or, in extreme cases, shut down. Such responses can lead to credit crunches in which access to credit for households and businesses is substantially impaired.

Funding risks expose the financial system to the possibility that investors will "run" by withdrawing their funds from a particular institution or sector. Many financial institutions raise funds from the public with a commitment to return their investors' money on short notice, but those institutions then invest much of the funds in illiquid assets that are hard to sell quickly or in assets that have a long maturity. This liquidity and maturity transformation can create an incentive for investors to withdraw funds quickly in adverse situations. Facing a run, financial institutions may need to sell assets quickly at "fire sale" prices, thereby incurring substantial losses and potentially even becoming insolvent. Historians and economists often refer to widespread investor runs as "financial panics."

The report was balanced, with some vulnerabilities flagged as potentially troublesome and others as less concerning. No clear and present dangers were identified. The report suggested that the Fed was somewhat worried about elevated asset valuations and levels of corporate borrowing but unconcerned about household borrowing, financial sector leverage, or funding risks.

The report noted that borrowing by households "has risen in line with incomes and is concentrated among low-credit-risk borrowers." Outstanding mortgage debt credit risk "appears to be generally solid." Further, financial-sector leverage has "been low in recent years." Perhaps most importantly, banks have "strong capital positions." Finally, broker-dealers and insurance companies have "strengthened their financial positions since the crisis" even as "there are signs of increased borrowing at other nonbank financial firms."

The report observed that elevated asset valuations reflected higher risk tolerance by investors as they reached for yield in the corporate bond market, buying higher-yielding bonds with lower credit ratings. As a result, credit-quality yield spreads were very narrow (Fig. 47). The forward price-to-earnings ratio (P/E) of the S&P 500 was above its historical mean, though still well below the bubble of the late 1990s.[256]

The upshot of the 38 pages was that financial stability had markedly improved since the days leading up to the Great Financial Crisis, which was news to no one. The decade-late report seemed to serve little purpose beyond covering the Fed's backside: If any of the risks materialized, Fed officials at least could say they had been aware of them and monitoring them.

The Fed's second *Financial Stability Report* was released during May 2019.[257] It had the same don't-worry-we-are-on-it tone as the first report. However, credit quality had clearly eroded in the corporate bond market. The second report observed:

> [T]he distribution of ratings among nonfinancial investment-grade corporate bonds has deteriorated. The share of bonds rated at the lowest investment-grade level (for example, an S&P rating of triple-B) has reached near-record levels. As of the first quarter of 2019, a little more than 50 percent of investment-grade bonds outstanding were rated triple-B, amounting to about $1.9 trillion.

And there was some alarming news about leveraged loans:

> The risks associated with leveraged loans have also intensified, as a greater proportion are to borrowers with lower credit ratings and already high levels of debt. In addition, loan agreements contain fewer financial maintenance covenants, which effectively reduce the incentive to monitor obligors and the ability to influence their behavior. The Moody's Loan Covenant Quality Indicator suggests that the overall strictness of loan covenants is near its weakest level since the index began in 2012, and the fraction of so-called cov-lite leveraged loans (leveraged loans with no financial maintenance covenants) has risen substantially since the crisis.[258]

The good news was that the junk-bond default rate remained very low during the first half of 2019. The renewed decline in bond yields at that time certainly helped to ease financial conditions in the corporate debt markets. Nevertheless, both the November 2018 and the May 2019 reports warned that in a recession there would be widespread credit-quality downgrades of near-junk bonds to junk status. Some institutional investors who were restricted from holding noninvestment-grade bonds would be forced to sell into an illiquid market at distressed prices. The situation would be exacerbated if corporate bond mutual funds and ETFs were forced to sell their holdings as a result of panic redemptions by individual investors. The resulting credit crunch for corporate borrowers would exacerbate the recession.

Undoubtedly influenced by May's *Financial Stability Report*, the minutes of the July 30–31, 2019 FOMC meeting included more discussion about financial stability than in previous recent meetings. For example:

> Several participants noted that high levels of corporate debt and leveraged lending posed some risks to the outlook. A few participants discussed the fast growth of private credit markets—a sector not subject to the same degree of regulatory scrutiny and requirements that applies in the banking sector—and commented that it was important to monitor this market.

There wasn't much said about potential vulnerabilities in private credit markets in May's *Financial Stability Report*, suggesting that private credit markets needed much more monitoring!

The Fed's third *Financial Stability Report* was dated November 2019. Like the previous two, it was relatively sanguine, but did warn about the mounting debts of nonfinancial corporations and their potential to destabilize the financial system. The report also acknowledged that historically low interest rates could undermine the stability of the financial sector: "If interest rates were to remain low for a prolonged period, the profitability of banks, insurers, and other financial intermediaries could come under stress and spur reach-for-yield behavior, thereby increasing the vulnerability of the financial sector to subsequent shocks."[259]

Zombie Apocalypse

The major central banks are inadvertently contributing to deflation, as I explained in the previous chapter. They are also destabilizing the financial system, as the Fed's own *Financial Stability Report* attests. As noted previously, the major central banks are run by either PhD macroeconomists or people who have spent their careers surrounded by PhD macroeconomists, such as Jerome Powell at the Fed and Christine Lagarde at the ECB. Most of the macroeconomists working at the central banks were trained as demand-side Keynesians. They believe that easy money should stimulate demand, which should revive inflation. That's their core belief, in fact.

More specifically, easy money should boost consumer spending on durables and housing. It should stimulate capital spending by businesses. When the economy runs out of slack, that's when it will run hot enough to heat up inflation. The central bankers admit that there has been more slack than they expected, but once the economy runs out of workers, wage inflation will rise, pushing price inflation higher, especially when capacity utilization gets to be tight enough. The Phillips curve model and output-gap models are variations of this demand-side view of the world.

There are two major flaws in such models: They fail to recognize the demand-side limitations to borrowers' ability to keep on buying stuff with credit. And they completely ignore the supply-side impact of easy money on borrowers' behavior.

First, let's look at the demand-side effects: When borrowers have plenty of capacity to take on more debt, easy money stimulates demand quite effectively. But when easy-money conditions persist for years, borrowers get tapped out, resulting in high debt-to-income ratios. They borrow to their credit limits, and the effectiveness of easy money to stimulate demand further diminishes. Then even historically low interest rates, which reduce the cost of servicing debt, fail to boost demand—which explains why interest rates are kept historically low.

Meanwhile, supply-side borrowers, who produce the goods and services purchased by demand-side borrowers, take advantage of easy money to refinance their debts at lower rates and to borrow to keep their businesses going. Among the most likely corporate borrowers are companies that would be out of business if they didn't have access to easy money. In other words, they are zombie businesses, the living-dead companies that don't die only because they are resuscitated by cash infusions from lenders. As long as they live on, they create deflationary pressures by producing more goods and services than the market needs, as discussed in Chapter 11.

And why are lenders willing to lend to the zombies? Instead of stimulating demand by borrowers, historically low interest rates incite a reach-for-yield frenzy among lenders. They are willing to accept more credit risk for the higher returns offered by the zombies. Besides, if enough zombies fail, then surely the central banks will come up with some sort of rescue plan.

It's interesting to compare the borrowing binge in home mortgages that led to the Great Financial Crisis and the current borrowing binge in nonfinancial corporate (NFC) debt, including bonds and loans. At the start of 1990, the amount outstanding of both equaled around $2.4 trillion each (Fig. 48). Home mortgages then soared by 378%, or $9.0 trillion, to a record $11.3 trillion during the first half of 2008. Over the same period, NFC debt rose 162%, or $4.0 trillion to $6.4 trillion.

After peaking, home mortgages outstanding fell $1.4 trillion through the first quarter of 2015, and then increased by $1.1 trillion to $11.0 trillion by the second quarter of 2019. That was still slightly below the record high. Over the same period, NFC debt rose 55%, or $3.5 trillion, to a record $10.0 trillion.

During the third quarter of 2019, NFC bonds outstanding rose to a record $5.8 trillion (Fig. 49). NFC loans held by banks rose to a record $1.1 trillion, while "other loans" (which are mostly leveraged loans) rose to a record $1.8 trillion (Fig. 50). The NFC data are less alarming when scaled by nominal GDP (Fig. 51 and Fig. 52). Home mortgages outstanding peaked at a record 77% of GDP during the first quarter of 2009. NFC debt rose to a record high of 47% of GDP during the third quarter of 2019.

My interpretation of the data is that excessively easy credit conditions fueled the mortgage borrowing binge and housing boom that ended with the Great Financial Crisis. The strong debt-financed demand for homes stimulated economic activity and caused home prices to soar. Since the Great Financial Crisis, the borrowing binge in NFC debt hasn't contributed much to economic growth, and consumer price inflation has remained subdued. Apparently, a significant percentage of NFC debt is attributable to zombie companies using most of the proceeds from their borrowing to stay in business.

During his October 30, 2019 press conference, Fed Chair Jerome Powell was asked about financial stability. He responded: "Obviously, plenty of households are not in great shape financially, but in the aggregate, the household sector's in a very good place. That leaves businesses which is where the issue has been. Leverage among corporations and other forms of business, private businesses, is historically high. We've been monitoring it carefully and taking appropriate steps."[260]

He didn't specify those steps. However, the Fed's three interest-rate cuts during 2019 undoubtedly kept lots of zombies alive and fed their appetite for more debt.

The result is that historically low interest rates will continue to cause investors to reach for yield while paying less attention to credit quality. Of the $7.1 trillion in US nonfinancial corporate debt (including bonds, loans, and revolving credit) at the start of 2019, $2.9 trillion was rated BBB (i.e., only one grade above junk) while $2.4 trillion was rated as junk, according to S&P Global.[261]

It's not hard to imagine that this pileup of dodgy debt could set the stage for a credit crunch that buries the walking-dead zombies, forcing them to shut down operations and let go of workers.

The good news is that unlike in 2008, the banks are in great shape. Furthermore, rising defaults by NFCs may not cause a credit crunch if distressed assets funds act as a shock absorber in the capital markets, as during the 2015 crunch.

In any event, for now, zombies are safe. The central banks continue to pump lots of liquidity into the global financial markets stimulating lots of reach-for-yield demand for the dodgy credits. It could all end badly, but is not likely to do so in 2020.

If you want to read a very frightening script of how this horror movie plays out, see the October 2019 *Global Financial Stability Report* prepared by the IMF. It is titled "Lower for Longer" but should have been titled "Is a zombie apocalypse coming?" Here is the disturbing conclusion: "In a material economic slowdown scenario, half as severe as the global financial crisis, corporate debt-at-risk (debt owed by firms that cannot cover their interest expenses with their earnings) could rise to $19 trillion—or nearly 40 percent of total corporate debt in major economies, and above post-crisis levels."[262]

That unsettling scenario didn't stop the S&P 500 from climbing to new record highs during the final three months of 2019. Apparently, investors expected that before doomsday arrives, the Fed will ride to the rescue, lowering interest rates close to zero yet again and allowing all the zombie borrowers to refinance their debts yet again—forestalling the zombie apocalypse.

Contrarians were put on high alert at the end of June 2017, when Fed Chair Janet Yellen said at a London conference: "Would I say there will never, ever be another financial crisis? You know probably that would be going too far, but I do think we're much safer, and I hope it will not be in our lifetimes, and I don't believe it will be." Yet she also described asset valuations as "somewhat rich if you use some traditional metrics like price earnings ratios."[263] Yellen turned 71 on August 13, 2017, so her lifetime may not continue for as long as those of other interested parties. For someone who tends to be very precise, her use of "our lifetimes" sure leaves room for interpretation! In any event, her comment is reminiscent of other ill-fated predictions by Fed chairs—like Greenspan's "once-in-a-century" technology and productivity revolution and Bernanke's no "significant spillovers" stance on the subprime mortgage debacle. I'll go out on a limb and predict that there will be another financial crisis in our lifetimes. However, like previous ones, it likely will offer a great opportunity for buying stocks.

Epilogue

Helicopter Money

So what's next?

The world's major central banks have tried numerous unconventional policies to boost inflation and stimulate faster economic growth, including zero interest rates, ultra-easy forward guidance, QE, and negative interest rates. These unconventional tools have become conventional since the Great Financial Crisis. Now there is chatter about the central banks considering "helicopter money" and embracing Modern Monetary Theory (MMT). These are the outer limits of monetary policy. At the same time as they are considering extreme options, the central bankers are increasingly admitting that monetary policy can't do much more, and that it's time for fiscal policy to either take over or at least supplement monetary policy.

Back in 1969, Milton Friedman coined the term "helicopter drop" in his book *The Optimum Quantity of Money*. The term gained currency after then-Fed Governor Ben Bernanke referenced it in his famous 2002 preventing-deflation speech, earning him the nickname "Helicopter Ben."[264]

Bernanke revisited the subject in detail in an April 2016 Brooking's series of posts titled: "What tools does the Fed have left?" He observed: "[S]o long as people have the option of holding currency, there are limits to how far the Fed or any central bank can depress interest rates. Moreover, the benefits of low rates may erode over time, while the costs are likely to increase." He concluded that when monetary policy is inadequate—especially when interest rates are "stuck" near zero—fiscal policy could be a "powerful alternative."[265]

In this scenario, the central bank could provide the money to finance either a tax cut or government spending. In his 2002 speech, Bernanke explained: "A money-financed tax cut is essentially equivalent to Milton Friedman's famous 'helicopter drop' of money." In a footnote, he elaborated:

> A tax cut financed by money creation is the equivalent of a bond-financed tax cut plus an open-market operation in bonds by the Fed, and so arguably no explicit coordination is needed. However, a pledge by the Fed to keep the Treasury's borrowing costs low, as would be the case under my preferred alternative of fixing portions of the Treasury yield curve, might increase the willingness of the fiscal authorities to cut taxes.[266]

An alternative to this private-sector approach is the public-sector approach where a central bank distributes interest-free funds to the government for the specific purpose of spending on fiscal projects like infrastructure. To protect the independence of the central bank, Bernanke proposed in his 2016 note that Congress could create a special Treasury account at the central bank, giving the bank the sole authority to "fill" the account. The central bank would add funds to the account only when a specified amount of funding was needed to achieve the bank's employment and inflation goals.

Outgoing ECB President Mario Draghi was asked about helicopter money in a discussion with European lawmakers on September 23, 2019. He mentioned an August 15 report, "Dealing with the next downturn: From unconventional monetary policy to unprecedented policy coordination." It was written by three executives at BlackRock Investment Institute along with Stanley Fischer, a senior adviser at the Institute. Recall that Fischer was the

Fed vice chair when Janet Yellen was the chair. When he taught at MIT, his students included Ben Bernanke and Mario Draghi. The man has been influential!

The BlackRock report observed: "Monetary policy is almost exhausted as global interest rates plunge towards zero or below." The authors considered using helicopter money to revive economic growth and boost inflation but concluded that doing so meant risking hyperinflation: "History as well as theory suggests large-scale injections of money are simply not a tool that can be fine-tuned for a modest increase in inflation." Instead, the BlackRock report proposed a facility like Bernanke's bank account for the fiscal-spending authorities that is replenished by the central bank as necessary to achieve its mandate.[267]

Draghi also suggested that European lawmakers should consider MMT to stimulate economic growth and boost inflation. The basic idea of MMT is that the government can borrow and spend without limit in its own currency because it can always print more money to service its debt. When inflation rebounds, then the government should stop doing so or raise taxes. In my opinion, MMT isn't modern, isn't monetary, and isn't a theory. Governments around the world have been borrowing like mad to fund fiscal spending and income redistribution programs, while inflation has remained subdued, allowing the central banks to enable the fiscal excesses with ultra-easy monetary policies.

The BlackRock analysts maintained that their proposal is far more disciplined. Debt-financed MMT amounts to helicopter money if the debt is monetized by the central bank through a QE program. Otherwise, it amounts to more government debt funding more government spending, which isn't a theory, but has been the reality for many years for many governments.

Punch Drunk

The nature of government bureaucracies is that over time they get bigger and more powerful. That generalization certainly applies to the Fed. The central bank was originally created on December 23, 1913 in response to the financial crisis of 1907. Its primary mission was to provide an "elastic" currency that would respond to the needs of the economy. It was created to provide financial stability to avoid financial crises, or at least to keep them from harming the economy. The Fed's original mandate, therefore, wasn't to moderate the business cycle, but rather to stabilize the financial system. By doing so, the Fed would presumably indirectly moderate the business cycle since financial crises tend to cause recessions.

Recall what Fed Chair William McChesney Martin famously said on October 19, 1955 in his punch-bowl speech:

> In the field of monetary and credit policy, precautionary action to prevent inflationary excesses is bound to have some onerous effects—if it did not it would be ineffective and futile. Those who have the task of making such policy don't expect you to applaud. The Federal Reserve, as one writer put it, after the recent increase in the discount rate, is in the position of the chaperone who has ordered the punch bowl removed just when the party was really warming up.

He wisely added:

> But a note should be made here that, while money policy can do a great deal, it is by no means all powerful. In other words, we should not place too heavy a burden on monetary policy. It must be accompanied by appropriate fiscal and budgetary measures if we are to achieve our aim of stable progress. If we ask too much of monetary policy, we will not only fail but we will also discredit this useful, and indeed indispensable, tool for shaping our economic development.[268]

Martin's speech indicated that the Fed's mandate had evolved from its original focus on financial stability to keeping a lid on "inflationary excesses," even if that required the Fed to slow the economy down by tightening monetary policy (i.e., by removing the punch bowl).

Since October 27, 1978, when President Carter signed the Humphrey–Hawkins Full Employment Act, the Fed has been mandated by law to keep the unemployment rate low and consistent with full employment, while achieving inflation so low that it amounts to price stability. Ever since then, virtually every monetary policy move by the Fed has been justified by Fed officials as necessary to meet their so-called "dual mandate."

And how has that been working out?

Not too well, in my opinion. In the late 1970s and early 1980s, achieving both low unemployment and low inflation was an impossible task. Volcker chose to break the back of inflation by pushing the economy into a severe recession. He was still an "old school" central banker taking away the punch bowl. His approach worked as he had expected. Much to almost everyone else's surprise, inflation came down much faster than expected and the economy was growing again by the mid-1980s.

Under Greenspan, from 1987 to 2006, price inflation remained low. During the early 2000s, Fed officials worried that it was too close to zero and bordering on deflation. So Greenspan didn't take the punch bowl away and in fact kept filling it up. The result was financial instability as asset bubbles inflated and burst. During the late 1980s, there was the S&L crisis. The bubble in technology stocks inflated during the late 1990s and burst in the early 2000s. Heightened fears of deflation and unemployment, especially after the September 11, 2001 terrorist attacks, led Fed officials to believe that the dual mandate required them to maintain easy monetary conditions, which set the stage for the housing boom and bust of the 2000s.

In response to the Great Financial Crisis and the Great Recession, Bernanke believed from 2006 to 2014 that the dual mandate unambiguously required ultra-easy monetary policy, with the federal funds rate pegged near zero and lots of QE. The punch bowl would be kept full for as long as necessary. Bernanke was doing everything in the Fed's power to get the party going again. All that liquidity did get the party going again in asset markets, as the prices of stocks, bonds, and real estate rebounded sharply during the 2010s.

However, the economic expansion remained lackluster, as did the recovery in the labor market. So Yellen, from 2014 to early 2018, also continued to provide plenty of punch, though she cut back on the rum a bit as the labor market improved during her term as Fed chair. In her opinion, the dual mandate required a gradual normalization of monetary policy. Powell stayed on the course charted by Yellen during 2018 and 2019, when adding more rum again to the punch bowl seemed appropriate, though it seemed to be provided mostly to keep the party in the stock market from fizzling out.

This brief recap suggests that the dual mandate has led to significant financial instability. It's good to see that the Fed started to monitor financial stability more formally in late 2018, with regular reports on it. However, the dual mandate is required by law—financial stability isn't. That doesn't mean that Fed officials can't work around that by arguing that achieving the dual mandate requires financial stability.

Fed officials should reassess their assumption that moderating the business cycle should be their main job. By doing so, they tend to inadvertently cause financial instability as lenders and borrowers take on too much risk in the belief that recessions are less likely to happen and any that do will be short and shallow. A good rum punch can easily cause that delusion to spread.

Cryptocurrencies: Beginning of the End?

End the Fed is a 2009 book by Ron Paul, a former Republican congressman from Texas and a vocal libertarian. The book advocates abolishing the Federal Reserve System. It debuted at number six on *The New York Times* Best Sellers list. The congressman blamed the Fed for the financial crisis of 2008. The Fed has had lots of critics over the years, especially among progressives, who believe it was founded by a cabal of bankers and remains that way. A lot of Germans feel the same way about the ECB.

In her 2017 book, *Fed Up*, Danielle DiMartino Booth argues that the Fed has morphed into a cabal of PhD macroeconomists who are clueless about how the economy works. The book's Amazon website states:

> Danielle DiMartino Booth was surprised to find herself recruited as an analyst at the Federal Reserve Bank of Dallas, one of the regional centers of our complicated and widely misunderstood Federal Reserve System. She was shocked to discover just how much tunnel vision, arrogance, liberal dogma, and abuse of power drove the core policies of the Fed. DiMartino Booth found a cabal of unelected academics who made decisions without the slightest understanding of the real world, just a slavish devotion to their theoretical models.

Unlike Ron Paul, she wants to amend the Fed, not end it. I'm sympathetic to that view. However, my focus from the beginning of my career has been on objective, rather than subjective, analysis. I'm not advocating either ending the Fed or changing it. My job is to watch the Fed—to understand the Fed and the other central bankers as they are, not as I think they should be—and to predict their actions accordingly. It's okay to judge the Fed too, just for fun, as long as doing so doesn't bias your objective, observation-based predictions.

Nevertheless, I do try occasionally to puzzle out whether technological innovation might put the central bankers out of business or radically change their modus operandi. I'm particularly intrigued by the impact of bitcoin and other cryptocurrencies on our monetary system. Blockchain, the software that runs these digital currencies, is allowing banks to eliminate clearinghouse intermediaries from transactions and to clear them much more rapidly. Smartphone apps allow consumers to use these digital devices to deposit checks and make payments. These innovations could reduce employment and bank branches in the financial services sector, much as Amazon is doing in the retail space. Central bankers are scrambling to understand the implications of bitcoin and blockchain. In time, central banks likely will incorporate these technologies into their operations, perhaps spawning bitdollars, biteuros, bityen, etc.

So far, the cybercurrencies have been too volatile and prone to speculative moves to function as elastic currencies. Bitcoin soared during 2017, leaving gold in the dust. It then came crashing down during 2018, only to rebound again during the first half of 2019 before sinking once again during the second half of the year (Fig. 53).

Libertarians might long for a day when central banks are replaced by a monetary system based on a digitized currency that is unregulated by governments. I doubt that the central monetary planners will allow that to happen. But who knows? Technology has disrupted major industries. Maybe it will disrupt central banking!

For now, we Fed watchers can continue to watch the Fed.

Acknowledgments

My colleagues at Yardeni Research deserve a great deal of credit for helping to put this book together. Debbie Johnson and Mali Quintana spent countless hours checking the data that are shown in the book's text and charts. Melissa Tagg and Joe Abbott provided insightful research and fact-checking assistance. Jackie Doherty provided numerous good editorial suggestions. Mary Fanslau helped to administer the project. Geoff Moore and Steve Rybka delivered great tech support.

Our in-house editor, Sandra Cohan, cheerfully and masterfully pulled double duty by editing the book and our daily commentary. Her dedication to making the book happen was impressive.

Tom Clemmons also provided great editorial support. Catherine Barr contributed as well, providing a thorough index of the book's contents. David Wogahn skillfully coordinated the production of the book.

Several professional friends also reviewed the manuscript and provided helpful guidance. They are Randy Alsman, Martin Barnes, Vineer Bhansali, Alan Blake, Robert Eiermann, Fred Fraenkel, Bill Hurt, Dec Mullarkey, Louie Navellier, Kent Shepherd, Jim Solloway, and Doug Tengdin. I take full responsibility for any remaining errors and omissions.

Appendix

1. Jackson Hole Economic Policy Symposium, 1978–Present
   https://www.yardenibook.com/pub/fed-appendix1.pdf

2. Chairs of the Fed's Board of Governors, 1936–Present
   https://www.yardenibook.com/pub/fed-appendix2.pdf

3. Chairs of the Council of Economic Advisers, 1946–Present
   https://www.yardenibook.com/pub/fed-appendix3.pdf

4. Bernanke's Fed and the Lehman Bankruptcy
   https://www.yardenibook.com/pub/fed-appendix4.pdf

5. Yellen on Fed Purchasing Corporate Bonds and Stocks
   https://www.yardenibook.com/pub/fed-appendix5.pdf

6. FOMC Projections for the Federal Funds Rate, 2017–2022
   https://www.yardenibook.com/pub/fed-appendix6.pdf

Author's Note

This book is another in a series of Topical Studies examining issues that I discussed in my book *Predicting the Markets: A Professional Autobiography* (2018), but in greater detail and on a more current basis. Previous studies in this series include:

Stock Buybacks: The True Story (2019)
The Yield Curve: What Is It Really Predicting? (2019)

The charts at the end of this study were current as of January 2020. Updates (in color), as well as linked Endnotes and Appendices, are available at **www.yardenibook.com/studies**.

Institutional investors are invited to sign up for Yardeni Research's service on a complimentary trial basis at **www.yardeni.com/trial-registration**.

Figure 1.

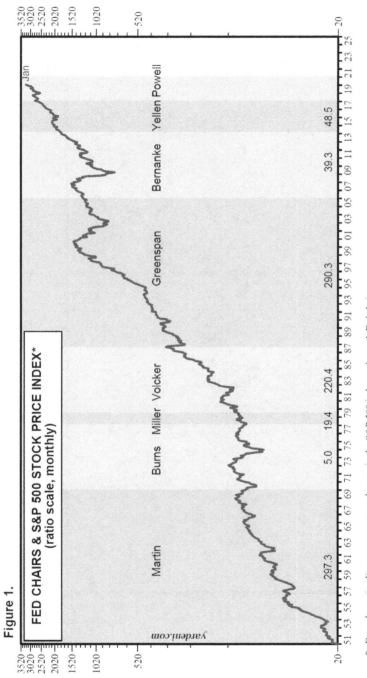

FED CHAIRS & S&P 500 STOCK PRICE INDEX*
(ratio scale, monthly)

* Data above timeline are percentage changes in the S&P 500 index under each Fed chair.
Note: Shades denote terms of Fed chairs.
Source: Standard & Poor's.

Figure 2.

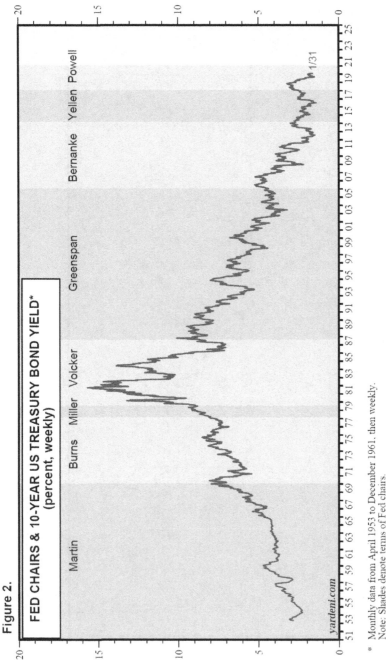

FED CHAIRS & 10-YEAR US TREASURY BOND YIELD*
(percent, weekly)

* Monthly data from April 1953 to December 1961, then weekly.
Note: Shades denote terms of Fed chairs.
Source: US Treasury.

Figure 3.

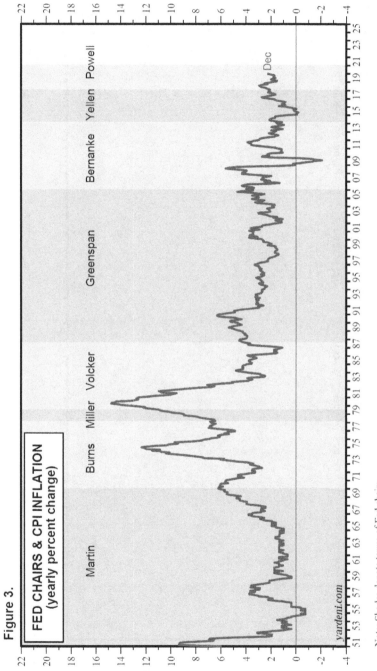

FED CHAIRS & CPI INFLATION
(yearly percent change)

Note: Shades denote terms of Fed chairs.
Source: Bureau of Labor Statistics.

Figure 4.

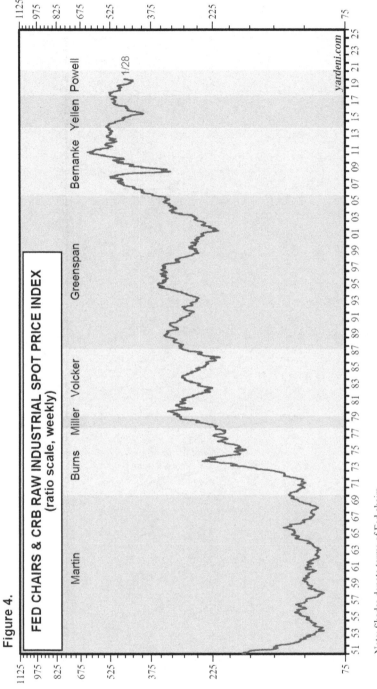

FED CHAIRS & CRB RAW INDUSTRIAL SPOT PRICE INDEX
(ratio scale, weekly)

Note: Shades denote terms of Fed chairs.
Source: Commodity Research Bureau.

Figure 5.

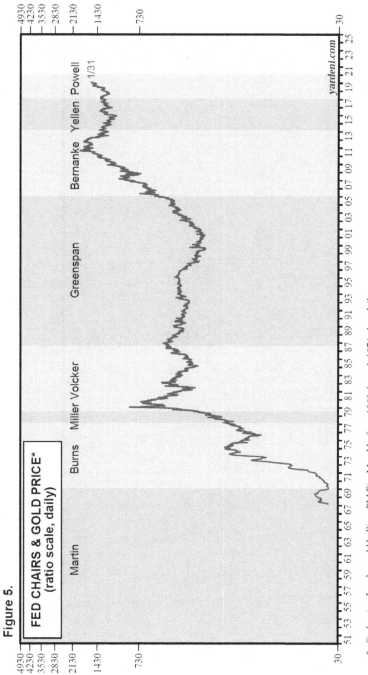

FED CHAIRS & GOLD PRICE*
(ratio scale, daily)

Martin   Burns   Miller Volcker   Greenspan   Bernanke Yellen Powell

* Cash price. London gold bullion. PM Fix. Monthly from 1968 through 1974, then daily.
Note: Shades denote terms of Fed chairs.
Source: Commodity Research Bureau.

yardeni.com

Figure 6.

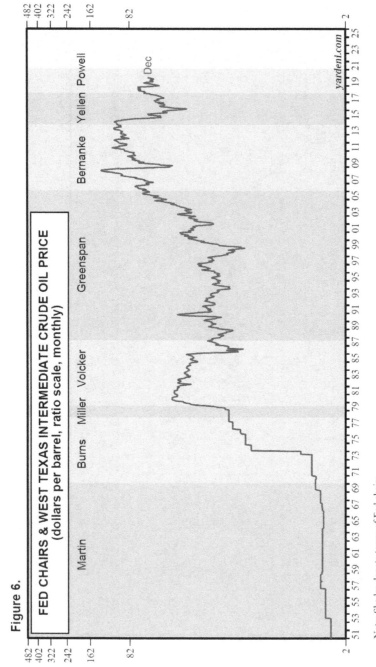

FED CHAIRS & WEST TEXAS INTERMEDIATE CRUDE OIL PRICE
(dollars per barrel, ratio scale, monthly)

Note: Shades denote terms of Fed chairs.
Source: Haver Analytics.

Figure 7.

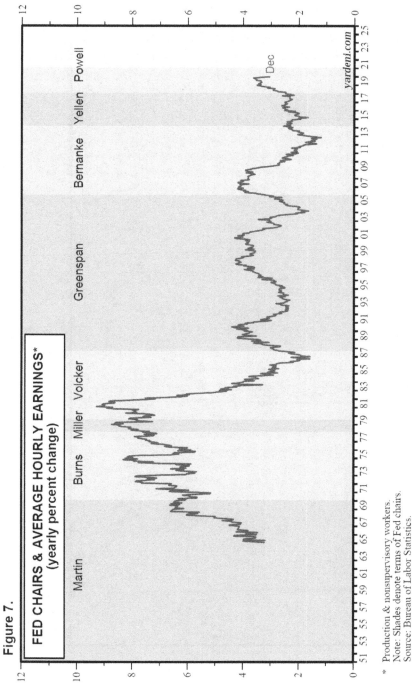

FED CHAIRS & AVERAGE HOURLY EARNINGS*
(yearly percent change)

* Production & nonsupervisory workers.
Note: Shades denote terms of Fed chairs.
Source: Bureau of Labor Statistics.

Figure 8.

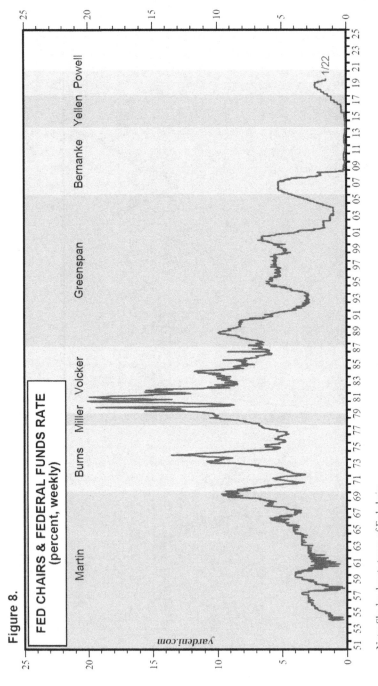

FED CHAIRS & FEDERAL FUNDS RATE
(percent, weekly)

Martin   Burns   Miller   Volcker   Greenspan   Bernanke   Yellen   Powell

yardeni.com

Note: Shades denote terms of Fed chairs.
Source: Federal Reserve Board.

Figure 9.

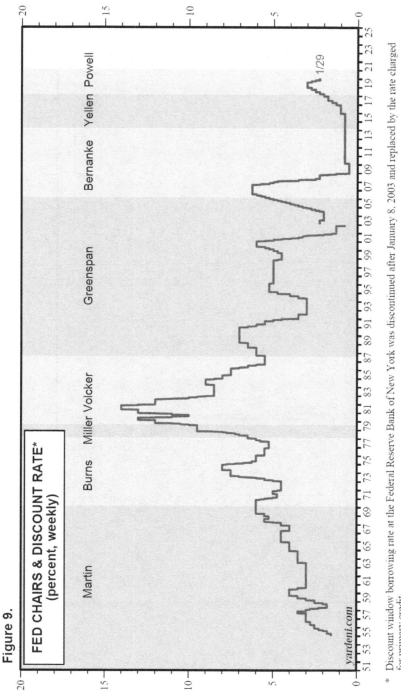

FED CHAIRS & DISCOUNT RATE*
(percent, weekly)

Martin   Burns   Miller Volcker   Greenspan   Bernanke Yellen Powell

*Discount window borrowing rate at the Federal Reserve Bank of New York was discontinued after January 8, 2003 and replaced by the rate charged
for primary credit.
Note: Shades denote terms of Fed chairs.
Source: Federal Reserve Board.

Figure 10.

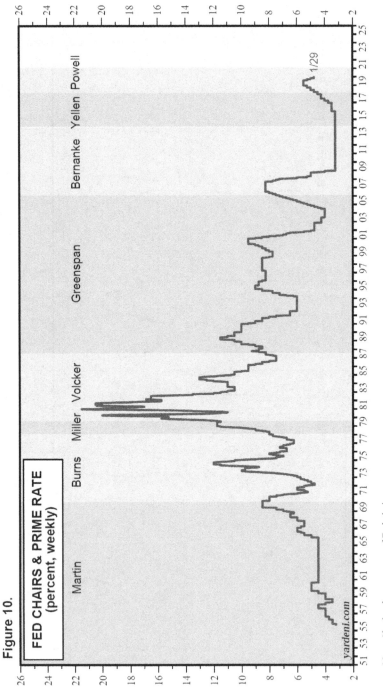

FED CHAIRS & PRIME RATE
(percent, weekly)

Martin   Burns   Miller   Volcker   Greenspan   Bernanke   Yellen   Powell

yardeni.com

Note: Shades denote terms of Fed chairs.
Source: Federal Reserve Board.

Figure 11.

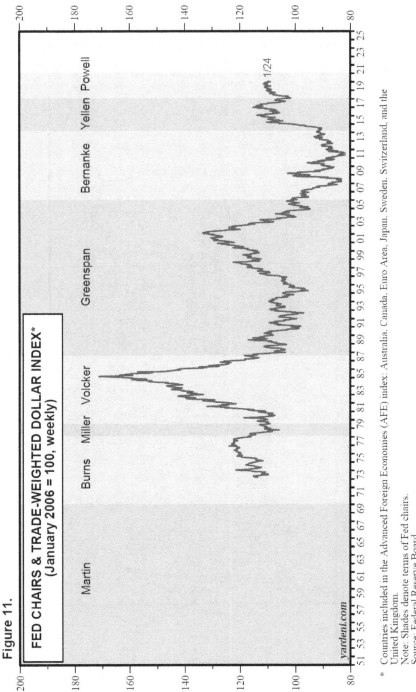

FED CHAIRS & TRADE-WEIGHTED DOLLAR INDEX*
(January 2006 = 100, weekly)

yardeni.com

* Countries included in the Advanced Foreign Economies (AFE) index: Australia, Canada, Euro Area, Japan, Sweden, Switzerland, and the United Kingdom.
Note: Shades denote terms of Fed chairs.
Source: Federal Reserve Board.

Figure 12.

FEDERAL FUNDS RATE & DISCOUNT RATE: 1979-1987
(percent, weekly)

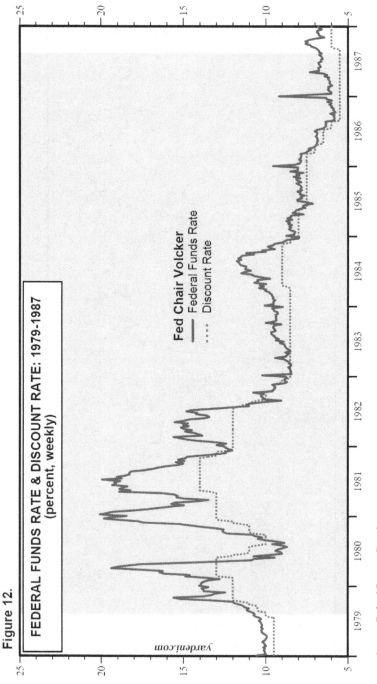

Fed Chair Volcker
—— Federal Funds Rate
..... Discount Rate

yardeni.com

Source: Federal Reserve Board.

Figure 13.

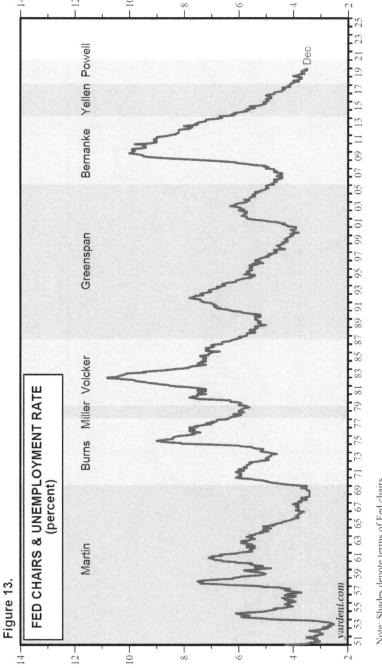

FED CHAIRS & UNEMPLOYMENT RATE
(percent)

Note: Shades denote terms of Fed chairs.
Source: Bureau of Labor Statistics.

Figure 14.

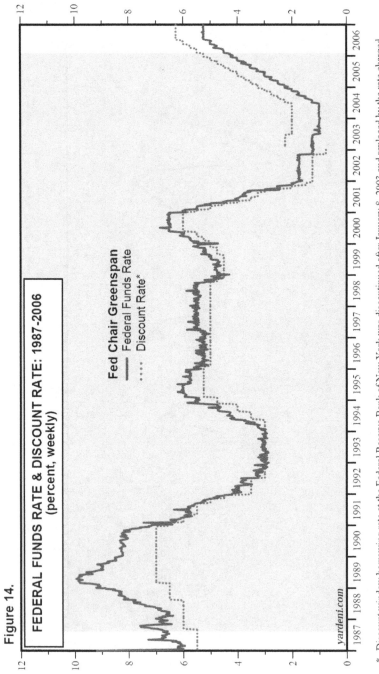

FEDERAL FUNDS RATE & DISCOUNT RATE: 1987-2006
(percent, weekly)

Fed Chair Greenspan
— Federal Funds Rate
····· Discount Rate*

yardeni.com

* Discount window borrowing rate at the Federal Reserve Bank of New York was discontinued after January 8, 2003 and replaced by the rate charged for primary credit.
Source: Federal Reserve Board.

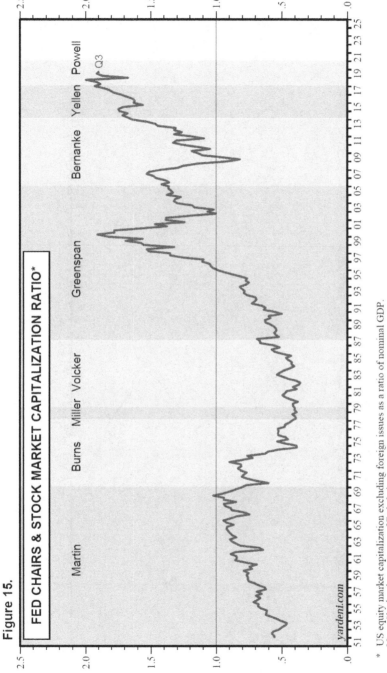

Figure 15.

FED CHAIRS & STOCK MARKET CAPITALIZATION RATIO*

* US equity market capitalization excluding foreign issues as a ratio of nominal GDP.
Note: Shades denote terms of Fed chairs.
Source: Federal Reserve Board Financial Accounts of the United States and Standard & Poor's.

Figure 16.

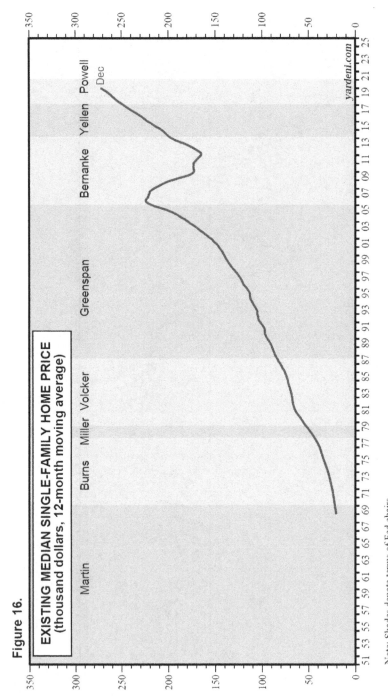

EXISTING MEDIAN SINGLE-FAMILY HOME PRICE
(thousand dollars, 12-month moving average)

Note: Shades denote terms of Fed chairs.
Source: National Association of Realtors.

yardeni.com

Figure 17.

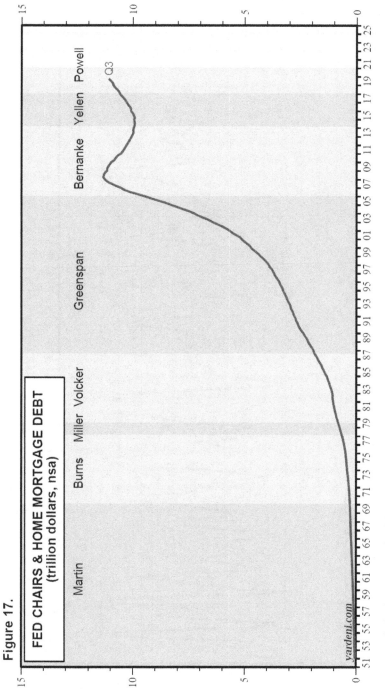

FED CHAIRS & HOME MORTGAGE DEBT
(trillion dollars, nsa)

Note: Shades denote terms of Fed chairs.
Source: Federal Reserve Board Financial Accounts of the United States.

Figure 18.

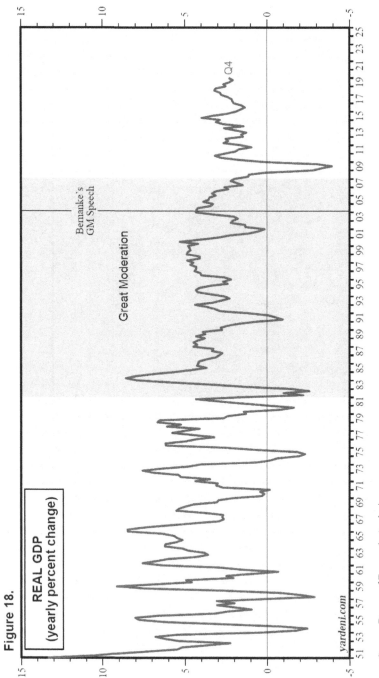

REAL GDP
(yearly percent change)

Great Moderation

Bernanke's
GM Speech

Q4

yardeni.com

Source: Bureau of Economic Analysis.

Figure 19.

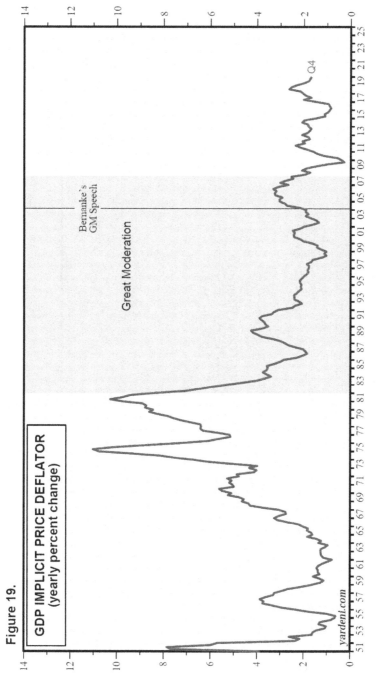

GDP IMPLICIT PRICE DEFLATOR
(yearly percent change)

Bernanke's
GM Speech

Great Moderation

Q4

yardeni.com

Source: Bureau of Economic Analysis.

Figure 20.

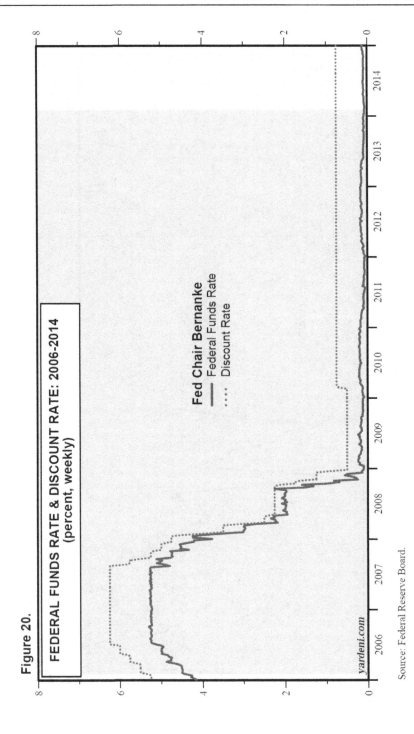

FEDERAL FUNDS RATE & DISCOUNT RATE: 2006-2014
(percent, weekly)

Fed Chair Bernanke
— Federal Funds Rate
····· Discount Rate

yardeni.com

Source: Federal Reserve Board.

Figure 21.

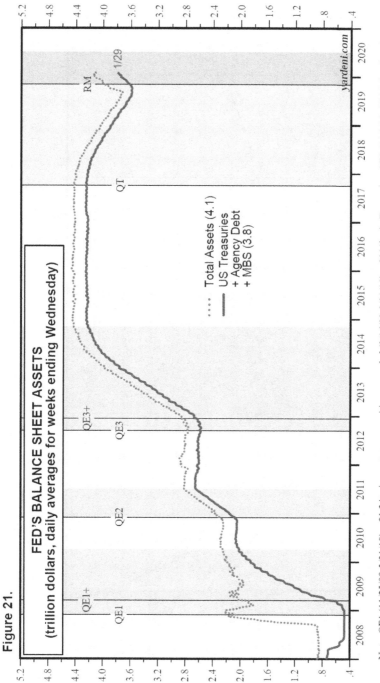

FED'S BALANCE SHEET ASSETS
(trillion dollars, daily averages for weeks ending Wednesday)

Note: QE1 (11/25/08-3/31/10) = $1.24tn in mortgage securities; expanded (3/16/09-3/31/10) = $300bn in Treasuries. QE2 (11/3/10-6/30/11) = $600bn in Treasuries. QE3 (9/13/12-10/29/14) = $40bn/month in mortgage securities (open ended); expanded (12/12/12-10/1/14) = $45bn/month in Treasuries. QT (10/1/17-7/31/19) = balance sheet pared by $675bn. RM (11/1/19) = reserve management, $60bn/month in Treasury bills. Source: Federal Reserve Board.

Figure 22.

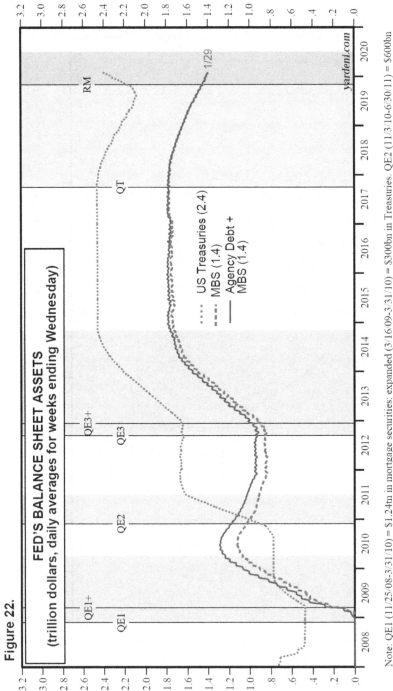

FED'S BALANCE SHEET ASSETS
(trillion dollars, daily averages for weeks ending Wednesday)

····· US Treasuries (2.4)
- - - MBS (1.4)
——— Agency Debt +
MBS (1.4)

yardeni.com

Note: QE1 (11/25/08-3/31/10) = $1.24tn in mortgage securities: expanded (3/16/09-3/31/10) = $300bn in Treasuries. QE2 (11/3/10-6/30/11) = $600bn in Treasuries. QE3 (9/13/12-10/29/14) = $40bn/month in mortgage securities (open ended); expanded (12/12/12-10/1/14) = $45bn/month in Treasuries. QT (10/1/17-7/31/19) = balance sheet pared by $675bn. RM (11/1/19) = reserve management. $60bn/month in Treasury bills.
Source: Federal Reserve Board.

Figure 23.

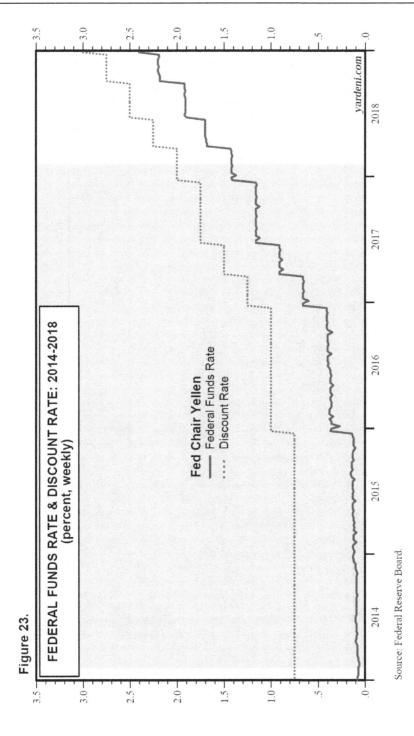

FEDERAL FUNDS RATE & DISCOUNT RATE: 2014-2018
(percent, weekly)

Fed Chair Yellen
— Federal Funds Rate
..... Discount Rate

Source: Federal Reserve Board.

yardeni.com

Figure 24.

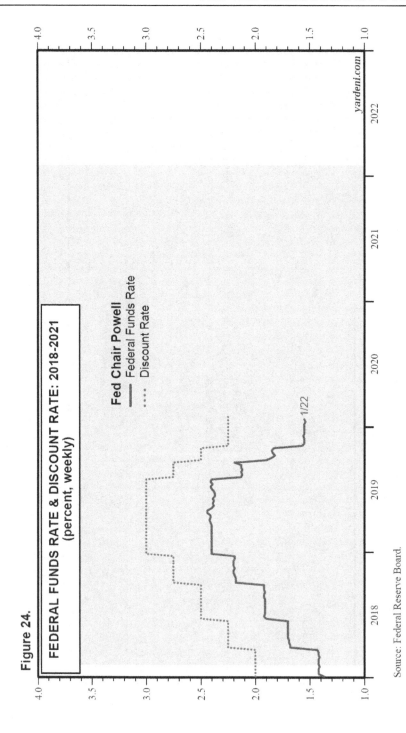

FEDERAL FUNDS RATE & DISCOUNT RATE: 2018-2021
(percent, weekly)

Fed Chair Powell
— Federal Funds Rate
····· Discount Rate

1/22

yardeni.com

Source: Federal Reserve Board.

Figure 25.

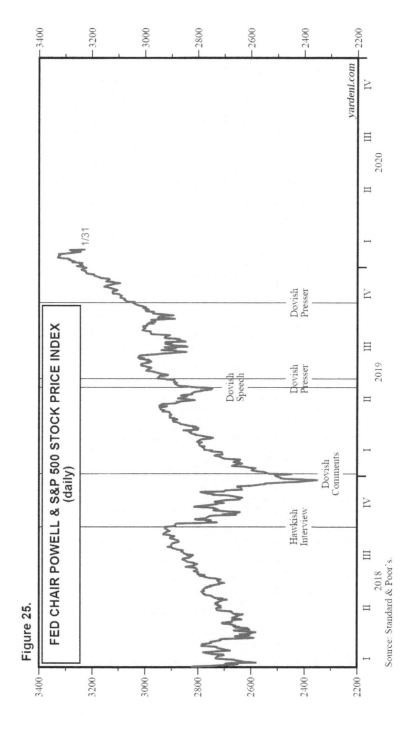

FED CHAIR POWELL & S&P 500 STOCK PRICE INDEX
(daily)

Source: Standard & Poor's.

Figure 26.

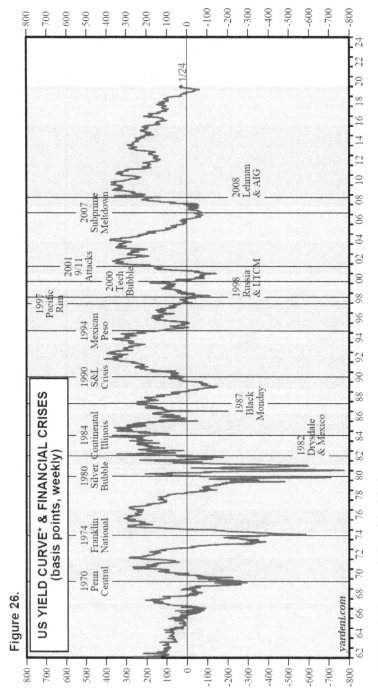

US YIELD CURVE* & FINANCIAL CRISES
(basis points, weekly)

yardeni.com

* 10-year US Treasury yield less federal funds rate.
Note: Blue shaded areas denote periods of monetary easing between cyclical peaks and troughs in the federal funds rate. Red shaded areas denote
monetary tightening periods.
Source: Federal Reserve Board.

Figure 27.

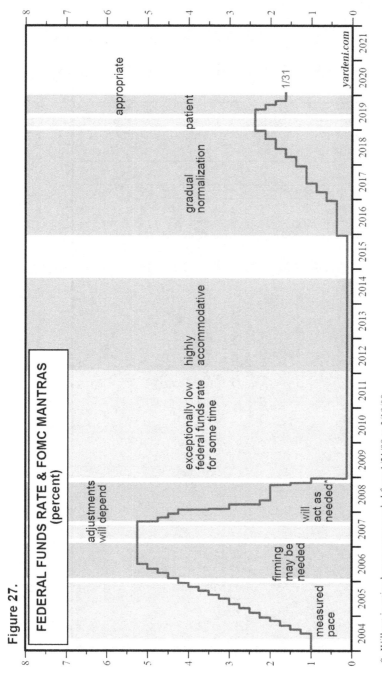

FEDERAL FUNDS RATE & FOMC MANTRAS
(percent)

* Will act in a timely manner as needed from 1/21/08 to 3/18/08.
Source: Federal Reserve Board.

Figure 28.

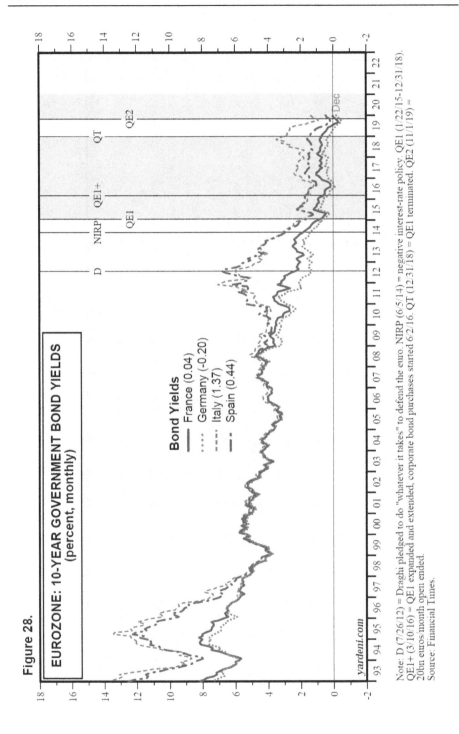

EUROZONE: 10-YEAR GOVERNMENT BOND YIELDS
(percent, monthly)

Bond Yields
—— France (0.04)
········ Germany (-0.20)
– – – Italy (1.37)
–·–· Spain (0.44)

yardeni.com

Note: D (7/26/12) = Draghi pledged to do "whatever it takes" to defend the euro. NIRP (6/5/14) = negative interest-rate policy. QE1 (1/22/15-12/31/18).
QE1+ (3/10/16) = QE1 expanded and extended, corporate bond purchases started 6/2/16. QT (12/31/18) = QE1 terminated. QE2 (11/1/19) =
20bn euros/month open ended.
Source: Financial Times.

Figure 29.

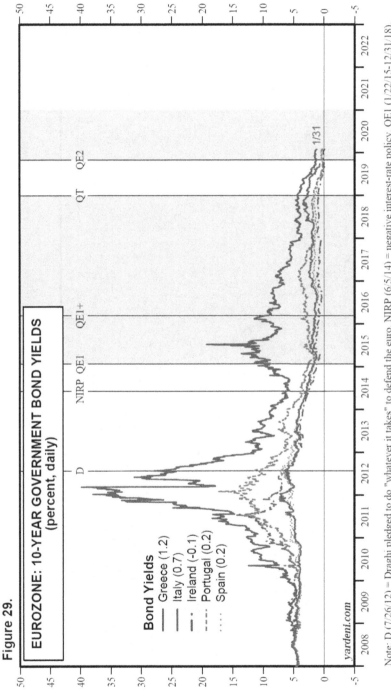

EUROZONE: 10-YEAR GOVERNMENT BOND YIELDS
(percent, daily)

Bond Yields
— Greece (1.2)
— Italy (0.7)
–·– Ireland (-0.1)
--- Portugal (0.2)
···· Spain (0.2)

yardeni.com

Note: D (7/26/12) = Draghi pledged to do "whatever it takes" to defend the euro. NIRP (6/5/14) = negative interest-rate policy. QE1 (1/22/15-12/31/18).
QE1+ (3/10/16) = QE1 expanded and extended, corporate bond purchases started 6/2/16. QT (12/31/18) = QE1 terminated. QE2 (11/1/19) =
20bn euros/month open ended.
Source: Financial Times.

Figure 30.

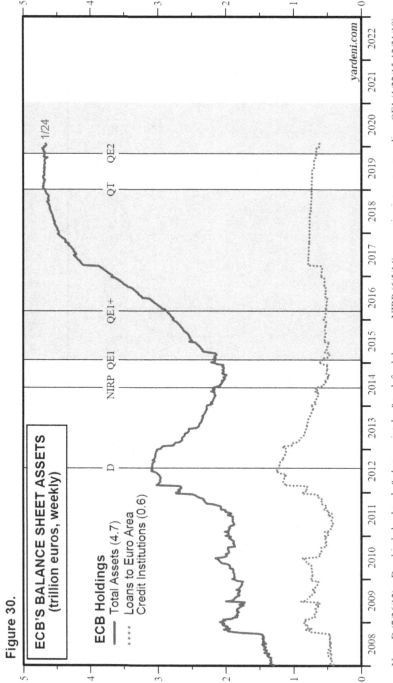

ECB'S BALANCE SHEET ASSETS
(trillion euros, weekly)

ECB Holdings
—— Total Assets (4.7)
······ Loans to Euro Area
       Credit Institutions (0.6)

yardeni.com

Note: D (7/26/12) = Draghi pledged to do "whatever it takes" to defend the euro. NIRP (6/5/14) = negative interest-rate policy. QE1 (1/22/15-12/31/18).
QE1+ (3/10/16) = QE1 expanded and extended, corporate bond purchases started 6/2/16. QT (12/31/18) = QE1 terminated. QE2 (11/1/19) =
20bn euros/month open ended.
Source: European Central Bank.

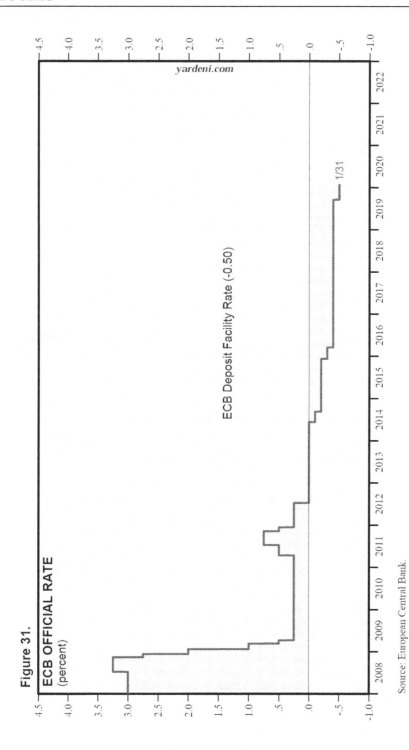

Figure 31.

ECB OFFICIAL RATE
(percent)

ECB Deposit Facility Rate (-0.50)

yardeni.com

1/31

Source: European Central Bank.

Figure 32.

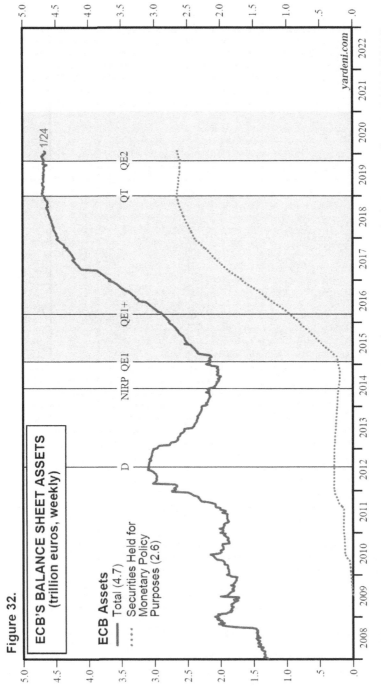

ECB'S BALANCE SHEET ASSETS
(trillion euros, weekly)

ECB Assets
—— Total (4.7)
······ Securities Held for
      Monetary Policy
      Purposes (2.6)

yardeni.com

Note: D (7/26/12) = Draghi pledged to do "whatever it takes" to defend the euro. NIRP (6/5/14) = negative interest-rate policy. QE1 (1/22/15-12/31/18).
QE1+ (3/10/16) = QE1 expanded and extended, corporate bond purchases started 6/2/16. QT (12/31/18) = QE1 terminated. QE2 (11/1/19) =
20bn euros/month open ended.
Source: European Central Bank.

Figure 33.

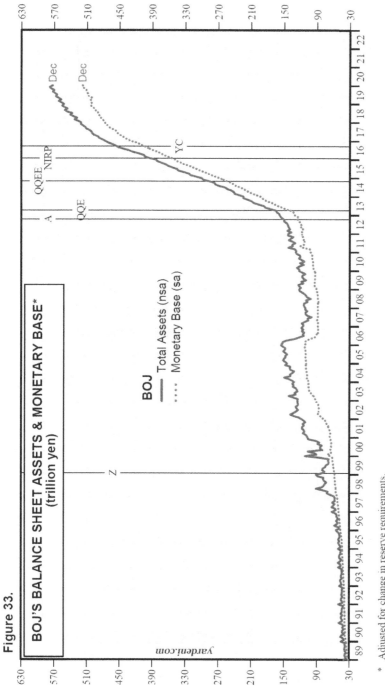

BOJ'S BALANCE SHEET ASSETS & MONETARY BASE*
(trillion yen)

BOJ
——— Total Assets (nsa)
······· Monetary Base (sa)

yardeni.com

* Adjusted for change in reserve requirements.
Note: Z (2/12/99) = Zero interest rate policy. A = (10/12/12) = Markets start to anticipate Abenomics. QQE (4/4/13) = Quantitative and Qualitative
Easing. QQEE (10/31/14) = expanded and extended version of QQE. NIRP = (1/29/16) = Negative interest rate policy. YC (9/21/16) = Yield curve
targeting.
Source: Bank of Japan.

Figure 34.

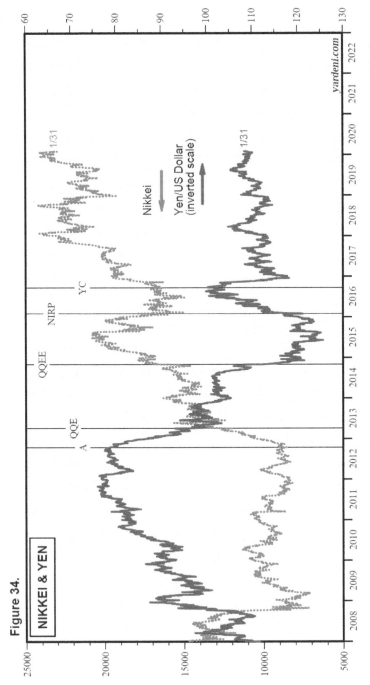

Note: A (10/12/12) = Markets start to anticipate Abenomics. QQE (4/4/13) = Quantitative and Qualitative Easing. QQEE (10/31/14) = expanded and extended version of QQE. NIRP (1/29/16) = Negative interest rate policy. YC (9/21/16) = Yield curve targeting.
Source: Haver Analytics.

Figure 35.

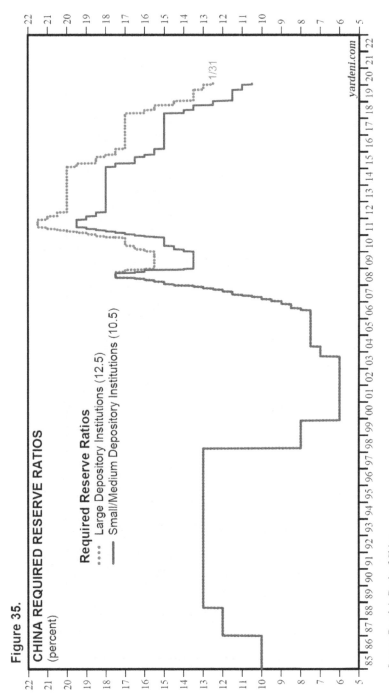

CHINA REQUIRED RESERVE RATIOS
(percent)

Required Reserve Ratios
• • • • Large Depository Institutions (12.5)
—— Small/Medium Depository Institutions (10.5)

Source: People's Bank of China.

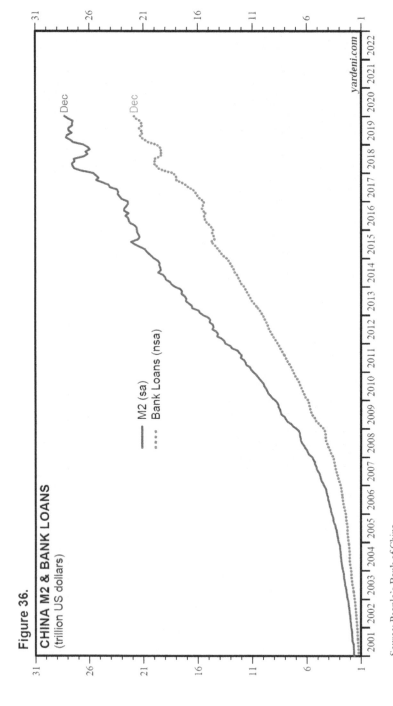

Figure 36.

CHINA M2 & BANK LOANS
(trillion US dollars)

M2 (sa)
Bank Loans (nsa)

Source: People's Bank of China.

yardeni.com

Figure 37.

CHINA INDUSTRIAL PRODUCTION / BANK LOANS*

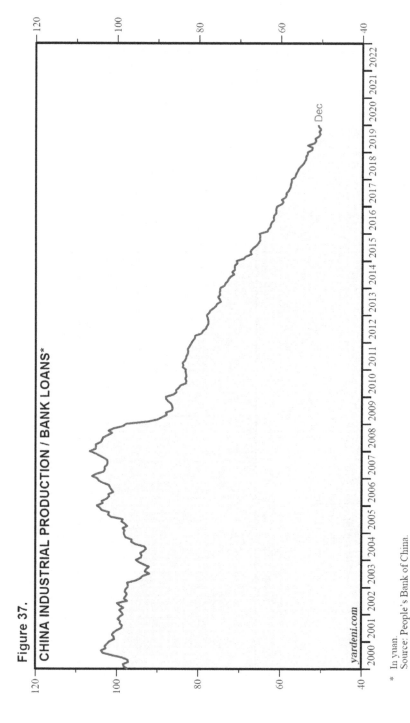

*In yuan.
Source: People's Bank of China.

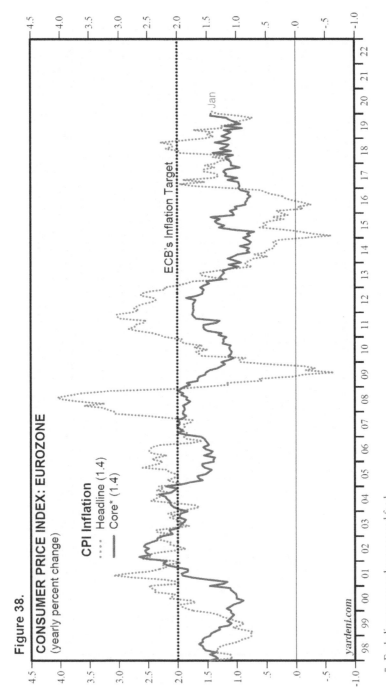

Figure 38.

CONSUMER PRICE INDEX: EUROZONE
(yearly percent change)

CPI Inflation
- - - - Headline (1.4)
——— Core* (1.4)

ECB's Inflation Target

Jan

yardeni.com

* Excluding energy and unprocessed food.
Source: Haver Analytics.

Figure 39.

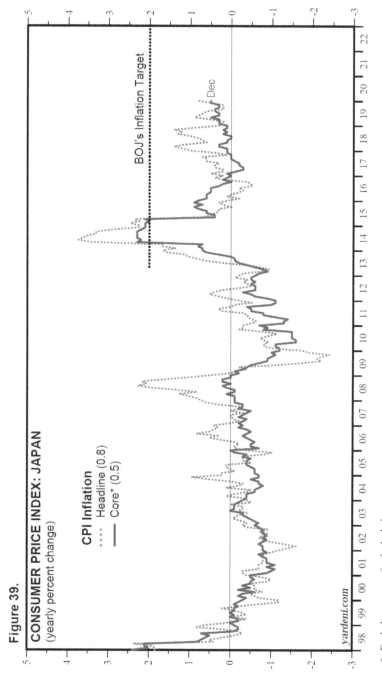

CONSUMER PRICE INDEX: JAPAN
(yearly percent change)

CPI Inflation
···· Headline (0.8)
—— Core* (0.5)

BOJ's Inflation Target

Dec

vardeni.com

* Excluding energy, food, alcohol.
Source: Ministry of Internal Affairs and Communications.

Figure 40.

PERSONAL CONSUMPTION EXPENDITURES DEFLATORS: UNITED STATES
(yearly percent change)

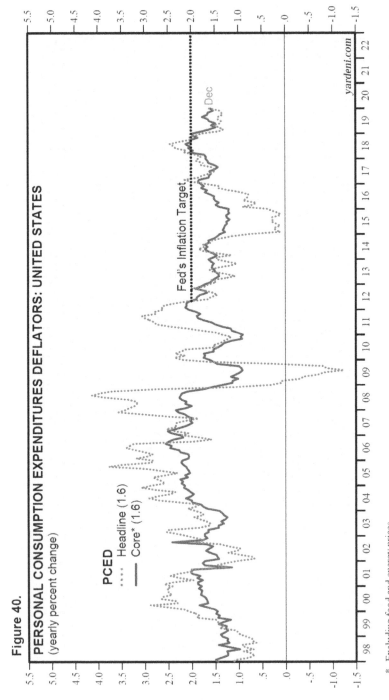

* Excluding food and energy prices.
Source: Bureau of Economic Analysis.

Figure 41.

PERSONAL CONSUMPTION EXPENDITURES DEFLATOR: UNITED STATES
(base period price Dec 2011 = 98, ratio scale)

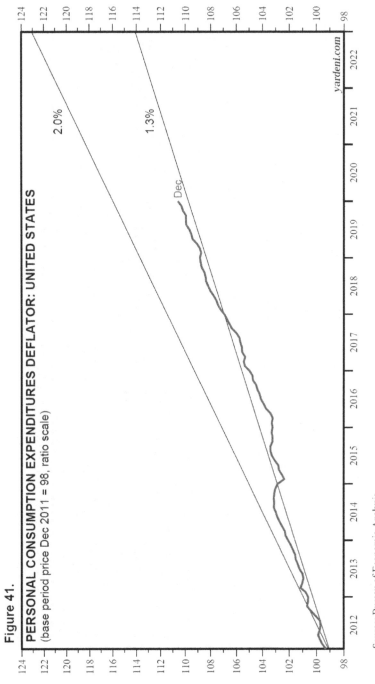

Source: Bureau of Economic Analysis.

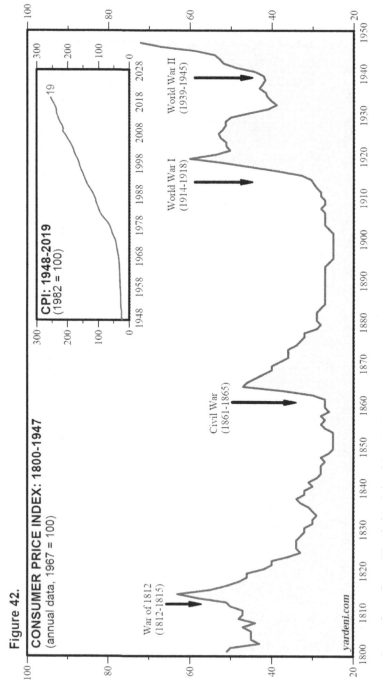

Figure 42.

CONSUMER PRICE INDEX: 1800-1947
(annual data, 1967 = 100)

CPI: 1948-2019
(1982 = 100)

War of 1812
(1812-1815)

Civil War
(1861-1865)

World War I
(1914-1918)

World War II
(1939-1945)

yardeni.com

Source: Census Bureau Historical Statistics of the United States.

Figure 43.

US MONEY MULTIPLIER
(M2 as a ratio of Monetary Base)

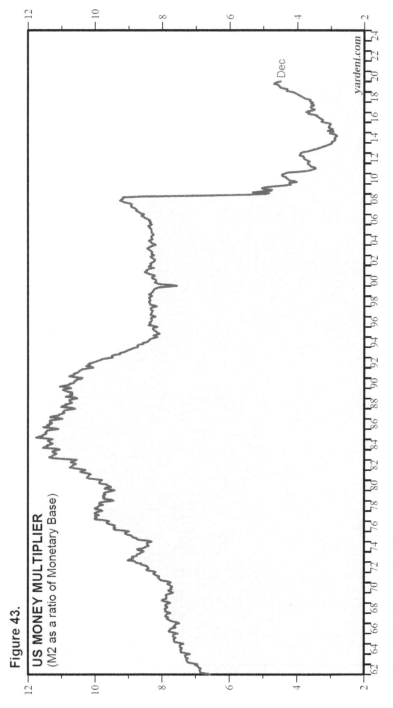

Source: Federal Reserve Board.

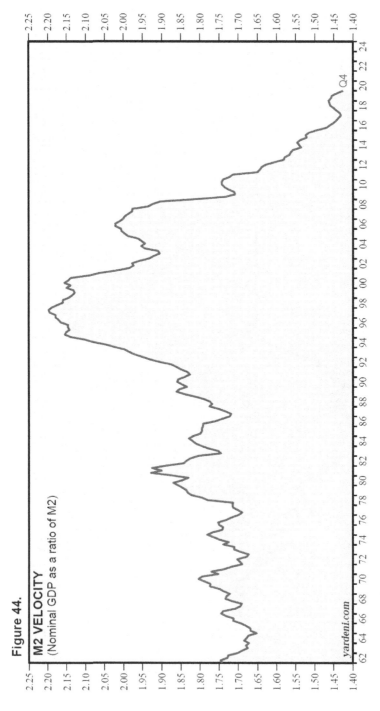

Figure 44.

M2 VELOCITY
(Nominal GDP as a ratio of M2)

yardeni.com

Source: Federal Reserve Board.

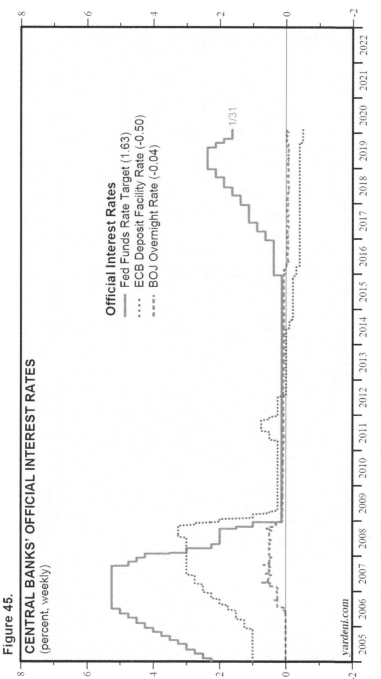

Figure 45.

CENTRAL BANKS' OFFICIAL INTEREST RATES
(percent, weekly)

Official Interest Rates
—— Fed Funds Rate Target (1.63)
······ ECB Deposit Facility Rate (-0.50)
– – – BOJ Overnight Rate (-0.04)

yardeni.com

Source: Federal Reserve Board, European Central Bank, and Bank of Japan.

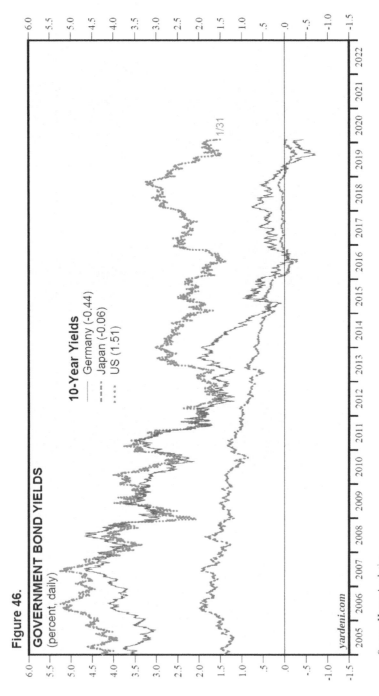

Figure 46.

GOVERNMENT BOND YIELDS
(percent, daily)

10-Year Yields
—— Germany (-0.44)
– – – Japan (-0.06)
· · · · US (1.51)

yardeni.com

Source: Haver Analytics.

Figure 47.

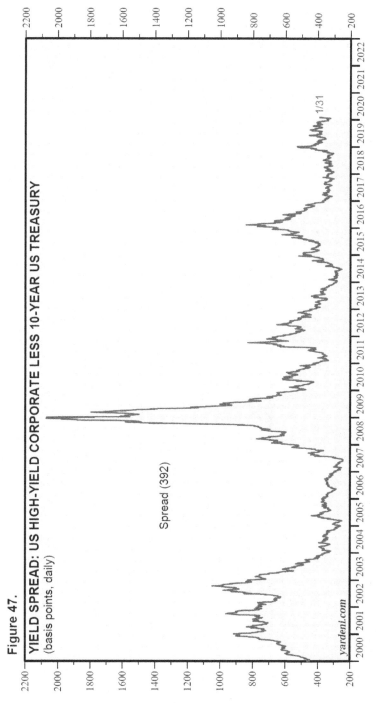

YIELD SPREAD: US HIGH-YIELD CORPORATE LESS 10-YEAR US TREASURY
(basis points, daily)

Spread (392)

1/31

yardeni.com

Source: Bank of America Merrill Lynch and Federal Reserve Board.

Figure 48.

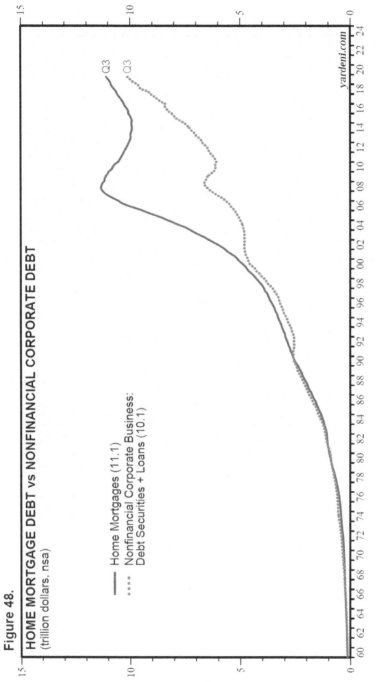

HOME MORTGAGE DEBT vs NONFINANCIAL CORPORATE DEBT
(trillion dollars, nsa)

—— Home Mortgages (11.1)
•••• Nonfinancial Corporate Business:
     Debt Securities + Loans (10.1)

Source: Federal Reserve Board Financial Accounts of the United States.

Figure 49.

NONFINANCIAL CORPORATE BONDS OUTSTANDING
(trillion dollars, nsa)

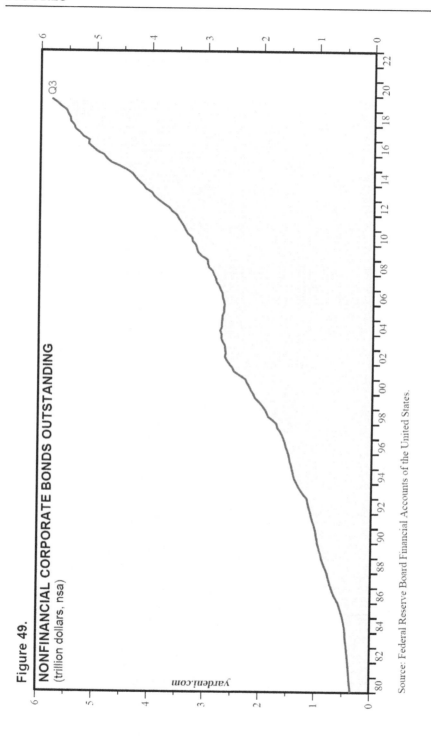

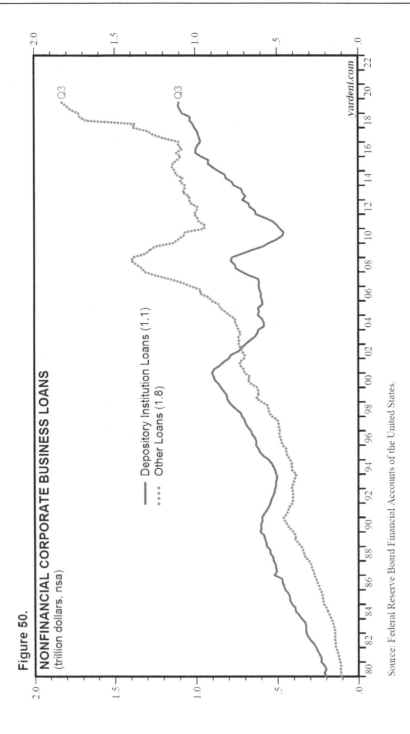

Figure 50.

NONFINANCIAL CORPORATE BUSINESS LOANS
(trillion dollars, nsa)

—— Depository Institution Loans (1.1)
••••• Other Loans (1.8)

yardeni.com

Source: Federal Reserve Board Financial Accounts of the United States.

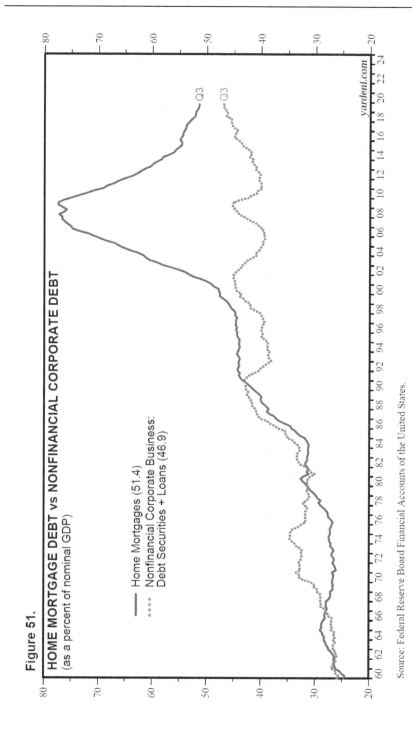

Figure 51.

HOME MORTGAGE DEBT vs NONFINANCIAL CORPORATE DEBT
(as a percent of nominal GDP)

Home Mortgages (51.4)
Nonfinancial Corporate Business:
Debt Securities + Loans (46.9)

yardeni.com

Source: Federal Reserve Board Financial Accounts of the United States.

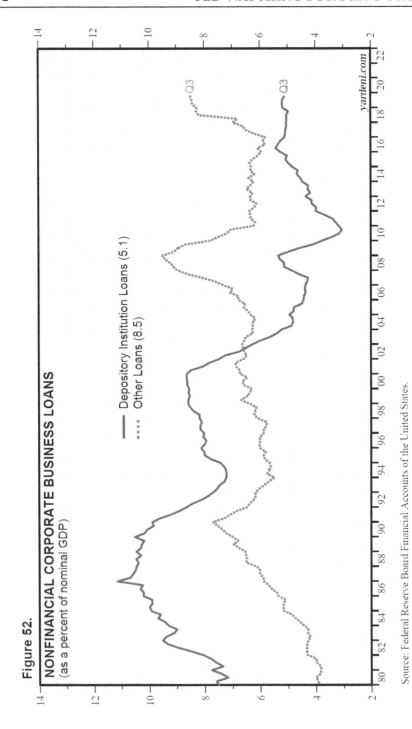

Figure 52.

NONFINANCIAL CORPORATE BUSINESS LOANS
(as a percent of nominal GDP)

— Depository Institution Loans (5.1)
···· Other Loans (8.5)

Source: Federal Reserve Board Financial Accounts of the United States.

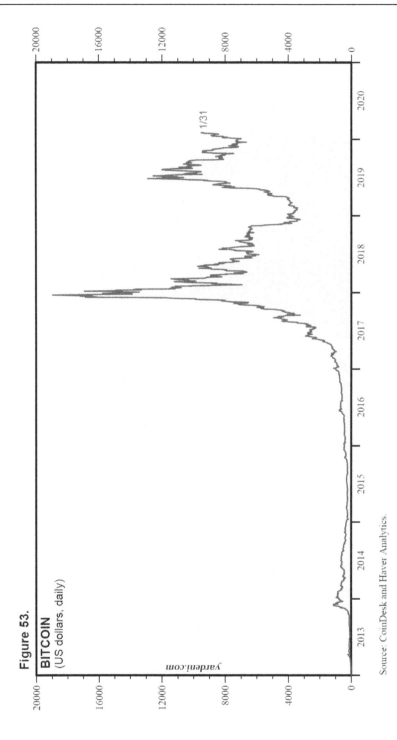

Figure 53.

BITCOIN
(US dollars, daily)

yardeni.com

Source: CoinDesk and Haver Analytics.

Endnotes

Introduction

1. See my profile on LinkedIn. My firm's website is www.yardeni.com.
2. Board of Governors of the Federal Reserve System, "Open market operations" webpage. See also Federal Reserve Bank of New York, "Open Market Operations" webpage.
3. Martin Zweig, *Winning on Wall Street* (New York: Warner Books, 1986), pp. 42–43.

Chapter 1

4. Board of Governors of the Federal Reserve System, *Monetary Policy Report* webpage (linking reports 1996–present).
5. Jon R. Moen and Ellis W. Tallman, "The Panic of 1907," Federal Reserve History webpage.
6. Board of Governors of the Federal Reserve System, "Federal Reserve Act" webpage.
7. Aaron Steelman. "Employment Act of 1946," Federal Reserve History webpage.
8. Aaron Steelman, "The Federal Reserve's 'Dual Mandate': The Evolution of an Idea," Federal Reserve Bank of Richmond, *Economic Brief*, December 2011.
9. By law, Board appointments must yield a "fair representation of the financial, agricultural, industrial, and commercial interests and geographical divisions of the country," and no two governors may come from the same Federal Reserve District.
10. Board of Governors of the Federal Reserve System, "Who are the members of the Federal Reserve Board, and how are they selected?" webpage.
11. The rotating seats are filled from the following four groups of Federal Reserve Banks, with one bank president from each group: Boston, Philadelphia, and Richmond; Cleveland and Chicago; Atlanta, St. Louis, and Dallas; and Minneapolis, Kansas City, and San Francisco.
12. The Fed district presidents are chosen by a search committee composed of the regional banks' directors. Once a candidate is formally appoint-

ed, he or she must be approved by the Board of Governors.

13. "A Short History of FOMC Communication," Dallas Federal Reserve Bank, September 2013.

14. See, for example, Board of Governors of the Federal Reserve System, "Implementing Note," July 31, 2009 press release.

15. Board of Governors of the Federal Reserve System, "The Discount Rate" webpage.

16. Board of Governors of the Federal Reserve System, "FOMC Meeting Calendars, Statements, and Minutes" webpage.

17. See, for example, "Summary of Economic Projections," September 18, 2019.

18. In 1993, Representative Henry B. Gonzalez (a Democrat from Texas and chair of the House Banking Committee) attacked the FOMC's disclosure policy on the grounds that the public deserved more detailed coverage of FOMC meetings. In response, the Federal Reserve instituted its current minutes policy and subsequently released historical transcripts, after light editing, with a five-year lag.

19. Yardeni Research, "FOMC Statements" (since 1997) webpage.

Chapter 2

20. Rich Miller, "Yalies Yellen-Hamada Put Tobin Twist Theory to Work in QE," Bloomberg, October 31, 2013.

21. The model was developed by John Hicks in 1937 and later extended by Alvin Hansen. It remains the leading framework shown in macroeconomic textbooks, as it has been since the 1940s.

22. "Rahm Emanuel on the Opportunities of Crisis," *The Wall Street Journal*, November 18, 2008.

23. If Emanuel's advice seems Machiavellian, well, it is. Sixteenth-century Italian political theorist Niccolò Machiavelli advised in his famous treatise *The Prince*: "Never waste the opportunity offered by a good crisis." However, it was Winston Churchill who reputedly popularized the sentiment.

24. Board of Governors of the Federal Reserve System, "Meet the Economists" webpage.

25. Justin Fox, "How Economics PhDs Took Over the Federal Reserve," *Harvard Business Review*, February 3, 2014.

26. Ben S. Bernanke, "On Milton Friedman's Ninetieth Birthday," November 8, 2002 speech at the Conference to Honor Milton Friedman, University of Chicago, Chicago, Illinois.

27. Board of Governors of the Federal Reserve System, "Leadership Structure: 1936–Present" webpage.

28. Robert L. Hetzel and Ralph F. Leach, "The Treasury-Fed Accord: A New Narrative Account," Federal Reserve Bank of Richmond *Economic*

Quarterly, Winter 2001.

29. Binyamin Appelbaum, *The Economists' Hour* (New York: Little, Brown and Company, 2019).

30. See the transcript of Martin's "Address before the New York Group of the Investment Bankers Association of America," October 19, 1955.

31. Paul A. Volcker and Christine Harper, *Keeping At It* (New York: Public Affairs, 2018).

Chapter 3

32. Arthur F. Burns and Wesley C. Mitchell, *Measuring Business Cycles* (National Bureau of Economic Research, 1946).

33. The NBER's Business Cycle Dating Committee webpage.

34. "Arthur F. Burns Is Dead at 83; A Shaper of Economic Policy," *The New York Times*, June 27, 1987.

35. Michael Bryan, "The Great Inflation: 1965–1982," Federal Reserve History webpage.

36. Binyamin Appelbaum, *The Economists' Hour* (New York: Little, Brown and Company, 2019).

37. FOMC Statement, November 21, 1978.

38. President Jimmy Carter, "Crisis of Confidence," July 15, 1979 speech.

39. Ezra Klein, "Jimmy Carter's 'Malaise' Speech Was Popular!" *The Washington Post*, August 9, 2013.

40. Binyamin Appelbaum and Robert D. Hershey Jr., "Paul A. Volcker, Fed Chairman Who Waged War on Inflation, Is Dead at 92," *The New York Times*, December 9, 2019.

Chapter 4

41. William Safire, *Before the Fall: An Inside View of the Pre-Watergate White House*, (New York: Doubleday & Company, Inc., 1975).

42. Paul A. Volcker and Christine Harper, *Keeping At It* (New York: Public Affairs, 2018).

43. FOMC Minutes, August 14, 1979. The minutes specified a range of 10 3/4% to 11 1/4%.

44. FOMC transcript, October 6, 1979.

45. Binyamin Appelbaum and Robert D. Hershey Jr., "Paul A. Volcker, Fed Chairman Who Waged War on Inflation, Is Dead at 92," *The New York Times*, December 9, 2019.

46. The original Saturday Night Massacre occurred on October 20, 1973, when Nixon ordered the firing of the special prosecutor investigating Watergate by his attorney general, who resigned rather than do so.

47. For more on Volcker's impactful October 6, 1979 monetary policy announcement, see the Federal Reserve Bank of San Francisco's Decem-

ber 3, 2004 *Economic Letter* titled simply "October 6, 1979." Also, see the collection of articles on this subject in the Federal Reserve Bank of St. Louis *Review*, March/April 2005.

48. The Dating Committee of the National Economic Bureau determined that there was a mini-recession from January to July 1980 followed by a brief expansion and another recession from July 1981 to November 1982. For most Americans, this "double-dip recession" felt like one long one. In his memoir, Volcker blamed the mini-recession on credit controls that the Carter administration had told the Fed to implement. The controls were terminated in July 1980.

49. Andrew Tobias, "A Talk With Paul Volcker," *The New York Times*, September 19, 1982.

50. Robert J. Cole, "Wall St. Securities Firm Files for Bankruptcy," *The New York Times*, August 13, 1982.

51. Market index values have been rounded to the nearest whole number at most mentions throughout the book.

52. FOMC transcript, October 5, 1982.

53. FOMC transcript, November 16, 1982.

54. Robert L. Hetzel, "What Remains of Milton Friedman's Monetarism?," Federal Reserve Bank of Richmond working paper, July 13, 2017.

55. Renee Haltom, "Failure of Continental Illinois," Federal Reserve History webpage.

56. FOMC transcript, May 21–22, 1984.

57. William R. Neikirk, "Volcker Resigns as Fed Chief," *Chicago Tribune*, June 3, 1987.

58. William L. Silber, *Volcker*, (New York: Bloomsbury Press, 2012).

59. Paul Volcker's remarks at *The Wall Street Journal's* Future of Finance conference, December 14, 2009.

Chapter 5

60. Nathaniel C. Nash, "Senate, by 91 to 2, Backs Greenspan as Fed Chief," *The New York Times*, August 4, 1987.

61. Jim McTague, "Dr. Greenspan's Amazing Invisible Thesis," *Barron's*, March 31, 2008.

62. Jim McTague, "Looking at Greenspan's Long-Lost Thesis," *Barron's*, April 28, 2008.

63. See Alan Greenspan, "Trade Deficit and Budget Deficit," C-SPAN video of a speech delivered at the Economic Club of New York, New York, June 14,1988 (quoted remark is 3 minutes, 20 seconds into the video).

64. Bob Woodward, *Maestro: Greenspan's Fed and the American Boom* (New York: Simon & Schuster Paperbacks, 2001).

65. I wrote about this in "That M&A Tax Scare Rattling the Markets," *The Wall Street Journal*, October 28, 1987.

66. For more details, see Mark Carlson, "A Brief History of the 1987 Stock Market Crash," Board of Governors of the Federal Reserve System, November 2006.

67. Alan Greenspan, February 2, 1988 congressional testimony before the Committee on Banking, Housing & Urban Affairs, United States Senate.

68. Alan Greenspan, "The Challenge of Central Banking in a Democratic Society," December 5, 1996 speech at the Annual Dinner and Francis Boyer Lecture of The American Enterprise Institute for Public Policy Research, Washington, D.C.

69. Alan Greenspan, "The Federal Reserve's semiannual monetary policy report, " July 22, 1997 congressional testimony before the Committee on Banking, Housing, and Urban Affairs, U.S. Senate.

70. Edward Yardeni, "The Technology Lottery," *Topical Study*, November 22, 1999.

71. Laurence H. Meyer, *A Term at the Fed: An Insider's View* (New York: HarperCollins Publishers, 2006), pages 6 and 16.

72. Meyer, page 18.

73. Meyer, page 38. The term "NAIRU" was first used by James Tobin in 1980. If the unemployment rate is at NAIRU, inflation should remain stable. According to this model, inflation should rise (fall) if the jobless rate remains below (above) NAIRU for a while.

74. Meyer, page 135.

75. Meyer, page 132.

76. Meyer, page 126.

77. Alan Greenspan, "Monetary policy and the economic outlook," June 17, 1999 congressional testimony before the Joint Economic Committee, U.S. Congress, June 17, 1999.

78. Ben Bernanke, "Deflation: Making Sure 'It' Doesn't Happen Here," November 21, 2002 speech.

79. Alan Greenspan, "Risk and Uncertainty in Monetary Policy," January 3, 2004 speech at the Meetings of the American Economic Association, San Diego, California.

80. Alan Greenspan, "Federal Reserve Board's Semiannual Monetary Policy Report to the Congress," February 16, 2005 congressional testimony before the Committee on Banking, Housing, and Urban Affairs, U.S. Senate.

81. Ben Bernanke, "The Global Saving Glut and the U.S. Current Account Deficit," March 10, 2005 speech.

82. Ben Bernanke, "Why Are Interest Rates So Low, Part 3: The Global Savings Glut," April 1, 2015 blog post.

83. Alan Greenspan, February 17, 2009 speech before The Economic Club of New York.

84. See The Board of Governors of the Federal Reserve System, "Application of the Commodity Exchange Act to Transactions in Over-the-Counter Derivatives," June 10, 1998 statement submitted before the House of Representatives Agricultural Committee's Subcommittee on Risk Management and Specialty Crops.

85. Alan Greenspan, "The Regulation of OTC Derivatives," July 24, 1998 congressional testimony before the Committee on Banking and Financial Services, US House of Representatives.

86. Alan Greenspan, "Over-the-Counter Derivatives," February 10, 2000 congressional testimony before the Committee on Agriculture, Nutrition and Forestry, United States Senate.

87. A CDO is a complex structured finance product that is backed by a pool of loans and other assets. A CDS is a derivative that allows one investor to swap credit default risk with another investor. For more, see "Credit Derivatives: Basic Definitions."

88. Alan Greenspan, "Understanding Household Debt Obligations," February 23, 2004 speech at the Credit Union National Association 2004 Governmental Affairs Conference, Washington, D.C.

89. Alan Greenspan, "Risk Transfer and Financial Stability," May 5, 2005 speech to the Federal Reserve Bank of Chicago's Forty-first Annual Conference on Bank Structure, Chicago, Illinois.

90. In an essay for *Fortune* in December 2001, Warren Buffett said: "For me, the message of that chart is this: If the percentage relationship falls to the 70% or 80% area, buying stocks is likely to work very well for you. If the ratio approaches 200%—as it did in 1999 and a part of 2000—you are playing with fire." During the latest bull market, Buffett remained bullish when his ratio rose back to 200% in 2017, observing that historically low inflation and interest rates were major considerations.

91. Alan Greenspan, Testimony before the Financial Crisis Inquiry Commission, April 7, 2010.

92. See "Testimony of Dr. Alan Greenspan," October 23, 2008 before the US House of Representatives' Committee of Government Oversight and Reform. The Q&A portion is available in an October 24, 2008 *Washington Times* article titled "He Found the Flaw?"

93. Alan Greenspan, February 17, 2009 speech before the Economic Club of New York.

94. "25 People to Blame for the Financial Crisis," *Time*.

Chapter 6

95. Ben Bernanke, "The Great Moderation," February 20, 2004 speech at the meetings of the Eastern Economic Association, Washington, D.C.

96. Milton Friedman and Anna Jacobson Schwartz, *A Monetary History of the United States, 1867–1960*, a study by the National Bureau of Econom-

ic Research (Princeton University Press, 1963).

97. Ben Bernanke, *Essays on the Great Depression* (Princeton University Press, 2000).

98. Ben Bernanke, "On Milton Friedman's Ninetieth Birthday," November 8, 2002 remarks at the Conference to Honor Milton Friedman, University of Chicago, Chicago, Illinois. In his first endnote, Bernanke wrote: "I hope the reader will forgive the many references to my own work in the list of references below. They arise because much of my own research has followed up leads from the Friedman-Schwartz agenda."

99. Barry Eichengreen, "The Political Economy of the Smoot-Hawley Tariff," NBER *Working Paper* No. 2001, August 1986.

100. Ben Bernanke, "The Federal Reserve and the Financial Crisis Origins and Mission of the Federal Reserve," March 20, 2012 lecture.

101. See Roger Lowenstein's article on Bernanke, "The Villain," *The Atlantic*, April 2012.

102. Ben Bernanke, "Deflation: Making Sure 'It' Doesn't Happen Here," November 21, 2002 speech before the National Economists Club, Washington, D.C.

103. Ben Bernanke, "Japanese Monetary Policy: A Case of Self-Induced Paralysis?" January 9, 2000 speech at the ASSA meetings, Boston, Massachusetts.

104. Ben Bernanke, "The Subprime Mortgage Market," May 17, 2007 speech at the Federal Reserve Bank of Chicago's 43rd Annual Conference on Bank Structure and Competition, Chicago, Illinois.

105. Ben Bernanke, Semiannual Monetary Policy Report to the Congress, July 18, 2007 congressional testimony before the Committee on Financial Services, U.S. House of Representatives.

106. FOMC Statement, October 31, 2007.

107. FOMC transcript of Conference Call on January 9, 2008.

108. FOMC transcript of Conference Call on January 21, 2008.

109. "What the Financial Crisis Commission Concluded About AIG's Failure," *Insurance Journal*, January 27, 2011.

110. Board of Governors of the Federal Reserve System, "Credit and Liquidity Programs and the Balance Sheet" and "Expired Policy Tools" webpages.

111. Yardeni Research, "Chronology of Fed's Quantitative Easing & Tightening" webpage.

112. Board of Governors of the Federal Reserve System, "What were the Federal Reserve's large-scale asset purchases?" webpage.

113. Ben Bernanke, "The Economic Outlook and Monetary Policy," August 27, 2010 speech at the Federal Reserve Bank of Kansas City Economic Symposium, Jackson Hole, Wyoming.

114. William Dudley, "The Outlook, Policy Choices and Our Mandate," Oc-

tober 1, 2010 remarks at the Society of American Business Editors and Writers Fall Conference, City University of New York, Graduate School of Journalism, New York City.

115. Ben Bernanke, "What the Fed Did and Why: Supporting the Recovery and Sustaining Price Stability," op-ed in *The Washington Post*, November 4, 2010.

116. Ben Bernanke, Press Conference, June 19, 2013.

117. FOMC Statement, September 18, 2013.

118. Ben S. Bernanke, *The Courage to Act: A Memoir of a Crisis and Its Aftermath* (New York: W.W. Norton & Company, Inc., 2015).

119. Ben Bernanke, "How the Fed Saved the Economy," op-ed in *The Wall Street Journal*, October 4, 2015.

Chapter 7

120. Janet Yellen, "Yale Economics in Washington," April 16, 1999 speech at Yale Economics Reunion New Haven, Connecticut.

121. Janet Yellen, Press Conference, March 19, 2014.

122. Janet Yellen, "What the Federal Reserve Is Doing to Promote a Stronger Job Market," March 31, 2014 speech at the 2014 National Interagency Community Reinvestment Conference, Chicago, Illinois.

123. Jon Hilsenrath, "Janet Yellen's Human Message Gets Clouded," *The Wall Street Journal*, April 1, 2014.

124. George Akerlof won the 2001 Nobel Prize in economics mostly for his work on asymmetrical information in an article titled "The Market for 'Lemons': Quality Uncertainty and the Market Mechanism," published in the *Quarterly Journal of Economics* in 1970. He shared the prize with Michael Spence and Joseph Stiglitz for their research related to asymmetric information.

125. Nicholas Lemann, "The Hand on the Lever," *The New Yorker*, July 21, 2014.

126. Ann Saphir, "Fed's Williams says sees 'smidgen' slower rate hikes," Reuters, January 29, 2016.

127. My PhD dissertation at Yale was titled *A Portfolio-Balance Model of Corporate Finance* (1976).

128. Janet Yellen, "Macroeconomic Research After the Crisis," October 14, 2016 speech at "The Elusive 'Great' Recovery: Causes and Implications for Future Business Cycle Dynamics" 60th annual economic conference sponsored by the Federal Reserve Bank of Boston, Boston, Massachusetts.

129. Board of Governors of the Federal Reserve System, *Beige Book* webpage.

130. See Yardeni Research chart book *Regional Business Surveys*.

131. The Fed's website explains: "The Federal Reserve generally conducts the survey quarterly, timing it so that results are available for the Janu-

ary/February, April/May, August, and October/ November meetings of the Federal Open Market Committee. The Federal Reserve occasionally conducts one or two additional surveys during the year. Questions cover changes in the standards and terms of the banks' lending and the state of business and household demand for loans. The survey often includes questions on one or two other topics of current interest." See the Fed's "Senior Loan Officer Opinion Survey on Bank Lending Practices."

132. See "Monetary Policy Rules and Their Role in the Federal Reserve's Policy Process," pp. 36–39 in the Fed's *Monetary Policy Report,* July 2017.

Chapter 8

133. Jerome Powell, Semiannual Monetary Policy Report to the Congress, February 27, 2018 congressional testimony before the Committee on Financial Services, US House of Representatives, Washington, D.C.

134. Federal Reserve Bank of Atlanta, Taylor Rule Utility webpage.

135. Jerome Powell, Press Conference, March 21, 2018.

136. Lael Brainard, "What Do We Mean by Neutral and What Role Does It Play in Monetary Policy?," September 12, 2018 speech at the Detroit Economic Club, Detroit, Michigan.

137. FOMC Minutes, September 25–26, 2018.

138. "Fed Chair Jay Powell: U.S. may be in a different era for workers' wages despite economic gains," PBS Newshour.org, October 3, 2018. Quoted remark is 11 minutes, 17 seconds into the videotape of the interview.

139. Federal Reserve Bank of Dallas, "Global Perspective with Jerome H. Powell," November 14, 2018.

140. Nick Timiraos, "Fed Shifts to a Less Predictable Approach to Policy Making," *The Wall Street Journal,* November 27, 2018.

141. Richard H. Clarida, "Data Dependence and U.S. Monetary Policy," September 27, 2018 speech at The Clearing House and The Bank Policy Institute Annual Conference, New York, New York.

142. Jerome Powell, "The Federal Reserve's Framework for Monitoring Financial Stability," November 28, 2018 speech at The Economic Club of New York, New York, New York.

143. FOMC Minutes, November 7–8, 2018.

144. Jerome Powell, Press Conference, December 19, 2018.

145. Jeff Cox, "Watch the Powell, Bernanke and Yellen roundtable live," CNBC, January 4, 2019.

146. Jerome Powell, Press Conference, January 30, 2019.

147. CNBC Exclusive: CNBC Transcript: Former Federal Reserve Chair Janet Yellen Speaks with CNBC's Steve Liesman Today, February 6, 2019.

148. Jerome H. Powell, Semiannual Monetary Policy Report to the Congress, February 26, 2019 congressional testimony before the Committee on

Banking, Housing, and Urban Affairs, U.S. Senate, Washington, D.C.

149. Jerome Powell, "Monetary Policy: Normalization and the Road Ahead," March 8, 2019 speech at the 2019 SIEPR Economic Summit, Stanford Institute of Economic Policy Research, Stanford, California.

150. The two images of Seurat's painting are shown in Figures 2 and 3 of Powell's March 8, 2019 speech: https://www.federalreserve.gov/newsevents/speech/powell20190308a.htm

151. Jerome Powell, "Opening Remarks," June 4, 2019 speech at the Conference on Monetary Policy Strategy, Tools, and Communications Practices, Federal Reserve Bank of Chicago, Chicago, Illinois.

152. Jerome Powell, "Monetary Policy: Normalization and the Road Ahead," March 8, 2019 speech at the 2019 SIEPR Economic Summit, Stanford Institute of Economic Policy Research, Stanford, California.

153. Jerome Powell, Press Conference, June 19, 2019.

154. FOMC Statement, June 19, 2019.

155. Jerome Powell, Semiannual Monetary Policy Report to the Congress, July 10, 2019 congressional testimony before the Committee on Financial Services, U.S. House of Representatives, Washington, D.C.

156. Jerome Powell, "Monetary Policy in the Post-Crisis Era," July 16, 2019 speech at "Bretton Woods: 75 Years Later—Thinking about the Next 75," a conference organized by the Banque de France and the French Ministry for the Economy and Finance, Paris, France.

157. John Williams, "Living Life Near the ZLB," July 18, 2019 speech at 2019 Annual Meeting of the Central Bank Research Association (CEBRA), New York City.

158. Richard Clarida interview on Fox Business News, July 18, 2019.

159. Jerome Powell, "Monetary Policy in the Post-Crisis Era," July 16, 2019, speech at "Bretton Woods: 75 Years Later—Thinking about the Next 75," a conference organized by the Banque de France and the French Ministry for the Economy and Finance, Paris, France.

160. FOMC Statement, July 31, 2019.

161. Jerome Powell, Press Conference, July 31, 2019.

162. Christopher Condon, "Here's a Timeline of Trump's Key Quotes on Powell and the Fed," Bloomberg, July 30, 2019.

163. Jeanna Smialek, "Trump Calls for Fed's 'Boneheads' to Slash Interest Rates Below Zero," *The New York Times*, September 11, 2019.

164. Alan S. Blinder, "When Presidents Pummel the Fed," *The Wall Street Journal*, September 18, 2019. By the way, a President does not have the legal authority to fire a Fed chair, even if he or she appointed the person.

165. Jerome Powell, Press Conference, September 18, 2019.

166. Edward Yardeni and Melissa Tagg, "The Yield Curve: What Is It Really Predicting?" July 2019.

167. Daniel Kruger and Sam Goldfarb, "Junk-Bond Sale Ends 40-Day Market Drought," *The Wall Street Journal*, January 10, 2019.
168. Fernando Avalos, Torsten Ehlers, and Egemen Eren, "September stress in dollar repo markets: passing or structural?," *BIS Quarterly Review*, December 8, 2019.
169. Jerome Powell, "Data-Dependent Monetary Policy in an Evolving Economy," October 8, 2019 speech at "Trucks and Terabytes: Integrating the 'Old' and 'New' Economies," the 61st Annual Meeting of the National Association for Business Economics, Denver, Colorado.
170. Board of Governors of the Federal Reserve System, "Balance Sheet Normalization Principles and Plans," March 20, 2019 press release.
171. Board of Governors of the Federal Reserve System, "Statement Regarding Monetary Policy Implementation," October 11, 2019 press release.
172. Federal Reserve Bank of New York, "Statement Regarding Treasury Bill Purchases and Repurchase Operations," October 11, 2019.

Chapter 9

173. Ben Bernanke, "Communication and Monetary Policy," November 19, 2013 speech at the National Economists Club Annual Dinner, Herbert Stein Memorial Lecture, Washington, D.C.
174. FOMC Statement, May 4, 2004.
175. FOMC Statement, December 13, 2005.
176. FOMC Statement, January 31, 2006 and FOMC Statement, March 28, 2006.
177. FOMC Statement, May 10, 2006.
178. FOMC Statement, June 29, 2006 and FOMC Statement, January 31, 2007.
179. FOMC Statement, September 18, 2007.
180. FOMC transcript of unscheduled conference call, January 21, 2008.
181. FOMC Statement, January 22, 2008.
182. FOMC Statement, April 30, 2008.
183. FOMC Statement, December 16, 2008.
184. FOMC Statement, September 23, 2009 and FOMC Statement, December 16, 2009.
185. FOMC Statement, June 22, 2011, FOMC Statement, August 9, 2011, FOMC Statement, January 25, 2012, and FOMC Statement, September 13, 2012.
186. FOMC Statement, December 12, 2012.
187. FOMC Statement, January 25, 2012.
188. FOMC Statement, January 30, 2013.
189. FOMC Statement, October 29, 2014.
190. FOMC Statement, October 28, 2015.
191. FOMC Statement, December 16, 2015.

192. FOMC Statement, January 30, 2019.

193. FOMC Statement, June 19, 2019.

194. Board of Governors of the Federal Reserve System, Timelines of Policy Actions and Communications: Forward Guidance about the Federal Funds Rate webpage.

Chapter 10

195. ECB, "Verbatim of the remarks made by Mario Draghi," July 26, 2012 transcript of speech at the Global Investment Conference in London.

196. Mario Draghi, Press Conference, August 2, 2012.

197. ECB, "Technical features of Outright Monetary Transactions," September 6, 2012 webpage.

198. ECB Governing Council, "Monetary policy decisions," June 5, 2014. See also Yardeni Research, "Chronology of ECB Monetary Policy Actions: 2014–Present" webpage.

199. ECB, "Targeted longer-term refinancing operations (TLTROs)" webpage.

200. Longer-term refinancing operations were first introduced by the ECB during March 2008 with a six-month maturity. Twelve-month LTROs were provided during June 2009. During December 2011, three-year LTROs were issued with banks' portfolios as collateral. A second auction of these loans occurred during February 2012.

201. "ECB announces expanded asset purchase programme," January 22, 2015 ECB press release.

202. ECB, "Monetary policy decisions," June 2, 2016.

203. Yardeni Research, "Chronology of ECB Monetary Policy Actions: 2014–Present" webpage.

204. ECB, "What is the expanded asset purchase programme?" March 31, 2016 webpage.

205. ECB, "Monetary policy decisions," December 13, 2018.

206. Mario Draghi, Press Conference, April 26, 2018.

207. Mario Draghi, Press Conference, June 14, 2018.

208. Mario Draghi, Press Conference, December 13, 2018.

209. Mario Draghi, Press Conference, March 7, 2019.

210. Mario Draghi, Press Conference, June 6, 2019.

211. ECB Governing Council, "Account of the monetary policy meeting," June 5–6, 2019.

212. Silvia Amaro, "Euro falls sharply as ECB's Draghi clears path for more stimulus," CNBC, June 18, 2019.

213. ECB Governing Council, "Account of the monetary policy meeting," July 24–25, 2019.

214. Mario Draghi, Press Conference, September 12, 2019.

215. "Christine Lagarde Pledges to Review ECB's Negative Rates," *The Wall*

Street Journal, September 4, 2019.

216. "ECB Launches Major Stimulus Package, Cuts Key Rate," *The Wall Street Journal*, September 12, 2019.

217. Christine Lagarde, "The future of the euro area economy," November 22, 2019 speech at the Frankfurt European Banking Congress.

218. Andy Sharp and Gonzalo Vina, "Kuroda Brings Oxford Mindset After Chicago-Alum Shirakawa," Bloomberg, March 14, 2013.

219. BOJ, "Introduction of the 'Quantitative and Qualitative Monetary Easing,'" April 4, 2013 press release on QQE program.

220. BOJ, "Expansion of the Quantitative and Qualitative Monetary Easing," October 31, 2014 press release on the expansion of QQE program.

221. Takashi Nakamichi, "Bank of Japan's Kuroda Channels Peter Pan's Happy Thoughts," *The Wall Street Journal*, June 4, 2015.

222. BOJ, "New Framework for Strengthening Monetary Easing: 'Quantitative and Qualitative Monetary Easing with Yield Curve Control,'" September 21, 2016 press release.

223. Haruhiko Kuroda, "Japan's Economy and Monetary Policy," December 7, 2017 speech.

224. "TIMELINE-Missing the Target: A timeline of Kuroda-nomics," Reuters, June 17, 2019.

225. IMF, *Global Financial Stability Report*, October 2019.

Chapter 11

226. "The ECB's monetary policy strategy," press release May 8, 2003.

227. "Bank of Japan sets 2% inflation target," *USA Today*, January 22, 2013.

228. See the first footnote in the Federal Reserve Board's *Monetary Policy Report* submitted to Congress on February 17, 2000.

229. Alan Greenspan, "Transparency in Monetary Policy," October 11, 2001 speech at the Federal Reserve Bank of St. Louis, Economic Policy Conference, St. Louis, Missouri (via videoconference).

230. Ben S. Bernanke, Thomas Laubach, Frederic S. Mishkin, and Adam S. Posen, *Inflation Targeting: Lessons from the International Experience* (Princeton University Press, 1999).

231. Fed Governor Frederic S. Mishkin, "Comfort Zones, Shmumfort Zones," March 27, 2008 speech.

232. "Federal Reserve issues FOMC statement of longer-run goals and policy strategy," January 25, 2012 press release.

233. Brendan Greeley, "US Federal Reserve considers letting inflation run above target," *Financial Times*, December 2, 2019.

234. Lael Brainard, "Federal Reserve Review of Monetary Policy Strategy, Tools, and Communications: Some Preliminary Views," November 26, 2019 speech at the Presentation of the 2019 William F. Butler Award New York Association for Business Economics, New York, New York.

235. Joseph Schumpeter, *Capitalism, Socialism and Democracy* (1942).
236. Federal Reserve Bank of Dallas, "Technology-Enabled Disruption: Implications for Business, Labor Markets and Monetary Policy," May 22–23, 2019 conference agenda.
237. Federal Reserve Bank of Dallas, "Technology-Enabled Disruption: Implications for Business, Labor Markets and Monetary Policy," May 22–23, 2019 conference overview.
238. Jerome Powell, "Monetary Policy in the Post-Crisis Era," July 16, 2019 speech at "Bretton Woods: 75 Years Later—Thinking about the Next 75," a conference organized by the Banque de France and the French Ministry for the Economy and Finance, Paris, France.
239. Daniel K. Tarullo, "Monetary Policy Without a Working Theory of Inflation," October 4, 2017 speech at the Hutchins Center on Fiscal & Monetary Policy at Brookings.
240. Claudio Borio, "Through the Looking Glass," September 22, 2017 speech at the Official Monetary and Financial Institutions Forum in London.

Chapter 12

241. Brian Blackstone, "Negative Rates, Designed as a Short-Term Jolt, Have Become an Addiction," *The Wall Street Journal*, May 20, 2019.
242. Mario Draghi, Press Conference, July 25, 2019.
243. Jens H.E. Christensen and Mark M. Spiegel, "Negative Interest Rates and Inflation Expectations in Japan," *FRBSF Economic Letter*, August 26, 2019.
244. Takashi Nakamichi, "Bank of Japan Faces a New Opponent on Negative Rates: Main Street," *The Wall Street Journal*, February 18, 2016.
245. Phil Molyneux, Alessio Reghezza, John Thornton, and Ru Xie, "Did Negative Interest Rates Improve Bank Lending?" *Journal of Financial Services Research*, July 30, 2019.
246. Phil Molyneux, Alessio Reghezza, John Thornton, and Ru Xie, "Bank margins and profits in a world of negative rates," *Journal of Banking & Finance*, October 2019.
247. "Negative interest rate policies are backfiring–new research," University of Bath, August 30, 2019.
248. FOMC Minutes, July 30–31, 2019.
249. "Federal Reserve to review strategies, tools, and communication practices it uses to pursue its mandate of maximum employment and price stability," November 15, 2018 press release.
250. Jerome Powell, Press Conference, September 18, 2019.
251. Swedish Riksbank, "Repo rate raised to zero per cent," December 19, 2019 press release.
252. Swedish Riksbank, *Monetary Policy Report*, December 19, 2019.

253. Board of Governors of the Federal Reserve System, *Financial Accounts of the United States* (current release). Especially useful are the links to all tables.

254. While it is widely believed that companies buy back their shares to boost their earnings per share and stock prices, Joseph Abbott and I found that most of this activity is driven by efforts to offset earnings dilution attributable to employee stock compensation plans. See our study *Stock Buybacks: The True Story* (2019).

255. Board of Governors of the Federal Reserve System, *Financial Stability Report*, November 2018.

256. The forward P/E is the time weighted average of industry analysts' consensus expectations for S&P 500 earnings during the current year and the coming year.

257. Board of Governors of the Federal Reserve System, *Financial Stability Report*, May 2019.

258. Board of Governors of the Federal Reserve System, *Financial Stability Report*, May 2019, p. 22.

259. Board of Governors of the Federal Reserve System, *Financial Stability Report*, November 2019, p. 28.

260. Jerome Powell, Press Conference, October 30, 2019.

261. S&P Global, "U.S. Corporate Debt Market: The State Of Play In 2019," May 17, 2019.

262. IMF, *Global Financial Stability Report: Lower for Longer*, October 2019.

263. Fed's Yellen expects no new financial crisis in 'our lifetimes', Reuters, June 27, 2017.

Epilogue

264. In his 2015 memoir, *The Courage to Act*, Bernanke lamented: "The deflation speech saddled me with the nickname 'Helicopter Ben.' In a discussion of hypothetical possibilities for combating deflation I mentioned an extreme tactic—a broad-based tax cut combined with money creation by the central bank to finance the cut. Milton Friedman had dubbed the approach a 'helicopter drop' of money. Dave Skidmore, the media relations officer . . . had advised me to delete the helicopter-drop metaphor . . . 'It's just not the sort of thing a central banker says,' he told me. I replied, 'Everybody knows Milton Friedman said it.' As it turned out, many Wall Street bond traders had apparently not delved deeply into Milton's oeuvre."

265. Ben Bernanke, "What tools does the Fed have left? Part 3: Helicopter money," April 11, 2016 Brookings post, April 11, 2016.

266. Ben Bernanke, "Deflation: Making Sure 'It' Doesn't Happen Here," November 21, 2002 speech before the National Economists Club, Washington, D.C.

267. Elga Bartsch, Jean Boivin, Stanley Fischer, and Philipp Hildebrand, "Dealing with the next downturn: From unconventional monetary policy to unprecedented policy coordination," BlackRock Investment Institute, August 2019.
268. See the transcript of Martin's "Address before the New York Group of the Investment Bankers Association of America," October 19, 1955.

Acronyms and Abbreviations

APP   asset purchase program
ARMs   adjustable-rate mortgages
BOJ   Bank of Japan
CDO   collateralized debt obligation
CDS   credit default swap
CEA   Council of Economic Advisers
CFTC   Commodity Futures Trading Commission
CPI   consumer price index
D   Democrat
DJIA   Dow Jones Industrial Average
ECB   European Central Bank
ELB   effective lower bound
EMU   European Monetary Union
ETF   exchange-traded fund
EU   European Union
FDIC   Federal Deposit Insurance Corporation
FDR   Franklin Delano Roosevelt
FOMC   Federal Open Market Committee
FRB   Federal Reserve Board
GDP   gross domestic product
GSE   government-sponsored enterprise
IMF   International Monetary Fund
JGB   Japanese Government Bond
LSAP   large-scale asset purchases
LTCM   Long-Term Capital Management

M&A merger(s) and acquisition(s)

MBS mortgage-backed security

NAIRU non-accelerating inflation rate of unemployment

NBER National Bureau of Economic Research

NFC nonfinancial corporation

NIRP negative-interest-rate policy

OECD Organisation for Economic Co-operation and Development

OMT outright monetary transactions

OPEC Organization of the Petroleum Exporting Countries

PBOC Peoples Bank of China

PCED personal consumption expenditures deflator

P/E price-to-earnings ratio

PIIGS Portugal, Ireland, Italy, Greece, Spain

QE quantitative easing

QQE qualitative and quantitative easing

R Republican

RM reserve management

RPI Retail Prices Index

S&L savings and loan association

S&P Standard & Poor's

SEC Securities and Exchange Commission

SEP Summary of Economic Projections

SMP securities market programme

SOMA System Open Market Account

TARP Troubled Asset Relief Program

TIPS Treasury Inflation-Protected Securities

TLTRO Targeted Longer-Term Refinancing Operations

UN United Nations

YRI Yardeni Research, Inc.

ZIRP zero-interest-rate policies

ZLB zero lower bound

Index

Italics indicate titles.

ALL CAPS indicate charts at end of book.

"f" in a page number (259f39) indicates a figure/chart at end of book.

A few acronyms are used to indicate origin: BOJ—Bank of Japan; ECB—European Central Bank; PBOC—People's Bank of China; UK—United Kingdom